Lecture Notes
in Business Information Processing　　149

Series Editors

Wil van der Aalst
Eindhoven Technical University, The Netherlands

John Mylopoulos
University of Trento, Italy

Michael Roseman
Queensland U　　　　　　　　　　　　　　　*'d, Australia*

Michael J. Shaw
University of Il

Clemens Szypersk
Microsoft Resea　　　　　*.., ..A, USA*

Hubert Baumeister
Barbara Weber (Eds.)

Agile Processes in Software Engineering and Extreme Programming

14th International Conference, XP 2013
Vienna, Austria, June 3-7, 2013
Proceedings

 Springer

Volume Editors

Hubert Baumeister
Technical University of Denmark
Department of Applied Mathematics and Computer Science
Lyngby, Denmark
E-mail: huba@dtu.dk

Barbara Weber
University of Innsbruck
Department of Computer Science
Innsbruck, Austria
E-mail: barbara.weber@uibk.ac.at

ISSN 1865-1348   e-ISSN 1865-1356
ISBN 978-3-642-38313-7   e-ISBN 978-3-642-38314-4
DOI 10.1007/978-3-642-38314-4
Springer Heidelberg Dordrecht London New York

Library of Congress Control Number: 2013938169

ACM Computing Classification (1998): D.2, K.6

Typesetting: Camera-ready by author, data conversion by Scientific Publishing Services, Chennai, India

Printed on acid-free paper

Springer is part of Springer Science+Business Media (www.springer.com)

Preface

In the last decade, interest in agile and lean software development has been continuously growing. Agile and lean software development has moved from a way of working—restricted in the beginning to some early adopters—to the mainstream way of developing software. Changing from traditional development processes to a more agile and lean mindset is not always easy. Companies often face big challenges during this transition process, and all too often benefits cannot be achieved as expected. A close collaboration between academia and practice is an important cornerstone to better understand all the various facets of agile and lean software development processes facilitating their adoption.

For the last 14 years, the XP conference series has actively participated in promoting agility and spreading the research results in this field. In addition, since the beginning, the XP conference series has been a place of close interaction between practitioners and researchers to meet and discuss new ideas, and experiences.

XP 2013 continued in the tradition of this conference series by providing an interesting and multifaceted program, including research papers, tutorials, workshops, panels, lightening talks, interactive presentations, experience reports, and open space.

These proceedings contain the selected research papers submitted to the research track of the conference, covering various themes related to agile and lean software development processes such as teaching and learning, development teams, agile practices, experiences and lessons learned, large-scale projects, and architecture and design.

All of the submitted research papers went through a rigorous peer-review process. Each paper was reviewed by at least three members of the Program Committee. Of the 52 papers submitted, only 17 were accepted (33%).

We hope that you find the proceedings of XP 2013 useful for your professional and academic activities.

We would like to thank everyone who contributed toward making XP 2013 a success including the authors, the sponsors, the reviewers, the volunteers, and the Chairs.

March 2013

Hubert Baumeister
Barbara Weber

Organization

General Chair	Ralph Miarka
Academic Chair	Hubert Baumeister, Barbara Weber
Industry and Practices	Michael Leber, Christian Hassa
Workshops and Tutorials	Charlie Poole, Martin Heider
Exceutives and Management	Diana Larsen
PhD Symposium	Johanna Hunt
Open Space	Charlie Poole, Diana Larsen
Panels	Steven Fraser
Event Management	Claudia Lembach
Student Volunteers	Johanna Hunt
Publicity	Olaf Lewitz

Research Program Committee

Muhammad Ali Babar	IT University of Copenhagen, Denmark
Hubert Baumeister	Technical University of Denmark, Denmark
Robert Biddle	Carleton University, Canada
Luigi Buglione	Engineering.IT / ETS, Italy
Ivica Crnkovic	Mälardalen University, Sweden
Simon Cromarty	Red Gate Software, UK
Torgeir Dingsøyr	SINTEF ICT, Norway
Tore Dybå	SINTEF and Department of Informatic, University of Oslo, Norway
Amr Elssamadisy	Gemba Systems, USA
Steven Fraser	Cisco, USA
Juan Garbajosa	Technical University of Madrid (UPM), Spain
Alfredo Goldman	University of São Paulo - USP, Brazil
Des Greer	Queens University Belfast, UK
Rashina Hoda	The University of Auckland, New Zealand
Helena Holmstrom Olsson	Gothenburg University, Sweden
Johanna Hunt	University of Sussex, UK
Kirsi Korhonen	NSN, Finland
Pasi Kuvaja	University of Oulu, Finland
Stig Larsson	Effective Change AB, Sweden
Casper Lassenius	Aalto University, Finland
Lech Madeyski	Wroclaw University of Technology, Porland
Michele Marchesi	DIEE - University of Cagliari, Italy
Grigori Melnik	Microsoft, Canada
Alok Mishra	Atilim University, Ankara, Turkey
Nils Brede Moe	SINTEF ICT, Norway

Ana Moreno	University Madrid, Spain
Oscar Nierstrasz	SCG - University of Bern, Switzerland
Maria Paasivaara	Helsinki University of Technology, Finland
Jennifer Perez	Technical University of Madrid (UPM), Spain
Kai Petersen	Blekinge Institute of Technology/Ericsson AB, Sweden
Adam Porter	University of Maryland, College Park, USA
Outi Salo	Nokia, Finland
Helen Sharp	The Open University, UK
Alberto Sillitti	Free University of Bozen-Bolzano, Italy
Darja Smite	Blekinge Institute of Technology, Sweden
Giancarlo Succi	Free University of Bozen-Bolzano, Italy
Marco Torchiano	Politecnico di Torino, Italy
Stefan Van Baelen	iMinds, Belgium
Xiaofeng Wang	Free University of Bozen-Bolzano, Italy
Hironori Washizaki	Waseda University, Japan
Barbara Weber	University of Innsbruck, Austria
Werner Wild	EVOLUTION, Austria
Laurie Williams	North Carolina State University, USA
Agustín Yagüe	Universidad Politecnica de Madrid, Spain

Additional Reviewers

Caracciolo, Andrea	Oliveira, Renan
Chis, Andrei	Santos, Viviane
Díaz, Jessica	Tonin, Graziela
Fernández Sánchez, Carlos	Wernli, Erwann
Kurs, Jan	

Sponsors

Boris Gloger

Cisco Research

Zühlke

Anecon

Techtalk

IdeaScale

Rally Software

Event MiLe GmbH

OBJEKTspektrum

Computerwelt

Austrian Computer Society

Austrian Airlines

Certum Airportservice

Table of Contents

Large Scale Projects

Architecture and Design

Barriers to Learning in Agile Software Development Projects

Jeffry S. Babb[1], Rashina Hoda[2], and Jacob Nørbjerg[3]

[1] Department of Computer Information and Decision Management, West Texas A&M
University, 2403 Russell Long Blvd. Canyon, Texas USA, 79016
jbabb@mail.wtamu.edu
[2] Electrical and Computer Engineering, The University of Auckland,
38 Princes St, Auckland, New Zealand
r.hoda@auckland.ac.nz
[3] Department of IT Management, Copenhagen Business School,
60 Howitzvej, 2000 Frederiksberg, Denmark
jno.itm@cbs.dk

Abstract. The adoption of agile methods promises many advantages for individual, team, and organizational learning. However, environmental, structural, and organizational/cultural constraints often find teams adapting agile software development methods rather than engaging in full adoption. We present results from two qualitative studies of teams and organizations that have, in many cases, adapted agile software methods to suit their needs through the omission or alteration of aspects of the method. In many cases, aspects of an agile method that are most related to learning were those that were modified or omitted. This paper utilizes the results of these studies to identify common and emergent barriers to learning. Often these barriers to learning exist according to organizational culture and the extent to which that culture influences attitudes, norms, and behaviors pertaining to learning. We present these barriers to learning and provide insight to the causes, effects, and potential ameliorations for these barriers.

Keywords: Agile software development, learning, organizational culture, XP, Scrum, Dialogical Action Research, Grounded Theory.

1   Introduction

Organizations and development teams adopting agile principles and practices are often faced with dilemmas governing the degree to which these practices should be adopted [5]. Moreover, given that many agile methods stress principles and practice over plan and prediction, Beck [6] asserts that, while the whole adoption of an agile method, such as XP, will realize a synergy that is greater than the sum or parts, strict orthodoxy in the use of the methods is not prescribed or mandated. As such, a wide range of choices, complications, and barriers exist for those who adopt an agile method. This paper is concerned with the implications of partial and modified adoption,

H. Baumeister and B. Weber (Eds.): XP 2013, LNBIP 149, pp. 1–15, 2013.

and the issues surrounding the effective utilization of agile methods as pertains to organizational culture and learning.

Some of the research questions we aim to answer are: How are XP and Scrum practices related to learning? Which practices support learning about the customer's needs and how the product under development will help meet those needs, and which practices support skills development (improving developers' capability, their knowledge about tools, change/improve processes and practices etc.)?

In this paper we share experiences from two studies, both conducted via engaged, action-oriented, and evidence-grounded methods, whereupon we seek to illuminate the issues highlighted in our research questions. This paper offers a post-hoc reflection on the outcomes of these studies as they relate to our research questions. Our first study focuses on the adoption issues related to individual and team learning in the adoption and adaptation of XP into the software practices of a small shop in Virginia, USA. Our second examines agile adoption and use among 58 practitioners in 23 different organizations, in both New Zealand and India. In both studies the analytic processes of Glaser's grounded theory research techniques are used to distill the patterns of attitudes and behaviors which inform our observations regarding the barriers to learning in the use of agile methods.

The common patterns which emerge between the two studies suggest that barriers to learning can be classified into four main areas: Multiple Goals (Projects), Excessive Iteration Pressure, Level of Customer Involvement, and Organizational Culture. As individual, team, and customer/organizational learning are each high probability outcomes of the utilization of agile methods, the emergence of barriers to this learning may be counter intuitive, given the inherent propensity for learning as a result of adoption [29]. However, in the two studies highlighted there were indeed various barriers to learning which emerged as the result of the adoption, and in some cases adaptation, of agile methods.

The rest of the paper is structured as follows: Section 2 presents the related work in this area, followed by the Research Design in section 3. We then present the Results of the two studies in section 4, followed by a discussion of the results and the Conclusion.

2   Related Works: Agile Methods, Knowledge and Learning

The agile approach to software development emphasize team-work, a situated, iterative and emerging solution process, and personalized knowledge capture and sharing [3,8, 9, 15, 18, 26, 27, 29]. Chau et al. [8] compare the strategies of agile and so-called traditional or Tayloristic software development and discuss how agile practices and principles support a personalized and team based approach to knowledge sharing and learning in software development.

Melnik and Maurer [25] argue the importance of direct personal relationships for effective knowledge exchange. Based on an experiment they argue that intermediaries and documentation based communication lead to distortions and information loss in when passing information from requirements analysts to software designers.

The implication is that agile software development projects must have direct personal interactions between different stakeholders; e.g. as expressed in the principles of customer-on-site (XP) and frequent and direct customer contact (Scrum).

Studies of agile practice show, however, that agile teams rarely adopt all agile practices, and that they will often adapt the practices they use to local circumstances and contexts [3, 7, 16, 17, 24, 31]. The question, therefore, arises how the adaptation, manifested as either non-use or modification, of particular agile practices impact knowledge building, sharing and learning in agile software development teams and projects. In this paper, we will explore this question through the analysis of agile practices.

Based on Schön's [30, 31] theory of the reflective practitioner, as well as on earlier research about knowledge in software development, we identify three kinds of knowledge building, sharing and reflection in agile software development projects: 1) knowledge about the product being developed, 2) the skills and experience required to build the product, 3) and ongoing reflection on the process itself. In the next section we will give a brief account of the underlying theory and concepts, and elaborate on our understanding of the three types of knowledge.

2.1   Knowledge and Learning in Agile Software Development

The agile development process is iterative, with several releases of intermediate products towards the culmination in a final product. The process embraces change as the developers' and the customer's understanding of the problem and the desired qualities of the solution emerge. Thus, agile software development processes resemble Schön's [30] description of how skilled designers solve difficult problems in areas such as architecture, management and industrial design [2, 13, 26]. According to this view on design and problem solving, problems are complex and multi-faceted and the properties of the "correct" or "best" solution are not easily determined beforehand. Nor can the solution be found through a pre-determined set of steps; i.e. a method. To solve such problems, the skilled designer, the *reflective practitioner,* engages in *reflection-in-action*, an "ongoing conversation with the situation", sketching and testing solutions against his understanding - or framing - of the problem, changing and evolving both the problem framing, the understanding of the desired properties of the solution, and the solution itself, in the process [30, 31].

Reflection-in-action depends upon the knowledge and skills of the practitioner and at the same time adds to this knowledge. As the process progresses, his understanding and framing of the problem and the solution change and deepen. In the process, he draws upon his *repertoire* of previous problems, fragments of solutions, tools and techniques. The *repertoire* influences both how he frames the problem, his solution process, and the solutions he develops in the process.

This description of design and problem solving, and how it relies on the knowledge and skills of the designer, resonates well with studies of software design practice. In a study of how software developers solve a difficult design problem, Guindon [12, 14] describes how previous experience and familiarity with specific programming techniques and design patterns formed the designer's appreciation of the problem and choice of a solution. She also observes how the designers' understanding of the problem and hence of the requirements for the solution, change and deepen as they repeatedly assess the evolving solution against the problem.

The agile development process is strongly related to *reflective* practice as stated above. One should bear in mind, however, that Schön [29] discusses the problem solving behaviour of the individual practitioner, whereas agile development is carried out by teams of developers in close collaboration with a customer. Thus, an agile development process must enable sharing of experience and skills within the developer team, as well as between the team and the customer. Agile software development practices, such as *customer-on-site, frequent releases, planning game, pair programming, user stories, acceptance tests*, and *refactoring* all support this goal [2, 15, 24, 26].

A software process that is not constantly monitored and improved risks *process erosion* [8] and ongoing learning, reflection and improvement are an intrinsic part of an agile team's responsibilities [8, 31]. Schön [30] uses the term *reflection-on-action* to describe how the practitioner reflects upon, and improves his solution process and its outcome. Like *reflection-in-action, reflection-on-action* is a personalized process that builds on and improves the individual practitioner's experience and expertise, but team-based *reflection-on-action* is implicitly supported by agile practices. Hazzan and Tomayko [14] demonstrate how the dialogue among developers and between developers and customers in agile practices such as *planning* game, *pair programming* and *refactoring* can induce team-based *reflection-on-action*. Likewise Babb and Nørbjerg [3] suggest adding techniques and tools to agile development practices in order to explicate *reflection-on-action* in agile development teams.

We derive three types of knowledge building, knowledge sharing, and learning from this account of the agile development process and reflective practice. We will use these three types in our discussion of barriers to knowledge sharing and learning in agile teams.

First, there is the knowledge about the problem and the solution that the developers and customer(s) build and share in the course of the agile project; i.e. the understandings and insights that evolve as they engage in *reflection-in-practice*. This includes an understanding of the problem and how the solution - the software - contributes to solving that problem. Note that this knowledge is not static but changes and evolves as the project progresses. Note also that this knowledge is not genuinely shared among all stakeholders: the customer cannot and should not understand all the technical details of the evolving software product, nor can the developers expect to completely share the customer's understanding of his world. Hence there is the need for ongoing dialogue between the development team and the customer.

The second type of knowledge concerns the expertise and skills that the stakeholders bring to the process - their *repertoire* Schön [30]. In the software development case this includes the developers' knowledge of software development techniques and tools, knowledge of previous solutions to "similar" problems, and their familiarity with software development practices. By sharing their *repertoire*, developers can learn from each other and thus increase the team's joint capabilities.

Finally, the agile development team must engage in *reflection-on-action* in order to learn from experiences and improve performance. The team may, for example, discuss how to improve the accuracy of their estimates during a Sprint planning meeting, or two programmers may reflect upon whether the process they just used to solve a problem can be transferred to other situations [15].

3   Research Design

This paper is based on the findings from two separate studies of agile practices: The first is a longitudinal Action Research study in a small software company in the USA [2, 3]. The other is a Grounded Theory study of agile practices in 23 different organizations in India and New Zealand [16, 17, 18].

At the time of study, all the organizations had introduced or were in the process of introducing agile practices based on either XP, Scrum, or a combination thereof. They would also adapt the agile practices based on local needs or constraints. In this context, adaptation means that the agile team may adopt a practice, but modify it or choose to not use it at all.

For the present paper we have identified adapted practices in both studies and the underlying causes; e.g. lack of customer involvement may be a cause for adaptation of the original "customer-on-site" practice. Through identification of common patterns, we were then able to group individual causes into a smaller set of common causes which are presented later in the results section. We now describe the research set-up of the two studies.

3.1   The Longitudinal Small-Shop Study

The small shop study is a longitudinal study of the introduction of agile practices and learning tools and techniques into SSC (a fictive name), a software company in the eastern USA consisting of the owner/founder and 4 developers.

The study used Dialogical Action Research [21] which uses practitioner and researcher dialog as the principle means by which interventions are introduced into the practitioner's setting. Dialogical AR - as action research in general - proceeds in cycles, each cycle contributes to solving the practitioner's problem as well as to the researcher's knowledge and thorough reporting to the research community in general.

During the practitioner-researcher partnership, the researcher conducted interviews with the practitioners and observed them in their daily work. Interviews and observations were documented in transcripts, supplemental documents, and field notes. During the 9 months of fieldwork the researcher was present onsite twice per week on average. Each visit usually lasted for a period of 1-4 hours. The data collected during this period consisted of:

- 26 recorded and transcribed dialogs with the company owner and lead developer, and various combinations of the team based on progress in a given iteration of the Dialogical AR cycle.
- Internal SSC documents
- Field notes taken while observing the practitioners' work

The data collected during the initial phase of the partnership were coded, using open, axial, and selective coding, in order to derive common themes related to SCC's method use. This initial analysis resulted in the recommendation to introduce XP into SSC and the method was introduced incrementally over the following months. The researcher continuously documented and analyzed how and why the practitioners adopted and adapted XP throughout this part of the project. It is the results from this latter analysis which forms the basis for the discussion in the present paper.

In the final phase of the Dialogical AR partnership, the researcher introduced explicit tools and techniques to support XP at SSC with on-going *reflection-on-action* at SSC. This is, however, beyond the scope of this paper and is described elsewhere [2].

3.2   The Grounded Theory Study

The Grounded Theory (GT) study was carried out over a period of 4 years using Glaser's classic GT method [11]. Using GT, the researcher – one of the authors of this paper – conducted iterative rounds of data collection and constant comparison method of text analysis. Data was collected from 58 agile practitioners in 23 different organizations in New Zealand and India through face-to-face, semi-structured interviews of approximately an hour each, using open-ended questions as well as observations of the workplaces and practices.

All participants used Scrum or a combination of Scrum and XP. All participants were practicing fundamental Agile practices such as iterative and incremental development (with varying iteration lengths), iteration planning, estimation and planning of user stories and tasks, testing, status report meetings (such as daily standup), frequent release of working software, and some form of retrospective meetings. A majority of the participants engaged in test-driven development and pair programming (on demand). Some participants were certified Scrum Masters. Participants belonged to organizations ranging from as small as 10 people to as large as 300,000 employees. Their domains ranged from health, telecommunications, entertainment, agriculture, energy, to software product development for multiple domains. The project duration varied from 2 to 12 months and team sizes ranged from 2 to 20 people on different projects. Participants varied in their levels of experience of using agile practices from novice to mature with several years' experience.

Data was analyzed using GT's open, selective, and theoretical coding procedures. Codes arising from one interview were constantly compared to those arising from all other interviews using the constant comparison method. This led to identifying common themes or patterns in data at increasing levels of abstraction. A number of findings were made from the GT study with respect to agile practices and have been described elsewhere [16, 17, 18].

We discovered a number of barriers to learning across the dimensions of *reflection-in-action*, *repertoire*, and *reflection-on-action* in the findings from both the -studies. We have analyzed examples of non-adherence or modifications to agile practices in order to identify the underlying causes of the adaptation/non-use. In each case we also identify the effect on learning and knowledge sharing. We describe these barriers in the next section.

4   Results: Barriers in Practice

In this section, we describe the categories of "barriers in practice" as identified in the two studies. These are: Multiple Goals (Projects), Excessive Iteration Pressure, Level of Customer Involvement, and Organizational Culture.

4.1   Multiple Goals (Projects)

In the longitudinal study, SSC is a small company with 20-40 individual customers at any given time. Furthermore, the company's projects spanned from as little as a week or two to three months (and beyond). The high number of customers and - very short - projects had implications for the adoption and adaptation of the practices of *pair programming* and *customer as team member*.

It was difficult for SSC to fully embrace the idea of *pair programming* although both the manager and the developers understood that this technique increases reflection and awareness among the developers and hence may contribute significantly to productivity. With each developer working on several projects simultaneously, and often only one person being active on a given project at a given point in time, it was infeasible in practice to apply *pair programming* in a systematic way. Programmers would, however, team up to explore and solve difficult programming problems and to create *spike solutions*. In this way the programmers used *pair programming* to improve their individual and shared knowledge of programming techniques and tools. This adaptation of *pair programming*, however, curtailed the adoption of *collective code ownership* and sharing.

SSC could not adopt the principle of *customer as team member* in the way prescribed by the XP method. With anywhere from 20 to 40 projects underway at varying stages of completion or maintenance, augmenting the "team" by 20 to 40 members was not realistic. Instead Daphne, the founder/owner, would act as a proxy for the customer and write u*ser stories*, and later a*cceptance tests*, based on her notes or her memory of a client's intentions. Thus, the customers' needs and intentions were not communicated directly to the developers in the customers' own language, but were mediated through Daphne's interpretations and language.

In the Grounded Theory study, we discovered a co-relation between team members being split across multiple projects and their ability to perform group programming – working together in an open-plan workspace while sharing the same code-base and collaborating closely. Group programming in agile teams provides opportunities for learning among team members.

"I think in our business, software developing, it's a complex subject and it's impossible for one person to know about everything, so it's a day-by-day thing...This is a normal step and everybody is learning each day." – Participant P14, Developer, New Zealand

Continuous learning involves different types of learning: learning Agile practices, learning new or complex technical skills, learning cross-functional skills, and learning from the team's own experiences - all of which fuel self-improvement. Where team members were split across multiple projects, their ability to perform group programming was curtailed.

"What I think a affected our project...[the developer] was working on another project, he didn't have enough time, so he didn't have the space to chat with anybody, to discuss ideas with anybody, to work with anybody, so he was really just on his own, and I think that really impacted a lot of the work he did in the last few months ... When you're working in a team like this [Agile team] and you've got to work quite closely, the individuals in the team matter." – Participant P21, Customer Rep, New Zealand

As a consequence the benefits of group programming, such as team-based reflection-in-action as a result of working together, were diminished. On the other hand, some other teams where members were largely dedicated to single projects at a time provided a strong learning environment, especially for new-comers who would pair up with more experienced members to learn new technologies.

"I had never worked on the Spring framework before, but in this project it's completely related to Spring framework, and Spring transaction management and all, so I started learning it...we were pairing each with other, that time it was beneficial because the other person was quite okay...and he knew about the Spring frame-work and he had done it before in some other project. So it helped me to learn it more faster, because he used to say: 'okay, you have to go with this stuff, and you can do it'. So that was a major advantage." – Participant P16, Developer, New Zealand.

It was obvious that while dedicated resources on projects performing group programming were able to benefit from enhanced learning opportunities, resources split across multiple projects suffered from diminished opportunities for learning.

4.2   Excessive Iteration Pressure

We defined "iteration pressure" as the pressure to deliver to a committed team goal every iteration. Iteration pressure, in itself, is not detrimental to the team, in fact some amount of iteration pressure is necessary to motivate teams to deliver their goals. Short iteration lengths or an extremely high and unsustainable development velocity, on the other hand, can cause excessive iteration pressure. For instance, in the GT study, a developer found one week iterations to be very demanding:

"I'm always feeling the need to rush, rush, rush!...after one week [iteration], we want to remove all these stickies [tasks] from the wall. So it's always pressure...if you have [longer] development time, then I can adjust my work like if we spent a little bit longer than we expected, I can catch up next week." – Participant P15, Developer, New Zealand

Creating and maintaining a continuous learning environment requires teams to set some explicit time aside for learning each iteration. Excessive iteration pressure, on the other hand, implies they may not have any extra time to spare for learning:

"I'd be interested to learn various agile techniques for requirements gathering, such as events and themes, and I'd love to try and use some of them in an Agile project. It's just [that] I haven't really had a lot of time to think about it. [Scrum] is very action oriented." - Participant P4, Business Analyst, New Zealand

"You need to actually allow time for other team members to learn what you do and for you to learn what they do. Often we tend to fill up our sprints with so much that a good teaching environment isn't necessarily there...they can see what you're doing but you need to be able to take the time to explain in really good detail." - Participant P8, Tester, New Zealand

Excessive iteration pressure was, therefore, found to be a barrier to learning in agile teams.

4.3   Customer Involvement

The original XP and Scrum practices to support customer collaboration are the 'on-site customer' and 'product owner' respectively. In practice, several factors contribute to less than ideal levels of customer involvement. These include skepticism towards agile practices, geographic distance including off-shoring setups, inability or unwillingness to collaborate, etc. [17].

In the longitudinal small-shop study, the change to XP increased the level of ongoing interaction with customers. Negotiating requirements with a key customer had previously been the responsibility of a key partner who was the main contractor. This had led to estimation and quality issues. After the introduction of XP, Daphne, the founder and CEO of SSC, insisted on engaging directly with the customer, using user stories to capture user requirements iteratively and respond to change. A drawback of this setup was that she was the prime – sometime only – liaison with customers. As such the repertoire of learning that can be derived from interactions with the customer was limited to Daphne, while the rest of the team did not get a chance to learn about the customer domain, business cases, and requirements in the same way.

Where the teams were suffering from inadequate customer involvement, a single team representative coordinating with the customer – or a *coordinator* role – emerged in most of the relatively new agile teams in the GT study [17]. It was mostly played by a business analyst or by developers. The *coordinator* was responsible for capturing customer requirements and relaying them to the team. Similarly, they would pass on questions from the team to the customer and elicit clarifications on requirements or prioritization. Another role identified in the GT study was that of a *translator* – a person responsible for understanding and translating between business language used by customers and the technical terminology used by the team, to improve communication between the two [18]. In relatively new agile teams, the *translator* role was mostly played by a single individual usually also playing the *coordinator* role. Both these roles involved close learning and in-depth understanding about the customer domain and requirements.

Lack of these roles altogether or where these roles are limited to individuals, becomes a barrier to learning for the whole agile team. Where the *coordinator* and *translator* roles were played by single individuals on new agile teams, they were useful in overcoming the challenges of inadequate customer involvement, however, it provided limited opportunities for other members to learn about the customer domain and requirements. In more mature teams – practicing agile for more than a year – most members of the team were able to play the *coordinator* and *translator* roles and interact directly with the customer. This provided better opportunities for all members of the team to develop a repertoire of learning about the customer and their requirements.

4.4   Organizational Culture

Organizational culture has been defined as *"a standard set of basic suppositions invented, discovered or developed by the group when learning to face problems of external adaptation and internal integration."* [18]. Senior management has a strong contribution in setting up overall corporate vision and values and maintaining the organization culture. Agile teams require organization structures that are informal in practice, where the boundaries of hierarchy do not prohibit free flow of information and feedback. In an informal organizational structure, the senior management encourages a strong learning environment with active mechanisms for knowledge management across the board.

In the longitudinal study, at the time when XP was introduced to SSC, the founder/CEO had all important knowledge about the company's processes, customers and products, and she would work hard to "mold" new employees into her ways of thinking:

"And even though we haven't written a formal methodology, which I guess is just in my head, and I have conformed Fred [a developer] to what's in my head...Luckily, he has been trainable and has listened to what I do... Fred was content with delivering back to me exactly what I asked for so I've molded Fred into my way of thinking, so I guess the methodology is in my head." – Daphne, CEO, SSC

This knowledge transfer process took time away from other important tasks and she hoped that having a formal method which everyone knew and could use, would take some of that pressure away from her. Her strong belief that her own knowledge and capabilities held the key to productivity and quality did, however, create obstacles for the kind of team learning intended in XP and other Agile methods. She saw the method as a more effective way to codify and transfer her ideas of best practices to the developers, rather than a vehicle for genuine knowledge sharing and skill development. This was evident in her approach to *pair programming, daily stand-up meetings,* and *user stories.* She immediately valued *pair programming* for skills development and saw developer pairing as a means for skills transfer from herself to one deveoper and through him to the next, and so on. Citing her own higher skill and experience level, Daphne saw *spike solutions* and *pair programming* as means to elevate her employees' skills until parity with her own skills was reached. On the other hand she was less confident to let the developers pair on their own without her guidance and support. She would be concerned that developers would "reinvent the wheel" and spend time finding solutions to problems she had solved already.. As a consequence - and also because of the resource and structural issues discussed above - she would neither support, nor endorse *pair programming* as a practice to be used across the board.

This view on learning as transferring knowledge and skills from management to developers, creates barriers to the team's own reflection and. It is feasible that *collective code ownership* will remain unachievable in SSC in practice.

Daphne's influence on the introduction and use of XP also had some positive impact on learning. To her, both *user stories* and *daily stand-up meetings* became means to monitor productivity and progress. She would, therefore, actively engage in these practices, thereby reinforcing their effect on learning and reflection.

In the GT study, we found that agile organizations, where all the teams operate using agile software development, are characterized by informal organizational structures. Informality in organizational structure promotes openness. Openness was one of the most common traits mentioned by participants, that made the organizational culture conducive for agile teams. In such organizations, team members are free to voice opinions, raise concerns, and freely share knowledge within and across teams. This was achieved in a few cases through knowledge repositories in the form internal project wikis where all important project information, domain knowledge, business cases, and technical tasks were recorded.

5   Discussion

Our discussion and analysis of the results of the two studies, as they related to the emerging theme of barriers to learning, will be presented in two steps: 1) an overview of adapted practices and the implications for learning, using the, and 2) discussion of the underlying causes of the adaptation/non-use.

We first summarize results, as they pertain to each identified barrier and the effect this has on learning and knowledge sharing within the agile teams. (See table 1)

Many of the barriers to learning and knowledge sharing emerge as the result of conflict and friction between constraints endogenous to the development team and, in some cases, the organization in which the development team is located. Company size, organizational culture, principle industry type, and team size, each play an influencing role concerning the adaptation of the agile method. Whereas agile methods are generally effective, they are not so codified that complete orthodox adoption is necessary. However, while ample instruction exists on the learning cycles inherent in XP and Scrum, experiences from both studies suggest that engagement in the reflective and learning-oriented practices are not always followed or are not sufficiently institutionalized. Thus there are structural and contextual hindrances for, knowledge sharing, reflection and learning in agile projects. Perhaps as profit is largely attached to the delivery and acceptance of working software, the learning cycles that improvement team and personal development may be eschewed in favor of moving forward to the next opportunities for billable hours, progress on projects, and productivity.

The learning that arises from the use of agile methods is also manifold. Some learning is related to improvements in a team's ability to understand the requirements of the project and to adapt the changes in requirements. Since these are productive aspects of agile methods which enable the delivery of working software (and thus revenue), this type of learning would be encouraged. Other learning relates to the improvement of developers' and teams' skills and expertise, and is perhaps, although counter-intuitively, reduced or omitted in favor of learning activities which are more directly related to the bottom line.

Table 1. Summary of Barriers to Learning and Knowledge Sharing in the Adaptation of Agile Methods

Barrier	Agile practices affected	Effect on learning and knowledge sharing
Multiple goals (projects)	Customer-on-site Pair programming Collective code ownership	**The product being developed:** Developers did not have direct access to the customer's needs and requirements. Developers did not share knowledge about the emerging product.
Excessive iteration pressure	Daily stand-up Retrospectives Pair programming	**Skills and experience:** The developers had insufficent time to experiement with new techniques and exchange new ideas. **Reflection-on-action:** Not enough time to reflect upon and improve practices and results.
Customer involvement	Customer-on-site	**The product being developed:** Developers did not have direct access to the customer's needs and requirements.
Organizational culture	Pair programming Spike solutions User stories Stand-up meetings	**Skills and experience:** Skills and experience transferred from a strong "expert" to other developers. No collective sharing **Reflection-on-action:** One person's view dominates reflection and improvement activities. Reduced team-based reflection and improvement.

Similar to Hazzan and Tomayko [15], we observe, that although practices in XP and other agile methods support reflection and learning, practical and contextual issues create barriers to learning which are not simple to resolve. That is, the learning that is possible from the utilization of agile methods is challenged by the natural entropy inherent in the particulars and context faced by a given team or organization. We conveniently characterize the constraints and proclivities of a given team as part and parcel of their organizational and/or managerial culture. Therefore, as agile methods emphasize knowledge sharing and learning at the team level, the team is situated within, influenced by, and perhaps, bound by, an organizational culture. There are many agile principles and practices, such as collective code ownershp, stand-up meetings, and retrospectives in which organizational culture is driving the barriers we identify from the highlighted studies.

Many of the barriers to learning, which resulted from ommission or partial engagement of learning-oriented agile practices, resulted from individual, team, and management dilemmas [33]. In the case of the longitundial study at SCC, many decisions made which were detrimental the realization of the full benefit of agile practices were cognizant of the potential costs. The dilemma was typically a matter of prioritizing other short-term or existential constraints. However, organizational culture can influence the degree to which a team benefits from an inherent culture or disposition towards the indoctination of learning practices.

Argyris and Schön [1] characterize the problem of cultural threats to learning as a Learning Paradox, wherein disconnect arises in what is discussable and not-discussable in the context of organizational norms. In the case of a small shop, such as SCC, there may be an involved owner who, rightfully insists on maintaining discretion on practices. Overall, organizational culture may have great impact on whether the team will engage in reflection-in-action and double-*loop learning* depending on what is *discussable*. This was evident in the Dialogical AR partnership at SSC where certain persistent problems related to one of their strategic partnerships precluded organizational learning for the team. This was so as SSC was too constrained by and codependent with their strategic partner to allow the not-discussable to enter into their reflections and learning.

This matter of organizational culture constitutes a particularly wicked problem as a learning culture - in spite of its seemingly problematic nature - may not be easily removed, since it is tied into the company's history, and - ultimately - the funder/owner's ambition to keep the company afloat. These sort of deeper structural problems which - in practice - limit the application of certain XP elements, are perhaps unavoidable. Evidence from the Grounded Theory studies also suggest many structural constraints which, at times, revealed the pace required for constant revenue-generating and forward-moving action, left some developers in a state where the productive trains of Scrum were dutifully engaged, while some of the more reflective and learning-oriented practices were curtailed.

We are left with a central question which is only partially answered by the evidence from our studies: what is the opportunity cost of trading the organizational and team learning aspects of agile methods for their productivity and adaptability aspects? In both studies, cracks and fissures in team learning were apparent. Certainly the implications these tradeoffs have for the long-term effectiveness of the team are worth further study. Perhaps metrics for learning and greater discipline for the specification of learning could be made more integral to the agile methods. However, it may be somewhat antithetical to the premise of agile methods that learning becomes a quantifiable metric. In any case, the importance of individual and team learning as a byproduct of agile method use is quite established, however, the mechanics to ensure that learning outcomes are inculcated as being concomitantly and equally important as product outcomes are perhaps not as integral to agile methods as we purport.

6   Conclusion

Even though software companies and practitioners aim to follow agile practices, they (or their managers) face challenging conditions as identified in our two studies. The answer to this is not, however, to insist that practitioners follow agile practices to the letter or abandon the agile practices altogether. Agile practitioners often end up adapting agile practices to different contexts and constraints, thus creating barriers to knowledge sharing and learning. For example, inadequate customer involvement leads to the emergence of adapted practices of using the coordinator and translator roles in place of 'on-site customer' or 'product owner'. When played strictly by single individuals on relatively new agile teams, these adapted roles limit the rest of the team's ability to acquire knowledge and enable learning about the customer domain.

Awareness of the barriers to learning described in this paper will help agile practitioners better grasp the risks associated with adapting agile practices and consciously include opportunities for learning and knowledge sharing when practicing agile. However, awareness alone may be insufficient as many of these barriers are structurally tied to the organizational context. The dilemmas and constraints that many agile teams and practitioners face may result in practices that forestall the learning mechanisms inherent in many agile practices. While more study into this area is needed, it seems that concepts related to reflective practice hold the most promise in allowing the individual practitioner opportunities to individually react and adjust to barriers to learning in the use of agile methods.

References

1. Argyris, C., Schön, D.: Organizational Learning II – Theory, Method, and Practice. Addison-Wesley, Boston (1996)
2. Babb, J.J.: Towards a reflective-agile learning model and method in the case of small shop software development: evidence from an action research study. PhD., Virginia Commonwealth University (2009)
3. Babb, J.J., Nørbjerg, J.: A Model for Reflective Learning in Small Shop Agile Development. In: Molka-Danielsen, J., Nicolajsen, H.W., Persson, J.S. (eds.) Engaged Scandinavian Research. Selected Papers of the Information Systems Research Seminar in Scandinavia, Molde, Norway, vol. 1, pp. 23–38. Tapir Akademisk Forlag (2010)
4. Bansler, J.P., Bødker, K.: A Reappraisal of Structured Analysis: Design in an Organizational Context. ACM Transactions on Information Systems 11(2), 165–193 (1993)
5. Boehm, B., Turner, R.: Balancing Agility and Discipline: A Guide for the Perplexed. Addison-Wesley, Boston (2004)
6. Beck, K.: Extreme Programming Explained. Addison-Wesley, Boston (2000)
7. Cao, L., Mohan, K., Xu, P., Ramesh, B.: A framework for adapting agile development methodologies. European Journal of Information Systems 18, 332–343 (2009)
8. Chau, T., Maurer, F., Melnik, G.: Knowledge Sharing: Agile Methods vs. Tayloristic Methods. In: Twelfth IEEE International Workshops on Enabling Technologies: Infrastructure for Collaborative Enterprises, WETICE 2003. IEEE Computer Society (2003)
9. Cockburn, A.: Agile Software Development. Addison-Wesley, Boston (2002)
10. Coleman, G., O'Connor, R.: Investigating software process in practice: A grounded theory perspective. J. Syst. Softw. 81(5), 772–784 (2008)
11. Fitzgerald, B., Russo, N.L., Stolterman, E.: Information Systems Development. Methods in Action. McGraw-Hill (2002)
12. Glaser, B., Strauss, A.L.: The Discovery of Grounded Theory. Aldine, Chicago (1967)
13. Guindon, R.: Designing the Design Process: Exploiting Opportunistic Thoughts. Human-Computer Interaction 5, 305–344 (1990)
14. Guindon, R.: Knowledge exploited by experts during software systems design. International Journal of Man-Machine Studies 33, 279–304 (1990)
15. Hazzan, O., Tomayko, J.: The Reflective Practitioner Perspective in eXtreme Programming. In: Maurer, F., Wells, D. (eds.) XP/Agile Universe 2003. LNCS, vol. 2753, pp. 51–61. Springer, Heidelberg (2003)
16. Hoda, R., Kruchten, P., Noble, J., Marshall, J.: Agility in Context. In: Object-Oriented Programming, Systmes, Languages and Applications Conference, OOPSLA 2010, Reno/Tahoe, NV. ACM (2010)

17. Hoda, R., Noble, J., Marshall, S.: Agile Undercover: When Customers Don't Collaborate. In: Sillitti, A., Martin, A., Wang, X., Whitworth, E. (eds.) XP 2010. LNBIP, vol. 48, pp. 73–87. Springer, Heidelberg (2010)
18. Holz, H., Maurer, F.: Knowledge Management Support for Distributed Agile Software Processes. In: Henninger, S., Maurer, F. (eds.) LSO 2003. LNCS, vol. 2640, pp. 60–80. Springer, Heidelberg (2003)
19. Humphrey, W.S.: Managing the Software Process. Addison-Wesley, Reading (1990)
20. Kautz, K., Madsen, S., Nørbjerg, J.: Persistent Problems and Practices in Information Systems Development. ISJ (2007) (accepted for publication)
21. Lee, A.S., Mårtensson, P.: Dialogical Action Research at Omega Corporation, Richmond, VA, pp. 1–39 (2004)
22. Madsen, S., Kautz, K., Vidgen, R.: A framework for understanding how a unique and local IS development method emerges in practice. European Journal of Information Systems 15, 225–238 (2006)
23. Mangalaraj, G., Mahapatra, R., Nerur, S.: Acceptance of software process innovations – the case of extreme programming. European Journal of Information Systems 18, 344–354 (2009)
24. Mathiassen, L., Pries-Heje, J., Ngwenyama, O. (eds.): Improving Software Organizations. From Principles to Practice, The Agile Software Development Series. Addison-Wesley, Boston (2002)
25. Melnik, G., Maurer, F.: Direct Verbal Communication as a Catalyst of Agile Knowledge Sharing. In: Agile Development Conference (ADC 2004). IEEE Computer Society (2004)
26. Moe, N.B., Dingsøyr, T., Dybå, T.: A teamwork model for understanding an agile team: A case study of a Scrum project. Information and Software Technology 52, 480–491 (2010)
27. Nerur, S., Balijepally, V.: Theoretical Reflections on Agile Development Methodologies. Commun. ACM 50(3), 79–83 (2007)
28. Rubin, K.S.: Essential Scrum: A Practical Guide to the Most Popular Agile Process. Addison-Wesley, Boston (2013)
29. Schein, E.H.: Oraganizational Culture and Leadership, 1st edn. Jossey-Bass Publishers, San Franciso (1985)
30. Schön, D.A.: The Reflective Practitioner. How Professionals Think in Action. Basic Books (1983)
31. Schön, D.A.: Designing as reflective conversation with the materials of a design situation. Knowledge-Based Systems 5(1), 3–13 (1992)
32. Senapathi, M., Srinivasan, A.: Understanding post-adoptive agile usage: An exploratory cross-case analysis. The Journal of Systems and Software 85, 1255–1268 (2012)
33. Steiner, L.: Organizational dilemmas as barriers to learning. The Learning Organization 5(4), 193–201 (1998)
34. Stolterman, E.: How System Designers Think about Design and Methods. Some Reflections Based on an Interview Study. Scandinavian Journal of Information Systems 3, 137 (1991)

Early Start in Software Coaching

Thomas Vikberg, Arto Vihavainen, Matti Luukkainen, and Jaakko Kurhila

Department of Computer Science, University of Helsinki, Finland
{tvikberg,avihavai,mluukkai,kurhila}@cs.helsinki.fi
http://www.cs.helsinki.fi/rage

Abstract. The demand for software coaching and coaches is increasing. As our programming courses are organized according to the Extreme Apprenticeship method, it is relatively safe and straightforward to allow students to participate as coaches in our CS1 course even as early as their second semester. Safety is ensured by the hierarchical structure of CS1 course personnel that provides enough peer and faculty support for students undertaking the task of coaching. We briefly describe the Extreme Apprenticeship method as well as the organization and the learning objectives in our coaching environment. Results acquired from student coaches (N=46) indicate that the learning experience of coaching is highly valued and deemed especially educational for the coaches without harming the learning results of the coachees.

Keywords: agile software coaching, software engineering best practices, coach development, cognitive apprenticeship, extreme apprenticeship.

1 Introduction

Emergence of lean and agile methods [1,2,3] has led to an increasing demand for software engineers that are able to perform as *coaches* for individual developers and teams. To satisfy this demand, higher education institutions with software engineering (SE) education have to give their students opportunities to learn agile coaching skills as well as traditional hard SE skills. As coaching is about working with people [4], learning to coach requires educational structures which involve interaction and cooperation, i.e. opportunities to practice coaching. Time and experience are needed to become an effective agile coach [4]. Therefore, it is beneficial to start practicing it as early as possible, given that supporting conditions can be put in place.

An agile coach not only performs as a teacher, facilitator, collaborator and a mentor, but in addition, an important part is *being* a coach [5]. Coaches guide people on their path towards better expertise through emphasizing best software engineering practices. Acting as a coach requires skills outside the traditional CS degree that consists of e.g. mathematics, programming, databases and architecture design. Agile coaches perform as agents of change and rely upon teamwork-related skills as well as other social skills. These skills are typically embedded only within the "hidden curriculum" within CS degrees which means that their realization is often not assessed or developed.

H. Baumeister and B. Weber (Eds.): XP 2013, LNBIP 149, pp. 16–30, 2013.

A traditional approach for coping with the emerging need for coaches in formal higher education would be to offer lecture-based courses titled along the lines of "software engineering coaching". Such courses or modules would introduce the students to e.g. project management methods such as Scrum [1] and Kanban [6] by covering their main principles and practises. Another approach would be to place the students to coach e.g. capstone projects, possibly under the instruction of faculty members of the institution. Such courses can be completed only in the later part of a CS degree as students taking the course should have hands-on experience in larger software engineering projects before they can be put to coach and share the responsibility of capstone-projects (see e.g. [7,8]).

The approach to software coaching presented in this paper is a mix of hands-on experience with clearly stated learning objectives with a twist: coaching starts very early in the degree programme. The approach is a formal part of the degree. However, it is *not* a course in the traditional sense: there is no lecturing, and no summative assessment of the students; the only course structure is the *specific way that we organize our programming courses*. The course design includes heavy interaction between every participant and a hierarchy of people which allows team-teaching and participation of junior coaches.

Noteworthy is that in our approach to teaching programming, a significant part of our students (ca. 20%) act as coaches in introductory programming courses (CS1) at a very early stage of their studies, as early as their second semester. Working as a coach to novice programmers gives the student valuable experience on technical as well as inter- and intra-personal aspects in programming, e.g. communicating with people with different CS knowledge levels, experiencing and truly understanding the meaningfulness of best programming practices [9]. The coaches are being exposed to thousands and thousands of lines of code from different programmers and are taken into the *community of practice* [10,11] of a team of coaches. Students are given a chance and an explicit responsibility to see what it can be like to be on the other side of the "teaching podium"; this is expected to both empower the students as well as give insight into what it takes to facilitate learning.

Our approach for organizing coaching opportunities for the students intertwines with our apprenticeship-based method of organizing our programming courses. In the rest of the paper we first briefly describe the apprenticeship-based educational method. We continue by describing the coaching study path offered within our degree, where students are being coached and act as coaches. We then concentrate on the early coaching experiences of the students, and how the coaching opportunity is organized within our educational setting. Results are gathered and presented from 46 students, who have participated as junior coaches at an early stage of their studies.

2   Extreme Apprenticeship Education

There is a long tradition of apprenticeship-based education in CS, especially in learning to program (see e.g. [12,13]). As an ongoing effort we have developed a version of apprenticeship-based education called the Extreme Apprenticeship method (XA) that is in use in programming courses at our institution [14,15]. XA is based on contemporary interpretations of apprenticeship education in which the emphasis is on teaching crafts that require abstract thinking [16,17,18].

As is typical for apprenticeship education, XA is based on modeling, scaffolding and fading. First, the student is provided with a conceptual model of the programming process in the form of course material, screen casts and few a lectures. Second, students are exposed to tasks, i.e. exercises, that are to be completed under scaffolding. Here, scaffolding refers to temporary support given to students, which allows them to reach the intended learning objectives. A significant part of the process of scaffolding is given by instructors who perform as coaches for the students. Scaffolding is also built into the learning material and exercises which guide the students to discover the content knowledge that is part of the learning objectives of the programming course.

Students complete programming tasks from day one. They are allowed to experience feelings of satisfaction from completing the programming tasks by themselves. Those giving the support must restrain themselves from giving full answers to the exercises, rather, just enough hints so that the students are able to discover the answers themselves. In XA, the aim is to get everyone to succeed in getting started, and receive enough support to progress further in the course. Many students are spending numerous hours practicing in our XA computer labs. Scaffolding needs to be temporary, and the support given by instructors fades away after it has served its purpose. In the exercise material, this fading means progression to ever larger and more open-ended assignments.

In addition to the adaptations of the three phases described above, XA relies on two key principles: (1) The craft can only be mastered by actually practicing it, as long as it is necessary; and, (2) bi-directional continuous feedback between the learner and the instructor is of utmost importance, in order to make progress and show the progress to both parties [19].

A sufficient amount of practice is ensured by the fact that there are literally hundreds of exercises to be completed. The instructors play a crucial role when interacting with the students. They do not only help the students, but also gather necessary information which is used for continuously assessing the progress of learning in the course. XA relies on this information when the tasks for the upcoming weeks are selected and crafted.

XA has been successfully employed in several courses [19,20,21], recently also outside the XA's "home university" [22]. XA has also been adapted to teaching university mathematics [23].

3   Coaching as Part of the Degree

The software engineering (SE) track at the Department of Computer Science at the University of Helsinki offers various courses that incorporate people skills: SE; SE Project; Software Processes and Quality; Software Project Management and Group Dynamics. Coaching and Engaging in Global Agile Software Teams

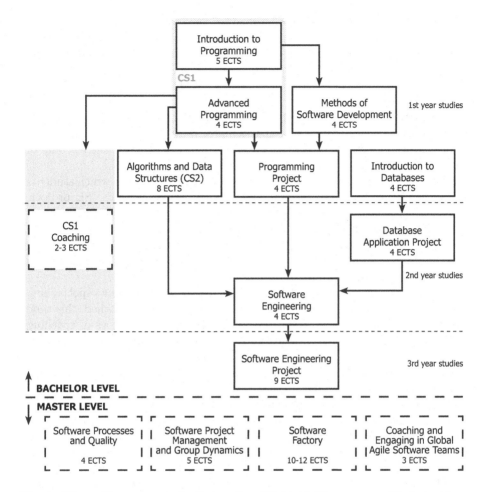

Fig. 1. SE-specific courses at the University of Helsinki. The courses with dashed borders are elective courses relevant for coaching. The arrows indicate prerequisites. The figure differs slightly from that in [20] due to minor curriculum updates.

is a specific coaching course targeted for students at the end of their Master's studies. Topics of the course are agile software development as a concept, agile methodology in distributed settings, and coaching of agile teams taught through problem- and case-based learning techniques. Students also have the opportunity to work under agile coaches in the Master's degree capstone project Software Factory [24]. Due to the technical prerequisites, all of these courses are offered quite late in the studies, see Fig. 1 for placement of the SE courses in the degree programme.

A purpose of the SE subtrack of the department is to educate experts on the path towards *software craftsmanship* [25,26,27]. This involves getting the students to focus on software quality, receive a broad understanding of the field and pursue continuous improvement. The courses forming our CS1 are purposefully designed and marketed to be the first steps on a road towards true SE expertise[1]. The emphasis is not only on learning to program, but also on how to program according to industry best practices with the intention to write understandable, easily maintainable and correctly working code. As even the first programming course emphasizes best practices in the industry, it is a suitable setting for our early start in software coaching[2].

In this way coaching is embedded in the curriculum early on. First, students are themselves coached when they participate in CS1. Then they can act as junior coaches in CS1. At this stage, coaching means facilitating the learning of a single CS1 participant.

A broader view of coaching is experienced in the SE Project in which students are coached by the faculty and graduate TAs. At the start of the SE project, the coach of each project group acts in the roles of product owner and scrum master, but during the project they gradually help project participants to take the responsibilities of these roles [20]. After participating in the SE project, many of the students showing interest and capability for coaching are hired as TAs to coach future SE projects.

After starting their Master's degree studies, many of the students specializing in SE take part in the Software Factory where they are again coached, this time by experienced agile coaches from our faculty. Besides experiences of coaching and being coached, the Master's degree studies contain many courses on topics related to coaching that give students more opportunities for self-reflection and deepening their theoretical knowledge on the topic. Of course not all CS students follow through the entire coaching track, but those who specialize in SE have the opportunity to experience coaching from multiple perspectives.

This interplay between observing a coach while *being coached* and *acting as coach* and thus modeling coaching to others throughout the studies, is fully embedded in the curriculum. It facilitates the progress to become an agile coach as "becoming an agile coach entails education, experience, and practice [...] 'being' an agile coach in all you do sets a powerful example for everyone you coach" [5].

4   Coaching "Course"

The early coaching approach is structured through a format that emphasizes active student engagement over everything else, selection of motivated coaching candidates, and scaffolding of coaches by senior faculty members. The structure is technically a course with study credit to formalize it as a genuine part of a

---

[1] The CS1 courses can be found as MOOCs at http://mooc.fi entitled Object-Oriented Programming with Java [21].

[2] In apprenticeship education, the term "coaching" has been used to refer to the activities of the course teacher (see e.g. [28,29]). We want to emphasize that coaching in our context is considered a different act from teaching, even if the coaches in CS1 perform as mentors and teaching assistants (TAs) [30]. Coaching is something that the *students* do, in order to learn coaching (in addition to helping fellow students to learn programming).

degree. (See Fig. 1 for the position of the course CS1 Coaching within the SE track.) It is important that coaching is a formal activity of the department, as it sets the message that the students are allowed and encouraged to participate, and that they are expected to learn from the experience, even if they are not taught in a traditional sense.

When XA-based CS1 courses began in 2010, the coaching course was not a part of the teaching organization of the course. The students received coaching by teaching assistants selected by the routine selection process of the department. The initial idea of giving students the opportunity to act as coaches as early as possible came from the students themselves. An eager student who had just finished XA-based CS1 approached the faculty in charge of the course and asked – even demanded – to be allowed to help in coaching the students in the next semester CS1 course. After realizing the additional benefits for our evolving CS curriculum SE track, in which agile software engineering principles and practices play a major role [20], the faculty welcomed the voluntary coaches. From the very beginning it was decided that the students' coaching involvement in the CS1 course was to be organized formally, i.e. students would earn study credits depending on the amount of their involvement.

Initially, this "coaching course" was not marketed nor included in the official study plan. Therefore, the first iterations had only a few participating junior coaches, based on word-of-mouth recruiting. After the initial experiment, the number of students has steadily increased: during the fall 2012 semester we had 26 students as junior coaches and 6 students as senior coaches, coaching our 185 new CS1 students. We aim to have roughly a 1:5 coach-to-student ratio in order to make sure that there are enough CS1 students to be coached in the XA computer labs.

4.1   Connecting Coaching to XA

There are clear similarities and synergies between XA education and students as future agile coaches. Fraser et al. state the most important purpose of agile coaching as "facilitating learning" [31]. This same goal is shared by instructors providing scaffolding for students in XA. A good agile coach tries to make herself unnecessary as soon as possible, i.e. helps the team and the team members to flourish [5] bridging directly to the idea of the scaffolding and fading phases in the teaching framework of apprenticeship-based teaching [17,29].

As XA is a form of apprenticeship education, the "pyramid" of the stakeholders is essential in organizing the CS1 programming course: (1) there are *responsible teachers* (tenured teachers also working as coaches) that are on the top of the pyramid, crafting material and exercises, coordinating and controlling the operation; (2) *senior coaches* (teaching assistants on a payroll) who work as coaches and contribute to exercises in addition to helping the students; (3) *junior coaches* (students taking the CS1 Coaching course), who learn to assist novice programmers by helping students in the XA labs and by being a part of the teaching team; and finally, (4) *students* of the CS1 course (potential junior coaches of future courses).

XA emphasizes individual efforts of students with continuous interaction between all parties, so using XA as a training ground for aspiring coaches is only natural. Junior coaches are typically students in a very early stage of their studies (the CS1 Coaching course can be taken after only one semester of studies); advancing to the stage of a senior coach might take as little as two semesters.

Apprenticeship-based learning stresses the importance of a situative view of learning, which emphasizes that learning activities should take place in the same context as they are practiced [16,11,18]. This is also considered in the coaching activities, which take learning of coaching into a genuine environment. All of the stakeholders in coaching, i.e. teachers in charge, senior and junior coaches, form a *community of practice* [10,11] of coaches for the duration of the course [30]. The community negotiates its meaning by supporting students and actually seeing the results of their participation in coaching.

4.2   Embedding Coaching Course into CS1

The ultimate goal of our SE curriculum is to educate proficient experts in the field of SE. Following the practice of constructive alignment [32] the CS1 Coaching course has its own formal learning objectives[3] that are available for the faculty and students alike. The learning objectives, arranged in a matrix (see Tab. 1), state the principal themes, prerequisites and the evaluation criteria as learning objectives.

The objectives are presented in the form of (1) *approaches the learning objective*, which states the minimum requirements for the activity, (2) *reaches the learning objectives* which mark the requirement of full completion of the course and (3) *deepens the learning objective* which states possible additional objectives and future directions that might be taken into consideration during the activity but are not required.

4.3   Selection of Coaches

The main requirements for participation in the CS1 Coaching course are the student's willingness to act as an instructor and a decent-to-good grade from CS1, ability to produce quality code and some technical skills (see Tab. 1).

Applications to register as a junior coach are sent well before the start of the term using an online application form. When applying, one needs to type in an open application as well as basic background information such as related grades. If the applicant passes initial filtering (good progress of studies so far), and not known to the course staff beforehand, the applicant is invited for an interview. The interview serves as a guarantee of the necessary people skills needed to be allowed to instruct novice programmers. So far, all applicants have been accepted. As CS1 is organized three times each academic year, it has been

---

[3] All mandatory and most of the steadily recurring courses have publicly available learning objective matrices, so students are familiar with them and expect them for every new course.

Table 1. Learning objectives for CS1 Coaching

Principal theme	Enhancing programming skills of peer-students	Instruction skills	Technical tools
Prerequisite knowledge	Good performance in CS1 and capability to produce quality code		Is capable of using VCS and other necessary tools
Approaches the learning objectives	Understands programming code that others have written Notices mistakes in the readability of code written by others Notices mistakes in the design of programs made by others	Is capable of instructing different kinds of people Gives and receives oral feedback Attends scheduled meetings and performs the instruction duties	Deepens the skills to use VCS and other tools Solves CS1 tasks and recognizes different kinds of mistakes in them
Reaches the learning objectives	Recognizes correct solutions of others, even if they differ from own solutions Can instruct mentored students, so that they are capable of correcting their problems with their programming code	Is encouraging Understands that people differ as learners Does not obtrude own solutions, but functions in a learner centered fashion Speaks less than the students Can function as a member of a team of instructors	Recognizes good and bad automated tests
Deepens the learning objectives	Is capable of creating useful tasks and automated tests for CS1 course material	Recognizes factors which help improvement as a teacher Makes students enthusiastic of programming	

possible to allocate most of the junior coach applicants; if not right away, then in the next cycle. It must be stressed that the selected junior coaches become a part of a teaching team and are not expected to perform coaching alone in the XA lab.

Senior coaches are recruited among the more experienced students from the department who have good grades and pace of studies and can show skills in coaching either through performing well as a junior coach, performing well as a teaching assistant in other duties at the department or through work- or hobby-related experience. Unlike the junior coaches, the senior coaches are employees of the department and are therefore subject to standard employement regulations.

4.4 What the Coaches Do

The junior coaches have enrolled voluntarily in an elective SE course. They are motivated and have shown willingness to improve as coaches of novice programmers. This *deliberate practice* [33,34] of coaching skills is the main tool used to pursue the learning objective of the CS1 Coaching course. In practice, the coaches obtain only little training prior to actual coaching, and are expected to learn while coaching.

The main task of the coaches is to be a vital part of the scaffolding that makes XA-based programming education possible [29,19,30]. The coaches support the students to learn programming by providing individual and interactive feedback to the students. This means that coaches help novice programmers make working software, review their code and point them towards necessary information. An important aspect is that the coaches are expected to embrace the ideas of the students and not obtrude their own solutions on the students, but function in a learner-centered fashion (see Tab. 1). In addition to the soft- and hard-skill related benefits, e.g. communication, experiencing the meaningfulness of best programming practices, we engage our new students in our department's community: the presence of young junior coaches is expected to make the transition from secondary school to the university easier for freshmen students [35].

In addition to the actual coaching, the coaches are encouraged to complete all the CS1 programming exercises before they are released to students. This strengthens their programming routine as well as helps them to direct more time to actual scaffolding instead of wasting time trying to remember what the exercises were about. To increase the formation of the community of coaches, the coaches are encouraged to discuss the exercises with each other, for example in IRC chat. This medium also serves as the main support mechanism for the coaches outside the XA computer lab and the weekly meetings.

An important aspect of the programming exercises of the CS1 course is that the solutions are automatically assessed by an assessment server through a plug-in in the IDE the students use (see [36] for details). The server runs automated tests in order to check for the correctness of the solutions and performs the bookkeeping of the course. This ensures that the coaches can concentrate on coaching, not on trivial correctness checks and error-prone human bookkeeping of student progress.

The junior coaches reflect on the upcoming material and act as beta-testers for the material and exercises by searching for weaknesses in automated tests and inconsistencies in course material. This gives the faculty an opportunity to do improvements before the exercises and course material are released to the course participants. It gives the coaches an opportunity to learn to recognize good and bad automated tests and also leads to a high-quality material as coaches help to make sure that there are no mistakes left in the exercises.

Before the first contact with the students, a 2-hour meeting is organized for the coaches. Faculty members together with the coaches (both junior and senior) go through necessary administrative issues as well as the most important pedagogical practices of coaching CS1. The most crucial information has been gathered in a coaches' set of guidelines and responsibilities that both the coaches and faculty members sign personally.

The guidelines are formulated in an instructive and inclusive manner so that the coaches should observe and proactively coach everyone in trouble. Feedback to the students needs to be constructive and positive. Coaches are instructed to be active even if the students do not ask any questions.

Coaches concentrate not only to the correctness but also to the style of the code: indentation; naming of variables, methods and classes; and method length. In addition, coaches push the students to refactor their code towards a clearer and more maintainable solution so that "the person sitting in the next seat should also understand the solution".

While interviewing the applicants for junior coaches, we have noticed that most, if not all, have a good sense of how an instructor is supposed to scaffold students in the CS1 course. Most of the applicants can already determine what type of coaching is beneficial to students and what is not, e.g. one should only nudge the student towards a correct solution and never give the solution. This is not surprising since all the students applying for the coaching course have so far participated in the XA-based CS1 course themselves.

Despite good prerequisites, the learning objectives could not be obtained without proper scaffolding of the juniors themselves. This scaffolding is conducted by the faculty member(s) in the form of meetings and peer-support. The faculty members as teachers in charge of the course are naturally also present in the XA labs. Students as coaches also perform implicit self-reflection with other coaches while instructing, as well as participate actively in discussions in an online chat.

During the course the responsible teachers organize biweekly face-to-face meetings where all participants of the coaching community are present. Meetings are typically organized as retrospectives, further introducing agile software development practices [3]. In the meetings, the teachers responsible for the course inspect and reflect on what has been done during the past two weeks, and bring up good and bad experiences and practices to the awareness of the whole team. The team identifies top good practices and marks them as *to-be-kept*, i.e. they should work also during the next weeks. Top bad practices are marked as *to-be-improved* that deserve special focus during the next few weeks. The goal is to have a few of the to-be-improved turned into good practices for the future.

5   Results and Evaluation

The results show that facilitating software coaching as an early part of a CS curriculum is possible. We started XA-based education in 2010 and the first junior coaches entered the stage in spring 2011. From the fall 2010 to fall 2012 semesters, we have had 101 persons working in our XA labs in different roles. Out of the 101 persons, 78 have served as junior coaches, and 59 as senior coaches (as some have served as both). During the two years, we have been able to offer 5468 hours of targeted hands-on guidance to our CS1 students. This has been done while improving the pass rate [37] and raising the demand level [20] of CS1.

In order to gain some sense of the learning from the junior coaching experiences, we posted a questionnaire to all the students that have been junior coaches in XA-based CS1. We received 46 replies which results in a response rate of 59%. Figure 2 shows the questions and the distribution of the coaches' answers.

One of the main themes of coaching is how to improve the programming skills of students in CS1. This puts some demand on the skills of the coaches themselves. To give appropriate feedback to CS1 students, the coach needs to learn

I have become more proficient ...

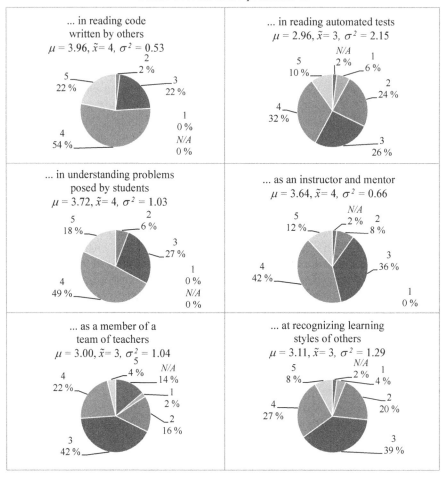

Fig. 2. Post-course survey of junior coaches (N=46) with Likert scale (1=not at all, 5=a lot). N/A stands for "cannot say" and is not considered in calculating the mean μ and variance σ^2. Median is denoted by $\tilde{x}$.

to communicate not only verbally but through written code. This is not only a valuable exercise for the coaches but also intended to make the coaches realize the importance of best programming practices. In the end, if the code is unreadable to others, the maintainability and the functionality of the code diminishes. The learning objective is therefore not only to recognize these problems but to be able to help other students overcome them. We can see in Fig. 2 that "I have become more proficient in reading program code written by others" scores uniformly high (μ=3.96), with low variance (σ^2=.53).

The other main theme of the course is improving coaching and instruction skills. Here, the learning objective is to encounter different kinds of learners and recognize their ways of thinking. This skill should make the junior coaches understand that their own ways of looking at things, e.g. tackling a programming task, might differ from those of others. As modern software development is done in teams, an understanding of different working habits and styles is crucial. This is further emphasized by the fact that the apprentices perform team teaching, i.e. coach together along with others, and have to agree with faculty about the practices of coaching and instruction. As we can see in Fig. 2, all of these interpersonal skills score relatively high ("member of a team", "understanding questions", "as instructor and mentor", "recognizing learning styles").

The junior coaches should also deepen their knowledge about the use of professional software development tools. The course material and exercises are maintained using a version control system, and automated testing plays a key role in how the course is formed [21,36]. We can see in Fig. 2 that "in reading automated tests" the score variance is very high ($\sigma^2=2.15$). This is probably due to the varying roles of the junior coaches as some take a more active role in creating and debugging tests. We do not view this as a problem *per se* as it is only natural for coaches to serve in different roles. Automated tests have been used in CS1 material only for a relatively short period of time and are evolving rapidly. It is expected that the role of automated tests will grow in future.

In addition to the Likert scale questions, coaches were able to tell if they had any coaching-related background. As expected, eager coaches tend to have *some* earlier experiences. Even though more than half reported something, background experiences were mostly minuscule, such as a week as a substitute teacher, or group leader in the boy scouts.

Open comments revealed that the coaching experience was highly valued. Quotes such as "coaching is hard but awesome!" crystallize the feelings of many coaches. Other, more targeted open comments included "learning to cope with chaos" and "learning to be more patient", as well as references to "learning to switch fast between mental tasks". Maybe the most insightful comment noted enhanced metacognitive skills:

> Coaching in the XA lab enhanced my view of programming. Afterwards I have noticed how beneficial it was to go through the whole problem solving process from the beginning with another person. That is, from reading the assignment given, all the way to completing the tests. Other people might start to tackle the problem from a completely other angle. This, of course, opens up new paths in my own way of programming.

6 Conclusions

We have been able to give our students an opportunity to act as coaches in a realistic setting at an early stage of their studies. The most important benefit for the students that are participating in coaching very early is the experience that can be used for reflection on upcoming coaching-related courses, as well as when being coached. The experience is also expected to help students to understand the importance of coaching as it pertains to software maintainability, development performance and sensed meaningfulness of software engineering.

In our earlier research, we have seen that the results of CS1 have been significantly improving when using the XA-based approach [19]. Deploying "rookie" students as coaches has not deteriorated the course results. In fact, the number of coaches has allowed us to significantly increase the amount of support and lab times available for our students.

Having a course where students are able to act as coaches during an early part of their studies is only one step. In our curriculum, the students are first coached in CS1, then become coaches, and later on are coached again. This interplay of roles is available throughout the curriculum, and becomes more "real" as the students proceed in their studies. After being a coach for individuals, students are coached as a part of a team, and later on have the opportunity to coach a team. Although there may be risks involved in our approach, e.g. related to the learning of the students, they are out of scope for this paper. For additional information, see [30].

As coaching is about guiding individuals and teams towards better working practises, it is important that all stakeholders are involved. In our approach, course instructors participate in the coaching activities, and coach the coaches as well as the students. All participants need to spend time in the changing environment to understand the need for change; adaptation should only happen after inspection and only if new practises can bring genuine additional value.

Coaching can be realized by e.g. leading by example, or by gently nudging the participants into a direction, where they are able to realize their mistakes and thus improve. In essense, it is about giving as much freedom as possible while providing scaffolding when needed. The goal is that the coached individuals and teams become self-directed entities that are able to respond to change, and strive to reach their full potential.

Acknowledgements. We thank the anonymous reviewers for their valuable feedback. We also wish to thank Mr. Matti Tahvanainen, who was the first eager student to demand the start of this activity as a formal way to be a part of XA-based education.

This work has been partly funded by a grant from the Centennial Foundation of Technology Industries in Finland.

References

1. Schwaber, K., Beedle, M.: Agile Software Development with SCRUM. Prentice Hall (2002)
2. Poppendieck, M., Poppendieck, T.: Lean Software Development: An Agile Toolkit. Addison-Wesley Professional (2003)
3. Beck, K., Andres, C.: Extreme Programming Explained: Embrace Change, 2nd edn. The XP Series. Addison-Wesley Professional (2004)
4. Davies, R., Sedley, L.: Agile Coaching. Pragmatic Bookshelf Series. Pragmatic Bookshelf (2009)

5. Adkins, L.: Coaching Agile Teams: A Companion for ScrumMasters, Agile Coaches, and Project Managers in Transition. Addison-Wesley Professional (2010)
6. Anderson, D.J.: Kanban. Blue Hole (2010)
7. Hedin, G., Bendix, L., Magnusson, B.: Coaching coaches. In: Marchesi, M., Succi, G. (eds.) XP 2003. LNCS, vol. 2675, pp. 154–160. Springer, Heidelberg (2003)
8. Hedin, G., Bendix, L., Magnusson, B.: Teaching extreme programming to large groups of students. Journal of Systems and Software 74(2), 133–146 (2005)
9. Martin, R.C.: Clean Code: A Handbook of Agile Software Craftsmanship. Robert C. Martin series. Prentice Hall (2009)
10. Wenger, E.: Communities of Practice: Learning, Meaning, and Identity. Learning in Doing Series. Cambridge University Press (1998)
11. Lave, J., Wenger, E.: Situated Learning: Legitimate Peripheral Participation. Learning in Doing. Cambridge University Press (1991)
12. Astrachan, O., Reed, D.: AAA and CS 1: The applied apprenticeship approach to CS 1. SIGCSE Bulletin 27, 1–5 (1995)
13. Kölling, M., Barnes, D.J.: Enhancing apprentice-based learning of Java. In: Proc. of the 35th SIGCSE Technical Symposium on Computer Science Education, SIGCSE 2004, pp. 286–290. ACM, New York (2004)
14. Vihavainen, A., Paksula, M., Luukkainen, M.: Extreme apprenticeship method in teaching programming for beginners. In: Proc. of the 42nd ACM Technical Symposium on Computer Science Education, SIGCSE 2011, pp. 93–98. ACM (2011)
15. Vihavainen, A., Paksula, M., Luukkainen, M., Kurhila, J.: Extreme apprenticeship method: key practices and upward scalability. In: Proc. of the 16th Annual Joint Conference on Innovation and Technology in Computer Science Education. ITiCSE 2011, pp. 273–277. ACM (2011)
16. Brown, J., Collins, A., Duguid, P.: Situated cognition culture of learning. Educational Researcher 18(1), 32 (1989)
17. Collins, A., Brown, J., Holum, A.: Cognitive apprenticeship: Making thinking visible. American Educator 15(3), 6–46 (1991)
18. Collins, A., Greeno, J.G.: Situative view of learning. In: Aukrust, V.G. (ed.) Learning and Cognition, pp. 64–68. Elsevier Science (2010)
19. Kurhila, J., Vihavainen, A.: Management, structures and tools to scale up personal advising in large programming courses. In: Proc. of the 2011 Conference on Information Technology Education, SIGITE 2011, pp. 3–8. ACM (2011)
20. Luukkainen, M., Vihavainen, A., Vikberg, T.: Three years of design-based research to reform a software engineering curriculum. In: Proc. of the 13th Annual Conference on Information Technology Education, SIGITE 2012, pp. 209–214. ACM (2012)
21. Vihavainen, A., Luukkainen, M., Kurhila, J.: Multi-faceted support for MOOC in programming. In: Proc. of the 13th Annual Conference on Information Technology Education, SIGITE 2012, pp. 171–176. ACM (2012)
22. Dodero, G., Di Cerbo, F.: Extreme apprenticeship goes blended: An experience. In: 12th IEEE International Conference on Advanced Learning Technologies, pp. 324–326 (2012)
23. Hautala, T., Romu, T., Rämö, J., Vikberg, T.: Extreme apprenticeship method in teaching university-level mathematics. In: Proc. of the 12th International Congress on Mathematical Education, International Commission on Mathematical Instruction (2012)
24. Abrahamsson, P., Kettunen, P., Fagerholm, F.: The set-up of a valuable software engineering research infrastructure of the 2010s. In: Workshop on Valuable Software Products (2010)

25. McBreen, P.: Software Craftsmanship: The New Imperative. Addison-Wesley Professional (2001)
26. Martin, R.C.: The Clean Coder: A Code of Conduct for Professional Programmers. Robert C. Martin Series. Prentice Hall (2011)
27. Luukkainen, M., Vihavainen, A., Vikberg, T.: A software craftsman's approach to data structures. In: Proc. of the 43rd ACM Technical Symposium on Computer Science Education, SIGCSE 2012, pp. 439–444. ACM (2012)
28. Bareiss, R., Radley, M.: Coaching via cognitive apprenticeship. In: Proc. of the 41st ACM Technical Symposium on Computer Science Education, SIGCSE 2010, pp. 162–166. ACM (2010)
29. Caspersen, M.E., Bennedsen, J.: Instructional design of a programming course: a learning theoretic approach. In: Proc. of the 3rd International Workshop on Computing Education Research, ICER 2007, pp. 111–122. ACM (2007)
30. Vihavainen, A., Vikberg, T., Luukkainen, M., Kurhila, J.: Massive increase in eager TAs: Experiences from extreme apprenticeship-based CS1. To appear in: Proc. of the 18th Annual Joint Conference on Innovation and Technology in Computer Science Education (July 2013)
31. Fraser, S., Lundh, E., Davies, R., Eckstein, J., Larsen, D., Vilkki, K.: Perspectives on agile coaching. In: Abrahamsson, P., Marchesi, M., Maurer, F. (eds.) XP 2009. LNBIP, vol. 31, pp. 271–276. Springer, Heidelberg (2009)
32. Biggs, J., Tang, C.: Teaching for quality learning at university: what the student does. Society for Research into Highter Education. McGraw-Hill (2007)
33. Ericsson, K.A., Krampe, R.T., Tesch-Romer, C.: The role of deliberate practice in the acquisition of expert performance. Psychological Review 100(3), 363–406 (1993)
34. Litzinger, T.A., Lattuca, L.R., Hadgraft, R.G., Newstetter, W.C.: Engineering education and the development of expertise. Journal of Engineering Education 100(1), 123–150 (2011)
35. Clark, M., Lovric, M.: Suggestion for a theoretical model for secondary-tertiary transition in mathematics. Mathematics Education Research Journal 20, 25–37 (2008)
36. Vihavainen, A., Vikberg, T., Luukkainen, M., Pärtel, M.: Scaffolding students' learning using Test My Code. To appear in: Proc. of the 17th Annual Joint Conference on Innovation and Technology in Computer Science Education (July 2013)
37. Vihavainen, A., Luukkainen, M.: Results from a three-year transition to the extreme apprenticeship method. To appear in: Proc. of the 13th IEEE International Conference on Advanced Learning Technologies (July 2013)

Introducing Programmers to Pair Programming: A Controlled Experiment

A.S.M. Sajeev[1] and Subhajit Datta[2]

[1] University of New England, Australia
sajeev@une.edu.au
http://mcs.une.edu.au/~sajeev
[2] IBM Research, Bangalore, India
subhajit.datta@acm.org
http://www.dattas.net

Abstract. Pair programming is a key characteristic of the Extreme Programming (XP) method. Through a controlled experiment we investigate pair programming behaviour of programmers without prior experience in XP. The factors investigated are: (a) characteristics of pair programming that are less favored (b) perceptions of team effectiveness and how they relate to product quality, and (c) whether it is better to train a pair by giving routine tasks first or by giving complex tasks first. Our results show that: (a) the least liked aspects of pair programming were having to share the screen, keyboard and mouse, and having to switch between the roles of driver and navigator (b) programmers solved complex problems more effectively in pairs compared to routine problems, however, perceptions of team effectiveness was higher when solving routine problems than when solving complex problems and (c) programmers who started pair programming with routine tasks and moved on to complex tasks were more effective than those who started with complex ones and moved on to routine ones. We discuss how these results will assist the industry in inducting programmers without prior pair-programming experience into XP process environments.

Keywords: pair programming, empirical software engineering, agile methods, extreme programming, software process, controlled experiment.

1   Introduction

Pair programming is one of the key concepts in agile methods such as XP. It involves two people working as a team to complete a programming task, usually involving, design, coding and testing of the task. One of the pair starts acting as the driver (who will do the keyboard activities) and the other as the navigator (who will watch, analyze, comment and, in general, guide the driver), and the two switch between these roles multiple times for the duration of the task.

Prior research has shown that pair programming when compared to solo programming can produce better outcomes (e.g. [1], [2]), even though others found the argument inconclusive (e.g. [3], [4]). Nevertheless, the popularity of agile

H. Baumeister and B. Weber (Eds.): XP 2013, LNBIP 149, pp. 31–45, 2013.

methods compared to heavy-weight processes means that increasingly more programmers and software engineers will be required to do pair programming. This includes both professionals with work experience and fresh graduates. The question then is what to expect when engineers without prior background in pair-programming are brought into the XP method and how best to "prepare" them to be effective pair programmers. Addressing such questions will assist the industry to fine tune their induction processes for new pair programmers. The main objective of this paper is to report on an empirical study that advances research in these directions.

We specifically address the following research questions:

- What aspects of pair programming are valued most and least by programmers that are new to pair programming?
- Do new pair programmers work better as a pair in routine problems or in complex problems?
- How best to prepare a pair? Are pairs that start with routine tasks and move on to complex tasks more effective than pairs that start with complex tasks and move on to routine tasks?

In order to address these research questions, we conducted a randomised controlled experiment. Compared to an observational study, a controlled experiment allows us to set controls in order to measure accurately the effect of treatment on the experimental group. It reduces the effect of confounding variables which otherwise could be present in observational studies were the researcher has little control over the events.

There is significant work in the literature on various aspects of pair programming. This involves both experienced pair programmers and those who are new to pair programming. However, as discussed in Section 6, the questions we investigate here have not been explored in the literature with the view of better understanding how programmers without pair-programming experience could be prepared for the method.

The rest of the paper is organized as follows. In the next section, we review the related literature. In Section 3, we describe the research method. Section 4 gives the results of the analysis and in Section 5 we discuss the limitations of the study. Finally, in Section 6 we conclude the paper by discussing the implications of our results for the Information Technology (IT) industry.

2   Literature Review

The literature related to our study can be roughly classified into three themes: those investigating models and frameworks for pair programming, those testing the question "is pair programming better than solo programming", and those investigating the benefits of pair programming.

In investigating frameworks, Fronza et al. collected data non-invasively in an industrial development team for 10 months to understand how pair programming helps the integration of novices in a team [5]. Using social network analysis techniques, the authors analyzed developer interactions and proposed a model for novice integration in teams engaged in spontaneous pair programming. Gallis et al., on the other hand, have pointed out the contradiction in the claims around pair programming, which they attribute to the lack of theoretical foundation supporting empirical research [6]. To address this situation, the authors presented a framework for pair programming research by identifying and categorizing important independent, dependent, and context variables, and exploring their relationships. This work was extended by Ally et al.based on a study of pair programming using the Delphi technique [7]. The authors concluded that Gallis et al.'s framework needed to include an additional category of factors relating to organizational matters.

A number of studies compared pair programming with solo programming. Lui and Chan [8] investigated the research question "do pairs outperform individuals in procedural solution tasks?" using Programming Aptitude Test [PAT] rather than traditional programming tasks; the reasoning was that PAT is independent of programming language proficiency and thus language proficiency would not become a confounding variable. They used a measure called REAP (Relative Effort Afforded by Pairs) to compare sole programming productivity with pair-programming productivity. Lui and Chan [8] also introduced the concept of repeat programming in studying pair programming; this is where the pairs repeated the same programming task multiple times. They used the term *novice* to mean that a programmer is doing a repeated task for the first time, and the term *expert* for one who has repeated the same task several times. They concluded that "novice-novice pairs against novice-solos are much more productive in terms of elapsed time and software quality than expert-expert pairs against expert solos". Madeyski investigated how pair programming fares vis-a-vis solo programming for thoroughness and fault detection effectiveness of test suites and did not find support for anecdotal evidence that the former facilitates these activities [4]. Arisholm et al [1] conducted a one-day controlled experiment to test the effectiveness of pair programming with respect to complex tasks. They used junior, intermediate and senior staff from local industries as subjects. They compared pair-programming with individual programming, as well as they studied effectiveness in using pair programming in simpler tasks versus complex tasks. Dybå et al. examined the fundamental assumption behind pair programming – that two heads are better than one – by conducting a meta-analysis of existing studies around pair programming's effects on quality, duration, and effort [2]. They concluded that whether two heads are indeed better than one is a nuanced question, and the answer depends on programming exercise and task complexity. They found empirical evidence that two heads can achieve higher correctness on complex programming tasks and be able to finish simpler tasks earlier. In a subsequent paper the authors extended their results and concluded that, higher quality on complex tasks comes with the price of higher effort and reduced completion time is offset by lower quality [9]. The authors emphasized the need for more attention to moderating factors while exploring the effects of pair programming. Vanhanen and Lessenius reported results from a study of three pair programming and two solo programming teams performing the same 400-hour fixed effort project with a focus on understanding the aspects of productivity, defects, design quality, knowledge transfer, and enjoyment of work [10]. They found that pairs have an initial "learning time" that increases the development effort upfront vis-a-vis solo programming. Although this difference tapers off later in the development cycle, it affects the overall productivity of the pairs. Complexity of tasks was found not to influence effort difference between pair and solo programming. Pair programmers delivered systems with higher number of defects, but had higher knowledge transfer; they also gave weak evidence for higher enjoyment of work. In a subsequent work, the authors studied the perceived effects of pair programming vis-a-vis solo programming in large scale, industrial software development [11]. They surveyed 28 developers and found pair programming's positive effects were maximum for learning, schedule adherence, knowing other developers, and team spirit. Vanhanen and Korpi summarize the experiences of extensive pair programming in an industrial project [12]. They found that frequent rotation between the driver/navigator roles improved knowledge transfer, and the developers perceived that pair programming was better suited for complex tasks rather than easy tasks. Xu and Rajlich conducted a case study with six students in a graduate software engineering course who were assigned to work on incremental changes to an application either individually or in pairs [13]. They found that the paired students delivered their change requests more quickly and with a higher quality. Similarly, Sison reported results from an experiment on the use of pair programming by undergraduate students in a software engineering course at a Philippine university [14]. The author found evidence that defect densities were significantly lower for programs written by pair programming vis-a-vis those written by non pair programming teams.

On the benefits of pair programming, Begel and Nagappan reported results from a longitudinal study of pair programming at Microsoft [15]. They found that pair-programming's biggest benefits were perceived to be fewer bugs, wider understanding of code, and overall higher code quality. Additionally, most of the study's participants were more amenable to a partner with complementary skills, flexibility, and good communication skills. Coman et al. examined the dynamics of the pairing process in a mature agile team of 16 developers in a three months study and found support for the claim that pair programming is useful for training and knowledge transfer [16].

3   Research Method

3.1   Participants

Our participants are 144 students of the two year Master of Technology (MTech) program at the International Institute of Information Technology, Bangalore (IIT-B); they were enrolled in a software engineering course mandatory for all MTech students. The experiment was conducted as part of programming skills assessments in the course for which they received credit. All students had an undergraduate computing degree in science or engineering. Sixty nine percent of the students had no work experience, 7% had less than a year's experience, and the remaining 24% had more than one year experience in the industry with maximum four years; 89% of those with work experience worked as programmers or software developers. Of the 144 subjects who participated in the study, only seven had prior experience with pair programming; these seven subjects participated in the experiment, but were excluded from the analysis of results. (One of them was part of the control and two formed a pair, the remaining four formed pairs with non-experienced subjects; those four non-experienced subjects were also excluded from the analyses in order to avoid their partners' pair-programming experience confounding the results.)

All participants were proficient (through work experience and/or prior coursework) in object oriented analysis, design and programming, and rated their Java programming skills at level 3 or above, on a scale of 0 = novice, 5 = expert. Even then, participants were allowed to complete their assigned programming tasks in either Java or C++. (There was only one submission in C++.)

Thus consistent with our research objectives, our subjects were a collection of fresh graduates and professionals with work experience up to four years, but none with prior experience in pair-programming.

3.2   Method

Our research method was a randomized concurrent controlled experiment spanning three sessions of programming. In a controlled experiment, one group acts as control (in our case, they consisted of solo programmers) and the other acts as the experimental group (in our case, pair programmers). In a randomized experiment, each participant is chosen at random to be in the control group or in the experimental group, and in a concurrent experiment, all groups do the activities (in technical terms, undergo the treatment) at the same time.

The subjects were randomly divided into an experimental group and a control group; this was done by drawing lots from a bowl. The experimental group consisted of 50 pairs of programmers whereas the control group consisted of 44 solo programmers. (As mentioned in the previous section, the pairs and controls that involved people with prior pair-programming experience were excluded from analysis thus resulting in 45 pairs and 43 controls.) Both the experimental group and the control group were further divided into two sub-groups in a two-factorial design; for reasons explained below, one subgroup was named Routine-to-Complex cohort, and the other, Complex-to-Routine cohort (See Figure 1).

3.3   Procedure

The experiment was organized as follows:

1. Approval to conduct the study was obtained by the second author from the institute authorities.

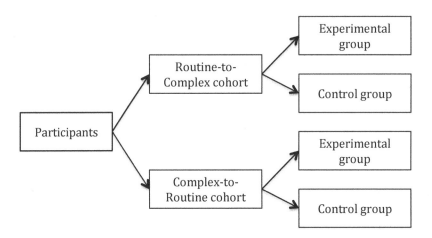

Fig. 1. Formation of experimental and control groups

2. An introductory lecture was given to all participants on pair-programming by the second author (who is an adjunct professor at the Institute) to ensure that all participants understood, in theory, the principles and practices of pair-programming.

3. An experiment is an event that occurs over a pre-defined time period. This means that we need to abstract real-world entities to fit into the framework of the experiment. In our case, we needed to model routine tasks and challenging tasks that pair programmers would encounter in the industry. We abstracted them into a set of programming problems of three levels of complexity (easy, moderately difficult and hard). The problems were selected from end of the chapter exercises of standard Java programming textbooks with appropriate modifications; each problem was annotated with a particular level of difficulty. In addition to that, the second author[1] and each of the four teaching assistants (TA) who assisted him solved the problems independently to confirm their differential level of complexity. For the easy level, we had four exercises that were interchangeable in terms of their difficulty, and similarly for the medium level. For the challenging level, we had two exercises that were interchangeable in terms of their difficulty. To ensure problems at the same level are of similar difficulty, they were selected from the same textbooks and further confirmed by ensuring they take similar amount of time to solve.

4. We prepared a set of test cases (input and expected output) for each problem. The subjects were given, in addition to the problem specification, a subset of the test cases to assist them in deciding when a task is complete. The full set of test cases were used by the researchers to give a quality score to the program produced. The quality score to the solution given was out of 10,

---

[1] Those interested in replicating the experiment may contact this author for the exercises.

where 0 means does not compile, 5 means means passes 50% of the tests and 10 means passes all tests.

5. The experiment was conducted in three sessions (see Figure 2). The Routine-to-Complex cohort was given the easy problems in the first session, then in Session 2, problems of medium complexity and finally in Session 3, a challenging problem. The Complex-to-Routine cohort solved problems in the other direction as shown in the figure. Since we selected a sufficient number of problems, those given in a session were not reused in another; this was to prevent subsequent sessions being affected by any discussions by the participants outside the experiment of solutions and problems they have worked on in a session.

6. At the end of each session, both a quantitative and qualitative evaluation of the groups were conducted. For quantitative evaluation, as mentioned above, the programs were tested for correctness; this was done by the TAs under the second author's supervision and a score of 0 to 10 is given. For qualitative evaluation, each individual in the experimental groups was given a team-effectiveness questionnaire. The questionnaire measured on a five point Likert scale (where $1 =$ disagree strongly, $3 =$ neither agree nor disagree and $5 =$ agree strongly) each programmer's perceptions on the effectiveness of pair programming. These perceptions were also analysed separately (as described in Section 4.1) to identify how the subjects favoured different pair programming practices.

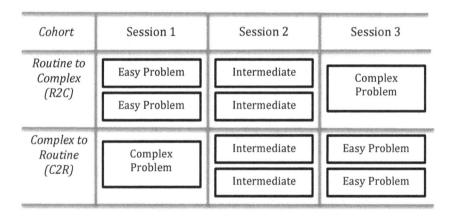

Fig. 2. Organization of the cohorts

3.4 Statistical Tests

For comparison between mean values of two groups, we used the independent samples t-tests [17]. The significance level, α was set at 0.05. Levene's test was used to check homogeneity of variances. The analysis were conducted using SPSS software package. We did not adjust for the potential Type-1 error increase from multiple tests; Bonferroni's adjustment, for instance, lowers the alpha level for multiple tests; however, some researchers recommend presenting the p-value instead of adjusting the alpha-level and let the readers decide on the results (for example, see [18]). Eta-squared was used to determine the effect size; a value of 0.01 is considered a small effect whereas 0.14 or above is a large effect [19].

4 Results

4.1 Pair Programming Characteristics

Figure 3 shows in descending order how the subjects favored different character-istics of pair programming. The explanation for the features is given in Table 1. The most favored ones were that *pair program allowed good discussions of the problems and solution strategies*, and that *it was helpful in developing teamwork skills*. The least favored characteristics were *the need to regularly swap the roles of driver and navigator* and *the need to share the screen, keyboard and mouse*. Also, the statement: *pair programming makes programming faster* was among the least agreed items.

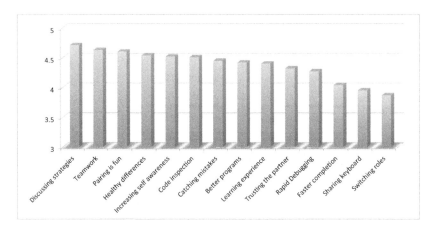

Fig. 3. Mean score on a 5-point Likert scale[3] for different pair programming character-istics (5 is strong agreement and 0 is strong disagreement)

4.2 Routine versus Challenging Development

Routine development is where programmers are familiar with the work and gen-erally know how to proceed to completion, whereas challenging development is where the task that the pair has to address needs lateral thinking and exploring

---

[3] Strictly speaking, Likert scale is ordinal, however, it is not uncommon for researchers to use it as an interval scale (for example: see [20]).

Table 1. Full form of the programming characteristics in charts

Programming Characteristics	Likert Item
Discussing strategies	Our team was good in discussing the problems and solution strategies
Teamwork	Pair programming is helpful in developing teamwork skills
Pairing is fun	I found pair programming fun
Healthy differences	In our team, we sorted out differences in a healthy manner
Increasing self awareness	Working with a partner makes it easy to understand what I am doing and why I am doing it
Code inspection	Having a partner is beneficial for learning to read another programmer's code
Catching mistakes	My partner and I caught each other's mistakes
Better programs	I believe, pair programming leads to better programs than individual programming
Learning experience	I have learned more working in pairs than when I have worked individually
Trusting the partner	My level of trust in my partner is very high
Rapid Debugging	My team found errors more rapidly than if we were working individually
Faster completion	Without pair programming I would have taken longer to complete the programming task(s)
Sharing keyboard	It was easy to share the keyboard, screen and mouse
Switching roles	In my team, we changed the role of 'driver' and 'navigator' fairly regularly

of different strategies in order to come up with a good solution. Intuitively, one could hypothesize that pair programming is more useful and effective for challenging tasks since it literally doubles the brain power. We tested this hypothesis by taking into consideration only the tasks completed in Session 1. The first session in our experiment is where new teams were formed. Not considering all sessions avoids any confounding influence of growing familiarity of partnerships on team effectiveness.

In Session 1, we had the R2C cohort (see Figure 2) solve easy problems and the C2R cohort solve a challenging problem; both cohorts consisted of an experimental group of pairs and a control group of solo programmers. In the discussion below, the pairs of the Session-1 R2C cohort are referred as the routine-group (that is, the group that solved easy problems) and the pairs of the Session-1 C2R cohort as the complex-group (that is, the group that solved a complex problem).

The questions we investigated are:

a) Is there a significant difference between the mean results of the routine-group and the complex-group?
b) Is the mean result of the routine-group significantly better than the mean result of the corresponding control group?
c) Is the mean result of the complex-group significantly better than the mean result of the corresponding control group?

The effectiveness of a group is measured using its (i) mean test score and (ii) mean team-effectiveness score. The answer to Question (a) could tell us which group has performed better, however, that answer would not be relevant unless that group has also performed better in test results than its corresponding control group; otherwise, we did not have to use pair programming to achieve the better results. Thus, answers to Questions (b) and (c) together with (a) should tell us which kinds of problems, pairing is better suited for.

With respect to mean test scores, there is significant difference between the routine-group and the complex-group with (as should be expected) the routine-group scoring much higher mean test scores ($M = 7.06, SD = 2.5$) than the complex-group ($M = 1.32, SD = 1.32$), $p < 0.0001$, $\eta^2 = 0.678$ There is also significant difference in perceived team effectiveness, with the routine group perceiving higher effectiveness ($M = 4.33, SD = 0.39$) than the complex group ($M = 3.99, SD = 0.5$), $p = 0.001$. The practical significance is also large ($\eta^2 = 0.126$). It may be the case that, when the teams are able to get better test scores (which is not unexpected with routine problems) they feel that their team is more effective. When the routine pairs were compared with their control group in test scores, however, there was no significant difference ($M = 7.06, SD = 2.5$ versus $M = 6.19, SD = 3.46; p = 0.306$). On the other hand, when the complex pairs were compared with their control group, there was significant difference albeit with a moderate effect size ($M = 1.32, SD = 1.32$ versus $M = 0.86, SD = 0.36; p = 0.025; \eta^2 = 0.07$). This is a very interesting result. *Pair programmers achieved significantly better results than their corresponding solo programmers in solving complex problems, however, they perceived pair programming to be less effective. On the other hand, pairs solving routine problems did not fare any better in test scores than solo programmers doing the same activity, even then, the routine pairs perceived their teams to be more effective than their complex counterparts.*

4.3   Training Pairs

The main challenges in the industry generally comes not from addressing routine tasks, but from having to solve complex tasks. Therefore, we tested what is a better approach in preparing new pairs to solve complex tasks. We explore the question of whether it is better to start new pairs with routine tasks and then move on to complex tasks, or start them with complex tasks. The reasoning behind the former approach is that with easy tasks there is likely to be less tension between the pairs and it gives them time to know each other better before moving on to complex ones. On the other hand, a possible reasoning behind starting pairs with complex tasks first could be that such a problem would force the pairs to put their heads together and work, whereas if a team is started with easy tasks, it might be a hindrance for the individuals to engage in teamwork thinking that "I could do this myself; having somebody sitting next to me is a distraction".

As explained in Section 3 and Figure 2, we had two cohorts of programming pairs, one cohort (the R2C cohort) started with easy problems and moved on to intermediate and complex problems whereas the other cohort (the C2R cohort) started with a complex problem and moved on to intermediate and easy problems. In other words, both cohorts did exactly the same number of easy, intermediate and complex problems, but in two different directions. For each cohort, as given in Figure 1 there was an experimental group and a control group.

As in the previous section, we tested whether there is a statistically significant difference in the test scores and team effectiveness scores between the R2C and C2R experimental groups in solving complex problems. We then compared each cohort independently with its control to test whether the effect is in fact from pair-programming.

Both in terms of test scores and team effectiveness scores, the cohort that started with easy problems (R2C) performed better in complex problem solving than the cohort that started straightaway with a complex problem (C2R) as shown in Table 2.

Table 2. Difference in scores between R2C and C2R cohorts

	Cohort	Mean	Std. Dev.	p	η^2
Test scores	Routine-to-Complex	3.89	2.01	< 0.0001	0.361
	Complex-to-Routine	1.36	1.35		
Team effectiveness	Routine-to-Complex	4.34	0.48	0.001	0.122
	Complex-to-Routine	3.97	0.51		

The difference in test scores between experimental and control groups in both R2C ($p=0.03$) and C2R ($p=0.044$) were significant indicating that pair programmers produced better outcomes than their solo counterparts in solving complex problems irrespective of whether they started with a complex problem or an easy problem.

5   Limitations

As in any empirical research there are several limitations to our study. It would have been ideal to conduct this experiment in an industrial setting with a mixture of fresh and experienced employees as participants. However, we believe, our choice of subjects does not invalidate the findings because even though the subjects come from a software engineering Masters degree program, their background makes them good proxies for fresh and experienced industry employees. Besides, when Höst et al. [21] compared the use of students with industry professionals, they found no significant differences in tasks involving software engineering judgment; they concluded that students can be used instead of professional software engineers if they are senior masters students rather than undergraduates.

Another limitation of the experiment is that we used graded Java exercises as proxies for routine, intermediate and complex industry tasks. The pair-programming tasks used in an industry generally will be part of a larger software product, whereas, the tasks we gave were standalone Java exercises. Since our aim is to identify pair programming behavior which is unlikely to be different whether the task is a standalone program or a well defined part of a larger software system, this abstraction is unlikely to have affected the external validity of the results.

Another threat to external validity is that we tested pair programming in isolation, whereas, in the industry, pair programming is likely to be only one part of the implementation of the Extreme Programming process. Any influence of other features of XP on pair programming is not included in our experiment.

We did not measure time of completion of tasks therefore were unable to measure success in terms of how fast the different cohorts completed their tasks.

We did not use the same tasks for more than one session; this was deliberately done to avoid the participants discussing the solution with other groups outside of the experiment. Instead, we chose several tasks of similar level of difficulty for different sessions. A threat to internal validity occurs if the level of difficulty varied; as explained in Section 3, we reduced this threat by independently solving each problem prior to the experiment and assessing their difficulty.

6   Discussions and Conclusion

Our study has similarities and differences with prior research discussed in Section 2. Our finding of the appropriateness of using new pairs for complex tasks concur with results of [1] and [2] which found experienced pair programmers also giving better outcomes in the case of complex tasks. Our primary focus, however, was not testing whether pair programming is "better" than solo programming; instead we used solo programmers as controls in identifying significant differences among cohorts of pair programmers. Additionally, we measured pair programming success both in terms of test results and perceived team effectiveness of pairs and compared the two measures, whereas prior literature largely measures effectiveness in terms of time and test results. Further, whereas prior work such as [15] investigated benefits of pair programming in general, we looked at the degree of acceptance of different features of pair programming with the view of identifying the ones that worries programmers new to the method.

As agile methods such as XP get increasingly adopted in the industry, software engineers and programmers who have not experienced the concept of pair-programming will need to be inducted into it. Our results, as discussed below, provide a number of guidelines for the software industry to make the induction smoother.

6.1   Pair-Programming Practices

While programmers appreciate the general benefits of pair programming such as the ability to discuss problem-solving strategies with the teammate, developing teamwork skills and learning to sort out differences in a healthy manner, it is the manual aspects of pair programming that needs attention. Aspects such as the need to work with a shared screen, keyboard and mouse and the need to switch roles between driver and navigator were comparatively less liked by our participants who were new to pair programming.

There are two ways to address these issues. One is education and practice: that is, while introducing pair programming to new programmers, it is not enough to tell them how it works, but also there should be sufficient training sessions for them to practice and become comfortable with its routine aspects such as sharing of the screen. Another way which industrial engineers and researchers could investigate is the possibility of having two screens duplicating the same information, and perhaps also having two keyboards and mice (where the input devices get locked and unlocked with a simple click as the pairs change roles). Further research is needed to see whether such technical solutions will help or hinder pair-programming outcomes.

6.2 Pair Programming Effectiveness

We found a dichotomy between team effectiveness and product quality. Perception of team effectiveness increased as pairs achieved success irrespective of whether the same success could be achieved through solo programming. Thus the pairs who were solving easy tasks found their teams to be more effective than the pairs who were solving complex problems. However, for managers, pair-programming can be considered effective, not just when it achieves better test results, but when it achieves better results *than what a solo programmer could achieve.* In our results, the pairs solving complex problems were getting significantly higher test scores than the solo programmers who were solving the same complex tasks, whereas, there was no statistically significant difference in the test scores between pairs and solo programmers who were solving easy tasks.

This demonstrates that, irrespective of how new pair programmers feel about their team effectiveness, pair programming results in better product quality when they are used for complex tasks. Thus new pairs attempting complex tasks may not feel that their team is working as effectively as it should, however, they are likely to produce significantly better results than solo programmers attempting the same tasks. On the other hand, for easy tasks, pair-programmers may feel that their team is working well, however, their performance in terms of test results is not significantly better than solo programmers, and therefore, it may not be worthwhile employing pairs in easy or routine tasks.

6.3 Training Pair Programmers

In the previous subsection, we mentioned that employing pairs in routine or easy tasks may not be worthwhile. However, there is one important reason to employ pairs in easy tasks, and that is to get them prepared for complex tasks. Whether new pairs programmed easy tasks first before moving on to complex tasks, or tackled complex tasks first, they performed significantly better in solving complex tasks than their solo counterparts. However, more important is the finding that the pairs who started with easy tasks first got better test and team-effectiveness outcomes when solving complex tasks, than the pairs which started with a complex task straightaway. The possible reason is that the former cohort got to work on their team-building skills while on easier tasks and therefore were better prepared to tackle the complex tasks as a team. Thus, when programmers are inducted into pair programming, it is likely to pay off if pairs are started with easy problems before moving on to complex ones. Throwing pairs in at the deep end thinking along the lines that a big challenge will encourage them to work together would not be an effective strategy.

In conclusion, successful induction of programmers into pair-programming depends on us understanding how programmers without prior experience would respond in such situations. This paper contributes to that effort by addressing a number of research questions on achieving effectiveness.

Acknowledgments. We thank the teaching assistants who helped us with the conducting of the experiment and the anonymous referees for their valuable reviews.

References

1. Arisholm, E., Gallis, H., Dybå, T., Sjøberg, D.: Evaluating pair programming with respect to system complexity and programmer expertise. IEEE Transactions on Software Engineering 33(2), 65–86 (2007)
2. Dybå, T., Arisholm, E., Sjøberg, D., Hannay, J., Shull, F.: Are two heads better than one? on the effectiveness of pair programming. IEEE Software 24(6), 12–15 (2007)
3. Hulkko, H., Abrahamsson, P.: A multiple case study on the impact of pair programming on product quality. In: Proceedings of the 27th International Conference on Software Engineering, pp. 495–504. ACM (2005)
4. Madeyski, L.: On the effects of pair programming on thoroughness and fault-finding effectiveness of unit tests. In: Münch, J., Abrahamsson, P. (eds.) PROFES 2007. LNCS, vol. 4589, pp. 207–221. Springer, Heidelberg (2007)
5. Fronza, I., Sillitti, A., Succi, G.: An interpretation of the results of the analysis of pair programming during novices integration in a team. In: Proceedings of the 3rd International Symposium on Empirical Software Engineering and Measurement, pp. 225–235. IEEE Computer Society (2009)
6. Gallis, H., Arisholm, E., Dyba, T.: An initial framework for research on pair programming. In: Proceedings of International Symposium on Empirical Software Engineering, pp. 132–142. IEEE (2003)
7. Ally, M., Darroch, F., Toleman, M.: A framework for understanding the factors influencing pair programming success. In: Baumeister, H., Marchesi, M., Holcombe, M. (eds.) XP 2005. LNCS, vol. 3556, pp. 82–91. Springer, Heidelberg (2005)
8. Lui, K., Chan, K.: Pair programming productivity: Novice–novice vs. expert–expert. International Journal of Human-Computer Studies 64(9), 915–925 (2006)
9. Hannay, J., Dybå, T., Arisholm, E., Sjøberg, D.: The effectiveness of pair programming: A meta-analysis. Information and Software Technology 51(7), 1110–1122 (2009)

10. Vanhanen, J., Lassenius, C.: Effects of pair programming at the development team level: an experiment. In: International Symposium on Empirical Software Engineering, 10 pages. IEEE (2005)
11. Vanhanen, J., Lassenius, C.: Perceived effects of pair programming in an industrial context. In: 33rd EUROMICRO Conference on Software Engineering and Advanced Applications, pp. 211–218. IEEE (2007)
12. Vanhanen, J., Korpi, H.: Experiences of using pair programming in an agile project. In: 40th Annual Hawaii International Conference on System Sciences, pp. 274b–274b. IEEE (2007)
13. Xu, S., Rajlich, V.: Pair programming in graduate software engineering course projects. In: Proceedings of the 35th Annual Conference on Frontiers in Education, pp. F1G–F1G. IEEE (2005)
14. Sison, R.: Investigating pair programming in a software engineering course in an asian setting. In: Proceedings of the 15th Asia-Pacific Software Engineering Conference, pp. 325–331. IEEE (2008)
15. Begel, A., Nagappan, N.: Pair programming: what's in it for me? In: Proceedings of the Second ACM-IEEE International Symposium on Empirical Software Engineering and Measurement, pp. 120–128. ACM (2008)
16. Coman, I.D., Sillitti, A., Succi, G.: Investigating the usefulness of pair-programming in a mature agile team. In: Abrahamsson, P., Baskerville, R., Conboy, K., Fitzgerald, B., Morgan, L., Wang, X. (eds.) XP 2008. LNBIP, vol. 9, pp. 127–136. Springer, Heidelberg (2008)
17. Moore, D.S., McCabe, G.P.: Introduction to the Practice of Statistics. W. H. Freeman & Co., New York (2006)
18. Perneger, T.: What's wrong with bonferroni adjustments. BMJ (British Medical Journal) 316(7139), 1236–1238 (1998)
19. Cohen, J.: Statistical power analysis for the behavioral sciences. Lawrence Erlbaum (1988)
20. Haag, S., Raja, M., Schkade, L.: Quality function deployment usage in software development. Communications of the ACM 39(1), 41–49 (1996)
21. Höst, M., Regnell, B., Wohlin, C.: Using students as subjects: a comparative study of students and professionals in lead-time impact assessment. Empirical Software Engineering 5(3), 201–214 (2000)

Team Performance in Agile Development Teams: Findings from 18 Focus Groups

Torgeir Dingsøyr[1,2] and Yngve Lindsjørn[3]

[1] SINTEF,
NO-7465 Trondheim, Norway
torgeird@sintef.no
[2] Department of Computer and Information Science,
Norwegian University of Science and Technology
[3] University of Oslo, Norway
ynglin@ifi.uio.no

Abstract. How to make teams perform well is increasingly important in software development, as agile development methods prescribe development in small teams. Team performance has been studied in a number of research fields, and there are many models of what enables team performance. A central question then is how relevant these models are for agile development teams. This article investigates the following research question: What factors do agile software practitioners perceive to influence effective teamwork, through a focus group study with 92 participants in 18 groups. The main findings are that what agile practitioners perceive foster and hinder team performance seems to comply well with what is stated in an existing research-based model. However, agile practitioners seem to place insufficient focus on backup behaviour. Agile practitioners place much emphasis on physical and technical infrastructure of the development team as enablers of team performance.

Keywords: team performance, agile software development, software engineering, software process improvement, focus group.

1   Introduction

Agile software development methods have led to a number of changes in the way software is developed [1]. One of the principles behind the agile manifesto states that "the best architectures, requirements, and designs emerge from self-organizing teams". While there are reports of major improvement with agile development methods over traditional development methods [2], team performance is still a challenge. Stray et al. [3] summarize the following challenges to teamwork: Team members solve the wrong tasks by working on low priority items, critical decisions are taken without team commitment due to a lack of communication, and many agile teams spend little time on reflecting on their work process, thus not releasing the potential of learning.

Team performance has been studied in a number of research fields, like management science and psychology, resulting in teamwork effectiveness models.

H. Baumeister and B. Weber (Eds.): XP 2013, LNBIP 149, pp. 46–60, 2013.

In this article, we are interested in what practitioners in agile development teams perceive as factors that influence team effectiveness. Are established models from other disciplines relevant for agile teams, or do we need to develop our own? This work is a part of a larger research programme on teamwork in agile development, and based on a focus group study, we ask the following research question: *What factors do agile software practitioners perceive to influence team performance?*

This article is structured as follows: In Section 2, we first present central definitions and related work regarding teamwork in general and in particular from the literature on agile software development. We then present the team performance model we use to structure the output from focus groups. Section 3 describes how focus groups were carried out, and how data was gathered and analysed. Section 4 describes the results and findings, in Section 5, we discuss the results through our research questions. In Section 6, we conclude, and state implications for practice, theory and further work.

2   Teamwork and Team Performance

A common definition of a team is "a small number of people with complementary skills who are committed to a common purpose, set of performance goals, and approach for which they hold themselves mutually accountable" [4]. In the second edition of the book describing XP, Beck and Andres states that "a variety of people work together in interlinking ways to make a project more effective. They have to work together as a group for each to be successful" [5].

There are a number of studies of teamwork in agile software development, on a range of topics. Some have focused on topics relevant for team composition, like personality [6] and individual characteristics [7]. Others have focused on establishing task-effective norms in groups [8], what motivates team members [9-11], and the importance of a team vision [12]. Yet others have focused on how teams use daily stand-up meetings to communicate [13], how teams make decisions [14], and how to achieve self-management [15, 16]. Some have suggested frameworks to assist improvement of teamwork [17, 18].

Another stream of research has focused on team performance in agile software development teams. Team performance refers to evaluations of the results of the teamwork. Such results are: The quality of the developed software, the ability of the team to meet project goals and budgets and the motivation of team members to work together in the future. Moe et al. used two team performance models to explain teamwork in a project adopting Scrum: The Salas et al. model [19] and the Dickinson McIntyre model [20]. Melo et al. used the "Input Process Output" model to identify team productivity factors in a multiple case study [21]. For a further discussion of team performance models, see [22].

In the general teamwork literature, we find a number of team performance models. Salas et al. [23] identify 136 models and frameworks in a literature review. However, there is a lack of consensus concerning the conceptual structure of teamwork behaviours [24]. Some have criticized that studies of teamwork have been fragmented and not suitable for practical use [25]. A recent review of this body of research by

Salas et al. [25] tries to answer this critique and make the studies practically usable, suggesting the "Big Five" core components of teamwork. Other strengths of the Salas model is that it originates from a solid literature review, and is one of the most cited team performance models.

Salas et al. [25] argue that teams require a complex mixture of factors that include organizational support and individual skills, and also teamwork skills. Therefore, Salas et al. have condensed the knowledge on teamwork into the "Big Five" framework. The five components are: team leadership, mutual performance monitoring, backup behaviour, adaptability, and team orientation. Each of the "Big Five" is required for team performance, but each component may be manifested differently across most teams task types because of constraints of team task and varying needs of the team [25]. The "Big Five" require three coordinating mechanisms: shared mental models, closed-looped communication, and mutual trust.

Building on the theoretically and empirically grounded "Big Five" framework, we describe each component of the framework in Table 1.

Table 1. Definitions of teamwork components in the "Big Five" teamwork model by Salas et al. [25]

Teamwork component	Definition
Team leadership	Ability to direct and coordinate the activities of other team members, assess team performance, assign tasks, develop team knowledge, skills, and abilities, motivate team members, plan and organize, and establish a positive atmosphere
Mutual performance monitoring	The ability to develop common understandings of the team environment and apply appropriate task strategies to accurately monitor team-mate performance
Backup behaviour	Ability to anticipate other team members' needs through accurate knowledge about their responsibilities. This includes the ability to shift workload among members to achieve balance during high periods of workload or pressure
Adaptability	Ability to adjust strategies based on information gathered from the environment through the use of backup behaviour and reallocation of intrateam resources. Altering a course of action or team repertoire in response to changing conditions (internal or external)
Team orientation	Propensity to take other's behaviour into account during group interaction and the belief in the importance of team goal's over individual members' goals
Shared mental models	An organizing knowledge structure of the relationships among the task the team is engaged in and how the team members will interact.
Mutual trust	The shared belief that team members will perform their roles and protect the interests of their team-mates
Closed-loop communication	The exchange of information between a sender and a receiver irrespective of the medium, where the information is received

3   Method

We conducted 18 focus group sessions to investigate our research question. Some of the advantages of focus groups include the ability to collect large and rich amounts of research data, that the researcher can interact directly with respondents for clarification of responses or follow-up questions and that focus group participants can react to and build upon responses from other focus group members [26]. Focus groups are applicable to quickly obtain information on emerging phenomena through structured, moderated discussions with groups of practitioners. We now describe the main steps of conducting the focus groups:

Planning: For each focus group, we developed a plan, which included the agenda of the day and a set of exercises for the participants. Each workshop was planned for 90 minutes and included the following agenda items:

1. Introduction: Purpose and overview of the workshop, motivation for the importance of teamwork in software development.
2. Group exercise 1: Brief introduction of all group members, completion of context questionnaire for each participant. Brainstorm on *"What fosters effective teamwork"* (documented on green stickers), and then on *"What hinders effective teamwork"* (documented on yellow stickers).
3. Presentation team performance model: The research-based Salas et al model.
4. Group exercise 2: Presentation of results from the brainstorm session within groups, categorization of stickers according to the model of team performance. Moderated discussions in the group on placement of stickers.
5. Summary: Presentation of results of the group, feedback on the workshop, information on minutes and further research on teamwork.

Recruitment: In total 92 persons participated in the 18 focus groups. Three were conducted at conferences on agile software development: Two at the Norwegian agile conference (Smidig 2011 and Smidig 2012), and one at XP2012. The participants signed up for a workshop on "Effective Agile Teamwork", and were divided into groups on arrival. Smidig 2012 had five groups, Smidig 2012 three, and XP2012 three. There were 4-6 participants in each focus group.

In addition we conducted focus groups within four companies that participated in a research project on effective teamwork in Norway. In two of the companies the participants included whole projects, while in one company we divided the whole development department into three focus groups. In the fourth company, participants were recruited for a focus group after working hours, which resulted in another two groups with members from a variety of projects.

From the context questionnaire that all participants filled out, we see that the participants were mainly software developers (39%), followed by Scrum masters (18%), team leaders (12%) and project managers (10%). Most of the participants were using the Scrum software development method (59%), followed by Kanban (22%), Lean software development (9%) and eXtreme Programming (8%). As for gender, 65% were male, and 35% female. The participants worked in teams with 3 to 20 members (average 8.4, standard deviation 3.2). The teams had on average 6.6 full time members (standard deviation 3.1). Further, the teams the participants worked in were collaborating with up to 35 other teams. However, 55 participants were working in teams that did not collaborate with other teams. The participants had on average 11.9 years of experience with software development (standard deviation 8.4), and 4.3 years with experience with agile software development (standard deviation 2.5).

Conducting the focus group: The rooms were set up with one table per group. Walls were covered with flip-over charts with numbered areas for grouping of stickers from the brainstorming session. Groups were given stickers in the right colour at the start of each task in order to avoid that participants confused the colours. An example of room set-up is given in Figure 1. At stage 4 in the agenda, groups were given a sheet explaining the teamwork model.

Fig. 1. Room set-up with one table per group and space for documenting results on flip-overs on walls

Moderation: The focus groups were moderated by the first author during agenda items 1, 3 and 4, and by both authors by discussing with groups during items 2 and 4. The discussions mainly involved deciding where to classify items in the team performance model.

Documentation of results, processing and analysis: We made minutes from all focus groups by taking pictures of the final results, showing groups of items that *foster* or *inhibit* team performance. This was documented for each teamwork component in the model, and we also documented items that did not fit into the model, see Figure 2 for example results from one group at the XP2012 conference workshop.

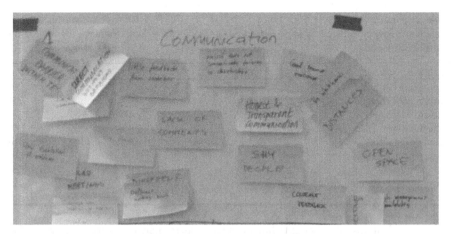

Fig. 2. Partial results of focus group for teamwork component "closed-loop communication" Items that *fosters* teamwork in green, items that *hinders* effective teamwork in yellow

In total, the groups found seven items that they were not able to fit into the model. These were classified by the researchers. Examples of such items were "teamsize" and "too difficult work tasks" what were moved to team leadership. The minutes were sent to all participants. Then, we recorded items, whether they were marked as *fostering* or *hindering* teamwork in a spreadsheet. The text on four stickers were unreadable in the minutes, and this left a total of 1183. These were first read to check that the topics identified was categorized into the right teamwork component. 17 items were moved from one component to another.

The questionnaire that all participants filled out was also coded in a spreadsheet, to provide descriptive statistics of the participant population.

Analysis included a quantitative and qualitative part. The quantitative analysis consisted of counting the number of items marked as fostering or hindering teamwork. The qualitative analysis consisted of thematic grouping of items marked within each teamwork component. For example, in Figure 2, the stickers "communication barriers within the team" and "direction communications without barriers" (in the upper left corner) were coded as teamwork component "closed-loop communication", while "distances" and "different working hours" were coded as sub-component "co-location. The names of sub-components were all stated as if they were factors that foster team performance, for example most of the stickers identified in the brainstorming for the subcomponent "planning" was aspects of "bad planning".

4   Results

The result of our grouping of items into teamwork components is shown in Table 2. In total 1183 items were placed in the eight teamwork component groups. We see that team leadership, closed-loop communication and team orientation received the highest numbers of stickers indicating items that foster team performance. Closed-loop communication, shared mental models and mutual trust received the largest

Table 2. Number of stickers with items *fostering* or *hindering* team performance, and the number of items considered as most *important* by the focus groups. Numbers are shown for each teamwork component.

Teamwork component	Foster	Hinder	Total
Team leadership	90	139	229
Mutual performance monitoring	49	22	71
Backup behaviour	44	57	101
Adaptability	46	50	96
Team orientation	91	65	156
Shared mental models	104	59	163
Mutual trust	97	58	155
Closed-loop communication	122	90	212
Sum	643	540	1183

numbers of items that could hinder team performance. Further, closed-loop communication mutual trust and shared mental models received the highest numbers of markers indicating that participants viewed these as important.

For the qualitative analysis, we have chosen to display results from the two groups with highest total number of items identified: Team leadership and closed-loop communication. Note that many stickers only shows that many are aware of this factor, it is not necessarily an important factor.

Team leadership: This component includes 139 items that foster effective teamwork, and 90 that hinders effective teamwork. 66 stickers simply described "leadership" (14 fostering and 52 hindering). See Table 3 and Figure 3 for a grouping of both fostering and hindering items.

Table 3. Main sub-components of team leadership, with selected items that foster and hinder team performance

Sub-Component	Items	
	Foster	Hinder
Planning	Good planning	Bad planning
	Participative planning	Too thorough planning
	Adequate planning	Short-sighted planning
Shielding from interruptions	Reduce unnecessary interruptions	Interruptions
	Shielding the team	Work day split up
	Someone protecting the team	Change the agreed content
Work processes	Slack to think big	Heavy process
	Responsibility process in place	Unnecessary processes
Adequate resources	Full time members	Part-time resources
	Capacity	Lack of resources
	Availability	Resource allocation
Infrastructure	Working infrastructure	Lack of tools
	Good work conditions	Lack of technical infrastructure
	Access to tools	Unnecessary tools

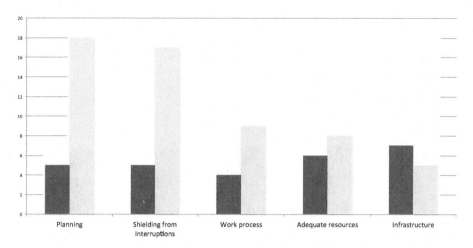

Fig. 3. Characteristics of *team leadership*. For each subcategory, the number of items marked as *fostering* to the left and the number of items marked as *hindering* to the right.

In addition we find the following groups with more than three items: "team members take responsibility", "team composition", "interesting work tasks", "social atmosphere", "well defined tasks", "engaged team members", "absence of conflicts", "balance between team members", "common goals", "frequent communication", "focus on setting priorities", "having the right focus", "self management", and "visualising status and progress".

Table 4. Main sub-components of closed-loop communication, with selected items that foster and hinder team performance

Sub-Component	Items	
	Foster	Hinder
Co-location	Physical presence Co-location Physically placed together	People are distributed Distance Not co-located
Openness	Open communication Openness in the team Open dialogue	Secrecy Retaining information
Infrastructure	Process support tools Suitable office spaces Tools that work	Bad tools Bad office facilities
Visualising status and progress	Informative workspace Visualise things that go well Whiteboard/taskboard	No whiteboards
Social atmosphere	Good atmosphere Fun Friendly tone	Scolding Antisocial environment Bad atmosphere

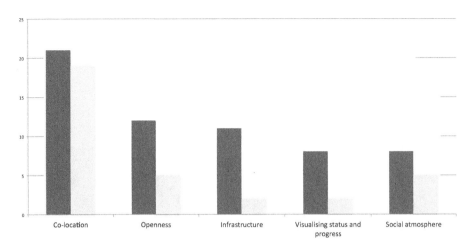

Fig. 4. Characteristics of *closed-loop communication*. For each subcategory, the number of items marked as *hindering* to the left and the number of items marked as *fostering* to the right.

Closed-loop communication: This component includes 90 items that foster effective teamwork, and 122 that hinder effective teamwork. Many stickers simply described "communication", in total 63 (23 hindering, and 40 fostering). See Table 4 and Figure 4 for a grouping of both fostering and hindering items. The sub-components that received the highest number of items indicating factors that both foster and hinder effective teamwork was "co-location", "openness", "infrastructure", "visualizing status and progress", and a "social atmosphere".

In addition to these five groups, we also find the following groups with three items or more: "frequent communication", "absence of conflicts", "absence of interruptions", "absence of introvert team members", "customer available", "common language and culture", "team leadership", "slow response" and "follow-up".

5   Discussion

We now proceed to discuss our research questions: *What factors do agile software practitioners perceive to influence effective teamwork?*

From the results section and Table 2, we see that the results of the focus groups fitted well into the general research-based model of team performance. The participants themselves only put 7 out of 1183 items in an "other" group, and these were later categorized by the researcher into the team components. If we interpret the number of stickers generated by all groups for a teamwork component as a sign of the perceived significance for team performance, we see that the components cluster in three groups: *Team leadership* and *closed-loop communication* have 229 and 212 items respectively. *Shared mental models*, *team orientation*, and *mutual trust* have around 160 items. The last group of components: *backup behaviour, adaptability* and *mutual performance monitoring* range from 71 to 101 items (Table 2).

In their description of the "Big Five" model, Salas et al. [25] suggest that *team leadership* and *team orientation* will be especially important in the initial stages of team development, when the team is exploring their task interrelationships and the roles of team members. If we divide teamwork into phases, Salas et al. hypothesize that *adaptability, team orientation* and *closed-loop communication* will be the most important before engaging in complex tasks. Then *mutual performance monitoring, backup behaviour* and *adaptability* are expected to increase in importance as the team is working on the tasks. It is interesting that there were not more stickers related to *adaptability*, as this is central in agile software development. Maybe this is something the participants take for granted in agile development.

The practitioners who participated in focus groups emphasized many of the same factors as Salas with *team leadership, closed-loop communication,* and *team orientation.* Components that are given attention by Salas, *adaptability, mutual performance monitoring,* and *backup behaviour* are given less attention by practitioners.

In a study of an agile development team introducing Scrum, Moe et al. [20] found that *team orientation, team leadership* and *backup behaviour* was particularly challenging. The first two are given much focus by practitioners, while the third receives less attention. A multiple case study in two companies by Stray et al. [3] discovered challenges related to communication (*closed-loop communication*), learning (*shared mental models, backup behaviour*) and selecting the tasks according to the priority list (*team orientation*). Compared to our focus group findings, we see that team orientation and closed-loop communication jointly receives much attention, while the practitioners place less emphasis on backup behaviour (shared mental models in the mid-range).

If we go further into details, we will compare the definition *team leadership* by Salas to the sub-components identified by agile development practitioners in the focus groups (Table 5). From the sub-components, we find a number of topics related to directing and coordinating the activities of team members, like "planning", "common goals", "self management", "focus on setting priorities", "frequent communication" and "visualising status and progress". The latter is also related to assessing team performance. Related to assigning tasks, we find "adequate resources", "well defined tasks" and "self management". We do not see sub-components that we can connect to "developing team knowledge, skills and abilities". Maybe this could be because many include this in their definition of a "self managing" team. As for motivating team members, we have "engaged team members", "interesting work tasks" and "absence of conflicts". The last item in Salas et al.´s list is to plan, organize and establish a positive atmosphere. Here we have "planning", "infrastructure", "team composition", "shielding from interruptions", "balance between team members", "work process" and "social atmosphere". In all, it seems like the participants in focus groups have an understanding of team leadership which is similar to the one described in Salas et al., with the exception of focus on "develop team knowledge, skills and abilities".

Table 5. Team leadership, definition by Salas et al. and sub-components identified in focus groups. The list of sub-components is according to frequency, with the sub-components with most items listed first.

Sub-components from focus group	Planning, shielding from interruptions, work process, adequate resources, infrastructure, team members take responsibility, team composition, interesting work tasks, social atmosphere, well defined tasks, engaged team members, absence of conflicts, balance between team members, common goals, frequent communication, focus on setting priorities, having the right focus, self management, visualising status and progress
Definition by Salas et al.	Ability to direct and coordinate the activities of other team members, assess team performance, assign tasks, develop team knowledge, skills, and abilities, motivate team members, plan and organize, and establish a positive atmosphere

If we do a detailed examination of *closed-loop communication*, the definition by Salas et al. is simply that a sender and a receiver exchanges information irrespective of medium (Table 6). The sub-component "co-location" received in total 40 stickers with either co-location promoting effective teamwork or the lack of co-location hindering effective teamwork. It seems then that many teams perceive co-location as important for good communication. Also, a number of other sub-components were related to the set-up of the team, like "infrastructure", "visualising status and progress". A number of sub-components focused on the quality of communication: "openness", "frequent communication", "absence of conflicts", "absence of interruptions", "customer available", and that there should not be "slow response". Some emphasized that good communication requires a "common language and culture" and a "social atmosphere". Some also included "follow-up" and "team leadership" here, the latter indicating a special role for a team leader with respect to ensuring good communication. To summarize, practitioners in agile development teams seem to place much emphasis on physical and technical infrastructure as enablers of closed-loop communication, shown by many stickers with topics in sub-components co-location, infrastructure, visualising status and progress.

Table 6. Closed-loop communication, definition by Salas et al. and sub-components identified in focus groups. The list of sub-components is according to frequency, with the sub-components with most items listed first.

Sub-components from focus group	Co-location, openness, infrastructure, visualising status and progress, social atmosphere, frequent communication, absence of conflicts, absence of interruptions, absence of introvert team members, customer available, common language and culture, team leadership, slow response, follow-up
Definition by Salas et al.	The exchange of information between a sender and a receiver irrespective of the medium

One question is what would have happened with our analysis if we had used another team performance model? Note that we conducted the brainstorming session on what fosterer and hinder effective teamwork (items 2 on the agenda) independent of any model. The model was first introduced when all items related to team performance had been introduced. We expected a larger number of items that the focus group participants would not be able to relate to the model, as the Salas et al. model is focused on a practical model with a limited number of factors. For example the "Input Mediator Output" model [27] has a far larger number of factors, like characteristics of team members with respect to diversity and emergent states of a team, like "empowerment" and "cohesion". However, it would be an interesting task to analyse the material with respect to other models to see if they are fitting equally well.

6   Conclusion

In this article, we report findings from a focus group study on how team performance is seen by practitioners in agile software development teams. We conducted 18 focus groups with a total of 92 participants, where participants brainstormed on factors that foster or hinder teamwork, and relate this to the Salas et al. model of team performance. We asked the following research question: *What factors do agile software practitioners perceive to influence effective teamwork?*

Our main findings are the following:

- The Salas model seem to fit well with what practitioners perceive as factors that affect team performance. Only 7 of 1183 stickers were not placed in the model by the groups (and all of these were later found to fit by the researchers).
- After number of stickers identified, the teamwork components cluster in three main groups: 1) *team leadership* and *closed-loop communication,* 2) *shared mental models, team orientation,* and *mutual trust,* 3) *mutual performance monitoring, backup behaviour* and *adaptability.*
- *Backup behaviour* has been found to be challenging in studies of agile development teams, and is one of the components with the lowest number of stickers. This could indicate a lack of awareness of this factor with respect to team performance.
- The practitioners understanding of *team leadership* seems similar to description in Salas et al. [25], except for a lack of focus on "develop team knowledge, skills and abilities".
- Further, practitioners in agile development teams seem to place much emphasis on physical and technical infrastructure as enablers of *closed-loop communication,* shown by many stickers with topics in sub-components co-location, infrastructure, visualising status and progress.

This study has the following implications for theory: First of all this study confirms previous findings from case studies showing that general theory on teamwork is of high relevance to agile software development teams. Second, this focus group suggests that team leadership is perceived as important, and practitioners' view of team leadership corresponds to how it is described in the team performance model of Salas et al.

Implications for practice are that much of the advice given in general team research will be relevant for agile software development teams. In particular what agile teams should focus more on in order to enable team performance is *backup behaviour*, which receives little attention in this study and has been shown in case studies to be problematic.

This focus group study has the following limitations: First of all, the opinions on team performance expressed by the focus groups might diverge from a representative sample of agile development practitioners. 67% of participants signed up voluntarily for the focus group workshops, either in a company or in one of the three conferences. Thus, our participants are likely to be more than averagely interested in teamwork. Second, focus groups are often criticized for enabling groupthink. For collecting items that foster or hinder team performance, we avoided this effect by individual brainstorming sessions. However, in the discussions where groups placed items in the Salas model, groupthink might influence placement. We tried to minimize this effect by critically examining the results of the groups and moving 17 items from one teamwork component to another. For the analysis, one could argue that the "Big Five" model should be replaced by another teamwork model, as agile teams are said to be self-managing and this model is not particularly tailored for self-managing teams. However, we argue that first of all, many teams that use agile development methods are not self-managing. Second, we can interpret the team leadership tasks as tasks that are the responsibility of the whole team and not of a team leader for teams that are self-managing.

In the future we plan to carry out a detailed analysis as we have done for the two main teamwork components for all teamwork components in the model. We hope then to be able to identify even further characteristics of what agile practitioners perceive as important in teamwork, and what might differentiate from what researchers or team members in other disciplines see as important.

Acknowledgments. We are very grateful to the 92 participants in our team performance focus groups who were willing to share their experience about teamwork. Also, we would like to thank Viktoria Gulliksen Stray at the University of Oslo for comments on a previous version of this article. This article was written in the TeamIT project, supported by the Research Council of Norway through grant 193236/I40.

References

[1] Dingsøyr, T., Nerur, S., Balijepally, V., Moe, N.B.: A Decade of Agile Methodologies: Towards Explaining Agile Software Development. Journal of Systems and Software 85, 1213–1221 (2012)

[2] Dybå, T., Dingsøyr, T.: Empirical Studies of Agile Software Development: A Systematic Review. Information and Software Technology 50, 833–859 (2008)

[3] Gulliksen Stray, V., Moe, N.B., Dingsøyr, T.: Challenges to Teamwork: A Multiple Case Study of Two Agile Teams. In: Sillitti, A., Hazzan, O., Bache, E., Albaladejo, X. (eds.) XP 2011. LNBIP, vol. 77, pp. 146–161. Springer, Heidelberg (2011)

[4] Katzenbach, J.R., Smith, D.K.: The Discipline of Teams. Harvard Business Review 71, 111–120 (1993)

[5] Beck, K., Andres, C.: Extreme Programming Explained: Embrace Chage, 2nd edn. Addison-Wesley (2004)

[6] Young, S.M., Edwards, H.M., McDonald, S., Thompson, J.B.: Personality Characteristics in an XP Team: A Repertory Grid Study. In: Proceedings of Human and Social Factors of Software Engineering, HSSE, St. Louis, Missouri, USA, pp. 1–7 (2005)

[7] Seger, T., Hazzan, O., Bar-Nahor, R.: Agile Orientation and Psychological Needs, Self-Efficacy, and Perceived Support: A Two Job-Level Comparison. In: Agile, Toronto, pp. 3–14 (2008)

[8] Teh, A., Baniassad, E., van Rooy, D., Boughton, C.: Social Psychology and Software Teams: Establishing Task-Effective Group Norms. IEEE Software 29, 53–58 (2012)

[9] Whitworth, E., Biddle, R.: The Social Nature of Agile Teams. In: Agile, Washington, DC, pp. 26–36 (2007)

[10] Beecham, S., Sharp, H., Baddoo, N., Hall, T., Robinson, H.: Does the XP environment meet the motivational needs of the software developer? An empirical study. In: Agile, Washington, DC, pp. 37–49 (2007)

[11] Tessem, B., Maurer, F.: Job Satisfaction and Motivation in a Large Agile Team. In: Concas, G., Damiani, E., Scotto, M., Succi, G. (eds.) XP 2007. LNCS, vol. 4536, pp. 54–61. Springer, Heidelberg (2007)

[12] Acuña, S.T., Gómez, M., Juristo, N.: Towards understanding the relationship between team climate and software quality—a quasi-experimental study. Empirical Software Engineering 13, 401–434 (2008)

[13] Stray, V.G., Moe, N.B., Aurum, A.: Investigating Daily Team Meetings in Agile Software Projects. In: Cortellessa, V., Muccini, H., Demirors, O. (eds.) 2012 38th Euromicro Conference on Software Engineering and Advanced Applications, pp. 274–281 (2012)

[14] Moe, N.B., Aurum, A., Dybå, T.: Challenges of shared decision-making: A multiple case study of agile software development. Information and Software Technology 54, 853–865 (2012)

[15] Hoda, R., Noble, J., Marshall, S.: Developing a grounded theory to explain the practices of self-organizing Agile teams. Empirical Software Engineering 17, 609–639 (2012)

[16] Moe, N.B., Dingsøyr, T., Dybå, T.: Overcoming Barriers to Self-Management in Software Teams. IEEE Software 26, 20–26 (2009)

[17] Moe, N.B., Dingsøyr, T., Røyrvik, E.A.: Putting Agile Teamwork to the Test – An Preliminary Instrument for Empirically Assessing and Improving Agile Software Development. In: Abrahamsson, P., Marchesi, M., Maurer, F. (eds.) XP 2009. LNBIP, vol. 31, pp. 114–123. Springer, Heidelberg (2009)

[18] Kettunen, P., Moilanen, S.: Sensing High-Performing Software Teams: Proposal of an Instrument for Self-monotoring. In: Wohlin, C. (ed.) XP 2012. LNBIP, vol. 111, pp. 77–92. Springer, Heidelberg (2012)

[19] Moe, N.B., Dingsøyr, T.: Scrum and team effectiveness: Theory and practice. In: 9th International Conference on Agile Processes in Software Engineering and Extreme Porgramming, Limerick, Ireland, pp. 11–20 (2008)

[20] Moe, N.B., Dingsøyr, T., Dybå, T.: A teamwork model for understanding an agile team: A case study of a Scrum project. Information and Software Technology 52, 480–491 (2010)

[21] de O. Melo, C., Cruzes, D.S., Kon, F., Conradi, R.: Interpretative case studies on agile team productivity and management. Information and Software Technology 55, 412–427 (2013)

[22] Dingsøyr, T., Dybå, T.: Team Effectiveness in Software Development: Human and Cooperative Aspects in Team Effectiveness Models and Priorities for Future Studies. In: Workshop on Co-operative and Human Aspects of Software Engineering, International Conference on Software Engineering, ICSE, Zürich, Switzerland, pp. 27–29 (2012)

[23] Salas, E., Stagl, K.C., Burke, C.S., Goodwin, G.F.: Fostering Team Effectiveness in Organizations: Toward an Integrative Theoretical Framework. In: 52nd Nebraska Symposium on Motivation, Lincoln, NE, pp. 185–243 (2007)

[24] Rousseau, V., Aube, C., Savoie, A.: Teamwork behaviors - A review and an integration of frameworks. Small Group Research 37, 540–570 (2006)

[25] Salas, E., Sims, D.E., Burke, S.C.: Is there a "Big five" in teamwork? Small Group Research 36, 555–599 (2005)

[26] Stewart, D.W., Shamdasani, P.N., Rook, D.: Focus Groups: Theory and Practice. Sage Publications (2007)

[27] Mathieu, J., Maynard, M.T., Rapp, T., Gilson, L.: Team effectiveness 1997-2007: A review of recent advancements and a glimpse into the future. Journal of Management 34, 410–476 (2008)

The Practice of Not Knowing for Sure:
How Agile Teams Manage Uncertainties

Denniz Dönmez and Gudela Grote

Department of Management, Technology, and Economics
ETH Zurich, Switzerland
{ddonmez,ggrote}@ethz.ch

Abstract. Uncertainties are ubiquitous in software development. They impact almost every aspect of a development project. Most uncertainties are viewed as threats to project efficiency and there are strong calls to their reduction. However, uncertainties can pose opportunities for creativity and innovation in some situations. The literature has been dominated by discussions that focus on requirements uncertainties. We aim to extend these discussions by drawing attention to additional types of uncertainties, namely resource, task, and output uncertainties. In this empirical study we investigate the potential of agile software development methods to manage these different types of uncertainties, and examine the mechanisms available to development teams. Our results reveal how some agile teams seized mechanisms to harvest positive and mitigate negative impacts of uncertainties. Drawing upon these results, we discuss several antecedents of successful uncertainty management.

Keywords: Uncertainties, Uncertainty Management, Agile Software Development Methods, Scrum, Empirical Study.

1 Introduction

In this study, we examine the potential of agile software development (ASD) methods to manage diverse uncertainties, which play a major role in software development projects [1,2,3]. Uncertainties have a significant impact on a project's performance as they result in situations that require adequate, oftentimes quick, reactions. They can be manifested in diverse conditions including unexpected events, or a lack of confidence in an estimation, and may consist of anything that is potentially important but not known for sure. Uncertainty is broadly defined as the absence of complete information [4] and linked to the inability of accurate predictions [5]. Because incomplete information can lead to costly delays, redundant work and other inefficiencies, uncertainties are unwanted impediments to most software developers and project managers. The elimination of uncertainties becomes feasible as more information becomes available during the course of a project [6,7] and has long been connected to reduced software project risks and costs [8,24]. However, in some situations, uncertainties can play an important role to foster innovation and productivity [9]. This is mostly the case when high levels of bureaucracy and exuberantly structured project management approaches suffocate creative thinking

H. Baumeister and B. Weber (Eds.): XP 2013, LNBIP 149, pp. 61–75, 2013.

and developers do not enjoy sufficient flexibility to react to dynamic problems and changing environments. Therefore, the adequate handling of uncertainties is crucial for a project's outcome. A team's capability to react adequately to unforeseen future events can result from well-managed uncertainties [10], whereas a highly structured project management approach may result in badly managed uncertainties [11]. Uncertainty management is not equivalent to the elimination of uncertainties. Uncertainties cannot be eliminated entirely in software development projects [10]. Instead, uncertainty management includes two main mechanisms; minimisation of uncertainties and coping with uncertainties [12]. In an attempt to establish the flexibility that is needed for this, many development teams have turned to agile development methods, which stress the importance of situation-dependent problem solving through an 'inspect-and-adapt' approach [10]. ASD methods, such as Scrum, deliberately encourage high flexibility and adaptability through iterative development processes, and foster communication among project stakeholders in order to enable quick and effective adaption to unexpected events. In this context, requirements uncertainties have been extensively studied, e. g. in [4], as the literature has been dominated by discussions that focus on technical aspects. Yet, little attention has been paid to identify the mechanisms that may be necessary to address different types of uncertainties, which exist in software development. We address this gap by studying additional types of uncertainties, which have been largely ignored. We aim to contribute to a more complete understanding of uncertainty management in software development by addressing four different types of uncertainties, namely resource, requirements, task and output uncertainties.

Resource uncertainties refer to incomplete information about the availability of resources that are required for the accomplishment of planned project tasks. Necessary but unavailable resources range from human resources subject to spontaneous temporal unavailability to process artefacts, such as delayed deliverables. **Requirements uncertainties** refer to ambiguous or changing customer demands. Requirements are a major source of uncertainties in software development and have been discussed by several authors [3,13,16], who argue that agile software development becomes especially important under conditions of frequent changes. **Task uncertainties** refer to a lack of clarity regarding the details of desired outcomes and appropriate solutions to problems. Uncertainty is high when tasks have unexpected dependencies or undiscovered problems with envisioned solutions exist. **Output uncertainties** result from incomplete information about the quantity or quality of product features that a team is able to implement in a given time. They are often linked to insufficient task or process knowledge resulting in unplanned delays.

The purpose of this paper is to examine the mechanisms that professional software development teams draw upon to manage these uncertainties. Thereby we shed light on different existing practices that are suggested by ASD methods, as well as established in extension to them, which are seized to approach a topic with significant influence on development projects. Apart from the identification of ASD practices, we present mechanisms that teams utilised to complement ASD methods in order to carry out their work. Our focus includes the potential of ASD to provide both the structure and flexibility necessary for the effective management of uncertainties.

2   Research Method

We applied qualitative methods for data collection and analysis, using mainly interview and observation techniques. In addition, project artefacts, such as documents and drawings, were collected during company visits. We applied observational techniques when we had the possibility to attend team meetings, witness conference calls (e. g. with clients and other project stakeholders) and conduct spontaneous informal interviews, for instance during lunch or coffee breaks. Field notes produced from these conversations were not included in the data analysis, but enriched our understanding of organisational and team processes and the projects' contextual settings.

2.1   Data Collection

Data collection took place in agile software development teams in three companies based in Switzerland. In total, 19 semi-structured interviews with individuals were conducted. Participants were members of 5 different teams and consisted of 15 men and 4 women, which reflects the teams' gender distribution. Table 1 summarises the data sources. The project teams are referred to by letters for confidentiality reasons.

We interviewed at least two and as many as five members of each team, including at least one person with official team leadership responsibility (i. e. Scrum Master, Product Owner, team or project leader). No stakeholders external to the teams were interviewed. This limitation was, however, mitigated through the fact that the teams had very close contact to them, because they worked for the same companies, and were informed about their perceptions concerning the projects. Interviews lasted from 20 minutes to one hour, with an average length of 38 minutes, and were audio-recorded. In addition, we had the chance to engage in informal conversations with almost all team members at multiple occasions as we visited each team several times.

During the interviews we focused on the interviewees' experiences with uncertain situations. We designed semi-structured interview questions that centred on different types of uncertainties. Each interview began with general questions, such as the current status of the project, and then moved to examples of recently experienced situations in which the team had to deal with incomplete information or unexpected events. We also collected experiences with negative, as well as positive outcomes of unexpected events. Interviewees were asked to describe situations they experienced (e. g., 'Could you give me an example of a situation in which your team faced the unexpected fallout of a team member?' or 'Please describe a situation in which you faced a task and it was not clear to you how to accomplish it') and how their team reacted to that particular situation. Special attention was paid to leadership and collaboration mechanisms including how decisions were made, and how communication took place. During the interviews we pursued interesting clues rather than strictly adhere to our interview guideline; we encouraged informants to wander freely in their answers and probed whenever possible.

The teams we approached apply Scrum in large company projects, mostly using sprint lengths of two weeks. According to the team members' expertise, several roles are established with overlapping responsibilities. Most teams employ specialised developers (e.g., front and back end), testers, designers (software architects), and requirements engineers. All teams are part of the IT development departments of their respective companies, and develop software solutions that are used by other departments of their organisations. The teams differed in several important aspect including not only characteristics, such as team size, but also their choice of leadership style and coordination mechanisms.

Team A is part of a telecom company. Its 19 team members are split into two sub-teams, which are collocated and share one Product Owner and Scrum Master. The team is interdisciplinary and pair programming is used for most development tasks. At the time of data collection, the team had been working together for one year. **Teams B and C** work for a bank. While Team C has 6 collocated developers, Team B consists of 11 developers who are dispersed over three locations (two in Switzerland, one in India). **Teams D and E** are employed by an insurance company and are all collocated. While Team D is the smallest team of our study (it consists of the 4 members who were interviewed), Team E counts 9 team members.

Table 1. An overview of project, team and study participant details

Team code	Project profile	Team size	Number of inter-viewees incl. roles
A	The project had been set up 2 years before data collection in order to develop an application for customer order management of future products. Scrum has been used from the beginning. Sprint lengths are 2 weeks.	19 team members split into 2 functional, collocated sub-teams.	*5 interviews:* A1-A5 developers; plus several informal interviews with the Scrum Master (A6)
B	The project was started 1.5 years earlier with the aim to develop and maintain several products for internal company use. Scrum has been used from the beginning with 2 week sprints.	12 team members	*4 interviews:* B1 Product Owner B2-B4 developers
C	Releases of a company-internal application are developed in cooperation with internal clients for the last 3 years, using Scrum since 2.5 years with 4 week sprints.	10 team members	*2 interviews:* C1 Scrum Master C2 developer
D	For the previous 2 years, Scrum was used to develop new versions of a customer management system. Sprint lengths were usually 2 weeks but varied sometimes.	8 team members	*4 interviews:* D1 Scrum Master D2 developer D3 Product Owner D4 developer
E	The project serves the development of new company communication technologies and started 1 year prior to data collection using Scrum. Sprints were 2 weeks in length.	5 team members and 1 Scrum coach	*4 interviews:* E1 Product Owner E2 developer E3 developer E4 Scrum coach
5 teams			*19 interviews*

2.2   Data Analysis

Transcripts of interviews constitute the primary data in this study. All interviews were coded to reflect different types of uncertainties, which resulted from earlier ethnographically informed [14] work, and mechanisms seized for their management. We coded the data openly until no new codes emerged, i. e. theoretical saturation [15] was reached. The codes were grouped according to the types of uncertainties they addressed, and summarised into concepts regarding the underlying uncertainty management practices. Those practices that were connected to organisational rather than team or project management characteristics, such as hiring power, were ignored, as not all teams were in the position to apply them.

3   Results

We present practices that are used by teams to manage different types of uncertainties. The results are grouped according to categories of uncertainties that were identified in the interviews. Some uncertainty management practices are related explicitly to agile software development (ASD), whereas others are not. Several practices are mutually dependent or contribute to the management of multiple uncertainties. Results are summarised in Table 1 at the end of the section.

3.1   Resource Uncertainties

Resources consist of technological artefacts or infrastructure, as well as human resources required in the development process. An inadequate level of resources results either from insufficient supply or excess demand for resources. Uncertain availability of resources causes threats to the success of a project.

Unavailability of Artefacts. The unavailability of technical infrastructure, software licenses, or other artefacts can render a team unproductive. Such threats need uncertainty management practices in order to reduce the risk of the inability to complete development tasks. Teams in this study routinely applied risk analysis techniques, however, some reported not to do so systematically. Participants stated they usually thought about risk in the moment when they find themselves in need to respond to an unexpected event and faced a strategic decision, such as to reduce product features or search for substitute functionality. One participant remarked:

"detailed planning would not have helped because the unexpected events were unexpected" (C1, Scrum Master)

Decision analysis was conducted according to *"a common sense process"* (C2, developer) by thinking about opportunities and possible consequences. One common practice was to call a team meeting in order to gather possible solutions for workarounds and make due as good as possible without satisfying their excess demand for the scarce resource.

Quality of Input. Resources available only in unpredictable levels of quality were named as one major source of dissatisfaction in Team A, where deliverables from external departments often were below the team's expected quality. This was especially the case when erroneous items were received that caused unexpected additional work. Team members could not successfully manage input quality uncertainty because causes were rooted in the organisational structure and differing team cultures. The team members complained about the number of bugs in systems they relied on and which were not improved by the supplier. To our knowledge, they did not try to engage their suppliers in close collaboration in an attempt to explain their quality requirements. Moderation was sought from higher level authorities, however, addressing the problem remained a recurring task of the Product Owner.

Availability of Human Resources. One central aspect of uncertainty management in software development is the management of human resources. It ranges from hiring to training and developing, and eventually letting go team members. The duration of an onboarding process (i. e. the phase of integration until a new team member becomes productive) significantly impacts project costs. New team members are required to learn a broad range of tasks reaching from administrative work to specific development tasks. To increase knowledge transfer, documentation of procedures and pair programming sessions were used in most teams.

Knowledge transfer is also crucial when a team member leaves, or is temporarily unavailable. Breaching functional separation of roles was seen as important by all teams, however, in some cases this was not feasible either due to expertise or individual differences of team members. We found that status and roles were created according to seniority and expertise, and had consequences based on team member expectations regarding decision-making and leadership toward conflict solving.

One developer reported that informal leadership structures collapsed after one dominant decision maker had left the team, and the developer was left in the in the unwanted role of his successor because he had become the most senior team member:

"the team dynamics changed completely after [the colleague] had left the team. [...] For me now the pressure is much bigger, because I am expected to take over his role now, but I am not this person. There is a lot more pressure for me, because a lot of requests come to me and I must make a lot more decisions now." (A1, developer)

When team members could anticipate their absence from work, or had regular absences because they did not work full time on the project, clusters of sub-teams were formed by the teams so that each team member had a functional substitute. Knowledge sharing and collaboration lied in the responsibilities of the team members and worked best in teams that used pair programming routinely. Team A had the policy that no pair could stay together for more than one task so that knowledge sharing would be maximised.

In one case, a developer was idle because of his inability to support his colleagues. This resulted from expertise differences and an unexpected difficulty which put his task on hold. The problem was solved by an anticipatory planning meeting with the Product Owner that was called to forecast future work packages and start anticipated tasks.

Team E reported that developers were disturbed frequently during their work by requests from other departments (in which they previously worked). The team solved this problem by extending the practice of process visualisation to include the external disturbers and transparently displaying the frequency of their requests:

"especially in the beginning of the development we were disturbed very often. That was really troublesome. [...] So we made a wall with who was disturbed more than 15 minutes and counted them, and that put them off so that they didn't come any more." (E1, Product Owner)

3.2 Requirements Uncertainties

Requirements uncertainties have been identified to cause irregularities and costly delays in many projects [16,25]. ASD teams use several mechanisms to manage requirements uncertainties, the effect of which we found to depend largely on communication effectiveness. Complementary to following the suggested collaborative sessions of the Scrum framework, all teams established additional communication structures that reflected their demand for information and integration of stakeholders into the project.

Lack of Details about Demanded Functionality or insufficient understanding of business context posed problems in several cases, which were addressed by customer representatives in the teams, i. e. either Product Owner or a developer with the mandate to communicate with a certain customer. As there is no substitute for business environment knowledge, one team had business representatives integrated as team members who were, however, not working full time with the team. This interdisciplinary not only increased the team's heterogeneity but also starkly increased the availability of rapid requirement clarifications compared to the other teams. Another team had the opposite problem of a customer not stopping to add items to the list of requested features. This was solved through the Product Owner centring discussions on a prototype:

"When you ship something, people start to imagine how they can do business with it. [...] the requirements phase was never ending. Instead, with a prototype, you stop discussions and then you can say: let's focus on this part." (B1, Product Owner)

Ambiguous Information was experienced as a major cause of uncertainty by many participants. Most teams had implemented the common Scrum policy of allowing work items to be commenced only when they were declared 'ready' for development after an evaluation of their ambiguity. When this was not the case, teams prepended investigative work to the requirements until they felt to have sufficiently clear information. Participants referred to such investigations as 'Spikes' (a time period with constrained duration that is used to expand knowledge and reduce requirements or task uncertainty by investigating a specific issue).

Requirement clarification meetings served to increase communication within teams as well as with external stakeholders, and to reduce ambiguities and, hence, uncertainties regarding requirements. One participant stressed the point that, with team autonomy, clarification lies in the responsibility of the team member. When information was required from unavailable stakeholders, other tasks needed to be turned to while awaiting reply. However, task idleness can become a process risk. One developer stressed the importance of repeatedly requesting required information:

"too many stories came in while too many others were idle. They were blocked and we did not inquire about them again, but this is important. [...] it is important to ask [the informants/customers] again, and ask again, and ask again [...] to keep bugging until something happens." (A2, developer)

Unexpected Requirement Changes were reported to occur seldom because of the rule that tasks are fixed during an iteration, which most teams adhered to. Requirements, such as product features, were exchanged only in emergency situations during an on-going sprint. With most teams running iterations of two weeks, project managers usually agreed to refrain from altering anything more than the priorities of tasks against the rhythm of the sprints. Instead, tasks were usually introduced through changing product backlog items and their priorities.

3.3   Task Uncertainties

Uncertainty concerning the best way to approach a task was a common theme during the interviews. The most frequently mentioned forms of task uncertainty were missing knowledge about the scope of a task, and lacking clues concerning the optimal solution, which resulted in time-consuming exploratory work.

Quality of a Solution. Finding the optimal solution to a problem requires skills, experience and oftentimes teamwork in order to pool knowledge and discuss possibilities and likely consequences. Expertise was shared with new team members through mentoring systems and pair programming sessions. Some teams by default implemented special task forces assigned to a problem, whereas others implemented frequent consultation meetings. Content specific knowledge was shared in order to qualify more team members to join discussions:

"in our team we do a bit of everything; design, development, testing... I'm just a regular team member and I have to adjust myself to every role" (A2, developer)

The functional separation of roles and responsibilities was less present than the separation according to expertise. Participants stressed that, despite the existence of distinct roles among team members, functional boundaries were often breached according to status resulting mainly from expertise:

"There are roles, sure. But sometimes they are not that strict. A tester who does only testing, a developer who does only development, a designer who does only design, these exist... but when you look at the team as a whole, then they don't – everybody here can work according to his skills" (A1, developer)

Unexpected Difficulties. Developers often got stuck due to lack of experience or task specific knowledge, or because unexpected difficulties arise with a work item.

Participants reported that clear signalling of task completion status helped within a system of transparent process visualisation (usually the task board or an online tool). When cards on a Scrum board were used, they were marked clearly as blocked. This signalled when help was needed or delays expected if demand for team member support remained unmet.

Task Sequence and Process Uncertainty results from incomplete information about a task's dependencies, which are intransparent especially in complex environments where no formal documentation is available. This requires (sometimes informal) meetings to understand the systemic environment. Participants reported that meetings, e.g. during coffee breaks and lunch, contributed significantly to their understanding of the overall process in which they worked. Consequently, some teams institutionalised common coffee breaks, e. g. once per day with the whole team.

Almost all teams tried to counteract a lack of process transparency using process visualisations including Scrum boards and keeping information visible on large sheets attached to a wall. Participants viewed it as the responsibility of the Scrum Master to prioritise tasks, sequentially order them, and make sure the tasks that are picked up belong to one story. Although team members were self-organised in their eyes, many relied on mechanisms that provided them with tasks to be completed. At the same time, developers felt they needed details about the overall process.

3.4   Output Uncertainties

The output a team can produce depends much on its resources and capabilities. Erroneous assumptions, unexpected difficulties or emergencies can force a team to deliver less than expected product features or result in diminished quality, e. g. when thorough testing is omitted.

Time Required to Accomplish a Task and Amount of Accomplishable Work. Output uncertainty was found in most teams in the form of a temporal uncertainty with regard to accomplishable work items in a given time period. Team members were stopped from working on a particular task because of unrelated emergencies that required immediate action, or because of underestimated required work effort. When tasks remained unfinished at the end of a sprint, most teams tried to break off unfinished parts into a new task, which was referred to the subsequent iteration, or they rescheduled the whole task. To mitigate the effects of distractions by emergencies, dependencies between tasks were minimised through assigning independent groups of developers to separated task bundles and formulating tasks as small as possible in size. This way, delays stemming from interdependent tasks could me avoided.

When uncertain about the amount of work that can be accomplished during an iteration, agile software developers usually rely on estimations. Estimation meetings served our participants to pool knowledge from all team members in order to predict the workload of an unknown task as accurately as possible. However, in many cases specific expertise impeded the participation of more than a few team members, while the remaining ones considered themselves disqualified for discussions and therefore blindly trusted their peers' judgements. All teams performed estimation meetings at the beginning of a sprint, and most re-estimated tasks on a regular basis (e. g., every second day) as new information became available. Conservative estimates served as uncertainty buffers. Participants reported that the accuracy of task estimations largely depended on technological expertise, knowledge about the business environment, and team cohesion, which is related to the time a team had spent together.

The extension of an iteration in the case of unfinished work was a solution applied by one team in order not to *"drag old tasks into a new sprint"* (D1, Scrum Master), but strongly discouraged by others, including a Scrum coach.

Project Status. All teams faced uncertainty about the amount of work remaining. Mitigation was largely drawn from daily status meetings in combination with a system established to signal transparently not only the status of task accomplishment but also the backlog of unattended work items. Daily status meetings were reported to reduce output uncertainties through the frequent possibility to monitor and report current output, as every developer gave a daily account for any completed and newly commenced task. This, however, was usually limited by the temporal horizon of one iteration. Long-term output was monitored and task distribution moderated by specially designated roles, such as the Product Owner, Scrum Master, or business representatives. In some situations, team members were drawn too deeply into daily activities that the overall direction fell into oblivion. One Product Owner reported that when she and the Scrum Master both were absent for a few days, the team

"lost track over its tasks and when [they] came back the team was way out of focus [...], they were taking tasks without tracking progress" (B1, Product Owner).

Quality. Variations in the delivered quality were mitigated by the attempt to involve customers in the testing, which focussed on the functionality important to them despite not being qualified software testers. Establishing mutual support among team members contributed to maintaining quality standards. When the team develops a sense of shared responsibility, developers are more likely to support their colleagues:

"I have the responsibility for the whole result and not just for my part" (A1, developer).

Code Errors were reported to be a frequent impediment. In order to avoid them, teams relied on early testing as much as possible, which was constrained by limited access to deployment systems in some cases. Several teams had successfully integrated the functional roles of developers and testers in their team, however, one interviewee warned that it might be detrimental if a developer tests his own code because he will have a narrow sense of the functionality and waste resources.

Unexpected errors during the release of a product were reported to appear less frequently when there is close collaboration with (external) stakeholders and their involvement in release planning activities. Having a release plan that is followed step-wise enables the team to identify the locus of errors quicker. One developer reported delays and decreased functionality of a released product version that could have been avoided if the affected database administrators had participated in a release kick off meeting organised by his team to have everybody on the same page.

Table 2. Uncertainties and applied practices to manage them. Practices that were employed as suggested ASD methods are denoted by (1): Scrum or (2): XP.

Type	Uncertainty or unexpected event	Uncertainty management practice
Resource	Availability of process artefacts	Discussing workarounds with the team in case necessary artefacts are missing, Analysing risks systematically.
	Quality of input	Collaborating closely with suppliers in order to develop understanding for differences[1,2].
	Availability of human resources	Working with redundant roles [1] and skills, Maintaining a knowledge base, Using transparency enhancing tools, such as publicly displayed charts or workflows [1,2].
	Duration for new team members to become productive	Recruiting within the organisation, Keeping documents of company and team procedures updated, Pair programming to support faster knowledge transfer [2].
Require-ment	Lack of details about demanded functionality	Integrating stakeholders into the project [1,2], Directly communicating with customers [1,2], Early prototyping to focus discussions [1,2].
	Ambiguous information	Performing investigative tasks until prev. defined clarity criteria are fulfilled [1].
	Unexpected changes	Allowing change requests only at certain points in time, i. e. not during sprints [1].
Task	Quality of a problem solution	Sharing of content specific knowledge among team to improve discussions, Pooling team members into task forces, Pair programming [2].
	Unexpected difficulties	Signalling of blocked tasks [1,2], Cultivating mutual team member support.
	Task sequence or process uncertainty	Improving processes via team reflections [1], Recognising the importance of informal meetings.
Output	Time required to accomplish a task	Minimising task sizes and dependencies, Matching levels of dependencies to developer availabilities.
	Amount of accomplishable work	Regularly updating task estimations [1,2].
	Project status	Separation of responsibilities according to temporal perspectives [1]; long-term planners moderate task distribution and prioritisation.
	Quality of the product	Early and frequent testing [1,2], Establishing shared team responsibility [1,2], Integration of functional roles [1], Involving external stakeholders through direct communication, esp. of plans [1,2].

4   Discussion

Agile software development (ASD) 'embraces' uncertainties by acknowledging the necessity to react flexibly to unforeseen and unforeseeable events during the course of a project. Our results reveal several mechanisms that are used by agile teams to address different types of uncertainties. The power to manage requirements uncertainties, for which ASD methods are well suited, was especially evident. In addition, ASD teams employ mechanisms to manage resource, task, and output uncertainties. However, in our study their management was complemented in many cases by practices that were not explicitly proposed by ASD methods.

Attempts to control uncertainties are less present in ASD than the emphasis on maintaining flexibility to cope with them. Flexibility is an important prerequisite for the effective management of uncertainties. Without flexibility, a team cannot mitigate the impact of unexpected difficulties or unforeseen dependencies. An inflexible team has insufficient capacity to react adequately to unexpected events, and limited access to a number of practices including the swapping of roles, or dynamically assigning the complementary skills of pair programmers to an emergent task. Positive effects of flexibility surface especially with regard to changing environments. For example, ineffective planning time is reduced when flexible task sequences allow the collection of information required for planning at the point in time at which it is needed.

Team autonomy and the redundancy of critical resources are important contributors to levels of flexibility that enable teams to become better uncertainty managers.

Team coordination and leadership style are closely connected to levels of autonomy and differ substantially between teams. Agile teams rely heavily on structures that support mechanisms for coordination and collaboration. On the basis of structural routines, ASD teams seize a variety of coordination and collaboration mechanisms that help them to collaborate on a wide range of issues [17]. Participants in our study profited from frequent status meetings, the use of physical artefacts and collocation. The benefit of having clearly defined roles and responsibilities, especially for tasks with shared responsibility, surfaced in situations of their absence. Explicitly defined routines provide important guidelines in situations where efficiency is crucial. The positive effects of collocation, and team members' redundant competence have already been discussed in previous research [18,19].

The relationship between flexibility and structure (also referred to as stability or stable structures) has been studied in the literature most prominently in connection with organisational exploration and exploitation [20]. Many authors believe that exploration and exploitation constitute opposite but complementary team characteristics. The notion of exploration refers to flexibility, the creation of knowledge and discovery of new solutions, as opposed to exploiting existing knowledge and solutions by relying on established structures.

It has been argued that a balance needs to be achieved between flexibility and structure in order to optimally address uncertainties [9]. On the one hand, flexibility is necessary to cope with the fast changes and the uncertainties that govern software development. On the other hand, structure needs to be established for efficient work processes and effective knowledge management. Teams who employ both display the ambidexterity that is important for creativity and innovation. These play a vital role in

ASD teams who are constantly pushed to deliver novel solutions. Teams must rely on the potential for creativity that is rooted in adequate collaborative processes [21]. Therefore, the same mechanisms that support the management of uncertainty foster creative thinking and create potential for innovation that requires the application of creative solutions to new problems. However, ASD methods themselves can also provide sources of uncertainties when the flexibility they create remains unmet by the establishment of adequate structures.

One way of seizing organisational ambidexterity is to move flexibly within the boundaries of structured work processes, or to use given structures that allow flexible reactions. Agile software developers routinely apply a number of concepts connected to uncertainty management that organisational researchers found in high-risk teams or action teams. For example, organisational bricolage (defined as 'making do by applying combinations of the resources at hand to new problems and opportunities' by [22]) was found in a study of fire fighters and film crews who routinely had to adapt to unexpected events [23]. One mechanism the teams used was to reorder the sequences of the work process by taking advantage of their knowledge of the work progression and how tasks fit together. Reordering the work involved changing the sequence in which pieces of the overall project were completed. Agile software teams routinely engage in similar practices by prioritising work tasks, evaluating their content and required estimated effort, and re-prioritising them in the event of an unexpected change. The sequential order of tasks is changed in case of unforeseen impediments. Formal roles exist in teams, but are not dominant. Instead, teams rely on a functional hierarchy that is characterised by informal roles according to skills and expertise, while responsibility often remains shared by the entire team. In order to ensure broad knowledge and capabilities across all team members, the breaching of formally assigned roles is common.

5   Limitations

In this study a small number of teams was studied. All teams operated in large company environments where additional contextual constraints apply that may not be generalizable to small firms with different organisational infrastructures. For example, large companies may have less difficulty to temporarily mitigate resource uncertainties in emergency situations because they have more access to resources.

Data collection was performed in a narrow period of time and did not allow us to observe the projects' developments on a larger scale. Our analysis is based mainly on interviews. In order to mitigate limiting factors to our analysis, we visited the teams in their work environments, in almost all cases more than once, and spoke with several team members and project managers to enhance our understanding of the projects.

6   Conclusion

In this paper, we addressed under-discussed aspects regarding different types of uncertainties in software development projects, and identified practices to manage them. We presented findings from an empirical study that involved five agile software development (ASD) teams. A total of 19 interviews were conducted to explore the teams' challenges associated with uncertainties. We investigated practices to manage four types of uncertainties; resource uncertainty (concerning the availability of human resources and process artefacts), requirements uncertainties (represented by customer demands), task uncertainty (referring to unexpected problems, such as dependencies on delayed input), and output uncertainty (incomplete information concerning the deliverable schedule and scope of the product). The identification of these practices extends our understanding of systematic uncertainty management and possible strategies that are available to teams, which is important in the face of increasing complexity of software projects and, hence, increasing sources of uncertainties. A key output from this study is a set of practices for the effective management of different types of uncertainties, the antecedents of which we discussed based on our insights.

ASD methods provide powerful tools to reduce a number of uncertainties, or cope with them in case they are not eliminable. For example, mechanisms exist to support the estimation of the time to finish a task with satisfactory accuracy, or to react to frequent changes of requirements. Still, agile teams sometimes have to go beyond the possibilities provided by ASD methods in order to adequately react to uncertainties. For uncertainties, such as the time required to make a new team member productive, ASD practices offer little specific advice, and self-organising agile teams have to complement them by missing mechanisms.

The potential to manage uncertainties depends not only on the structures that ASD methods provide, but also on the organisational context and the competence of the team itself. In order to design effective uncertainty management policies one must, therefore, keep in mind mutual dependencies among different types of uncertainties. We recommend that project managers pay attention to systemic dependencies and mutual relationships of uncertainties that affect the performance of a team.

In this study, we focused on the practice of uncertainty management through the lens of four types of uncertainties that were discussed with the participants of this and other studies in order to produce a representative set of uncertainties that ASD teams face. However, the possibility exists that our list is still incomplete and further types of uncertainties are of importance for other teams. We therefore suggest that future research concentrates on producing a complete taxonomy of uncertainties.

Acknowledgements. We thank the participants of this study and their managers for the possibility to explore their projects and spending much of their time explaining and answering questions. We also thank two anonymous reviewers who provided valuable comments and suggestions for this publication.

References

1. Williams, L., Cockburn, A.C.: Agile Software Development: It's about Feedback and Change. IEEE Computer 36 (2003)
2. Nerur, S., Mahapatra, R.K., Mangalaraj, G.: Challenges of Migrating to Agile Methodologies. Communications of the ACM 48, 73–78 (2005)
3. Laplante, P.A., Neill, C.J.: Uncertainty: A Meta-Property of Software. In: 29th Annual IEEE/NASA Software Engineering Workshop, pp. 228–233 (2005)

4. Nidumolu, S.: Standardization, Requirements Uncertainty and Software Project Performance. Information & Management 31, 135–150 (1996)
5. Milliken, F.J.: Three Types of Perceived Uncertainty about the Environment: State, Effect, and Response Uncertainty. The Academy of Management Review 12, 133–143 (1987)
6. McConnell, S.: Software Estimation: Demystifying the Black Art. Microsoft Press (2006)
7. Stutzke, R.D.: Estimating Software-Intensive Systems. Addison-Wesley Professional (2005)
8. Boehm, B.: Software Engineering Economics. IEEE Transactions on Software Engineering 10 (1984)
9. Grote, G., Kolbe, M., Waller, M.J.: On the Confluence of Leadership and Coordination in Balancing Stability and Flexibility in Teams. Paper presented at the 72nd Annual Meeting of the Academy of Management, Boston (2012)
10. Wang, X., Conboy, K.: Understanding Agility in Software Development through a Complex Adaptive Systems Perspective. Presented at the European Conference on Information Systems, December 1 (2009)
11. Boehm, B.W., Turner, R.: Balancing Agility and Discipline. Addison-Wesley (2004)
12. Grote, G.: Uncertainty Management at the Core of System Design. Annual Reviews in Control 28, 267–274 (2004)
13. Maruping, L.M., Venkatesh, V., Agarwal, R.: A Control Theory Perspective on Agile Methodology Use and Changing User Requirements. Information Systems Research 20, 377–399 (2009)
14. Robinson, H., Segal, J., Sharp, H.: Ethnographically-Informed Empirical Studies of Software Practice. Information and Software Technology 49, 540–551 (2007)
15. Glaser, B.G., Strauss, A.L.: The Discovery of Grounded Theory: Strategies for Qualitative Research. Sociology Press, Aldine (1967)
16. Ebert, C., De Man, J.: Requirements Uncertainty: Influencing Factors and Concrete Improvements. Presented at the 27th International Conference on Software Engineering, ICSE (2005)
17. Sharp, H., Robinson, H.: Collaboration and Co-ordination in mature eXtreme Programming Teams. International Journal of Human-Computer Studies 66, 506–518 (2008)
18. Moe, N., Dingsoyr, T., Dyba, T.: Overcoming Barriers to Self-management in Software Teams. IEEE Software (2009)
19. Dorairaj, S., Noble, J., Malik, P.: Understanding Team Dynamics in Distributed Agile Software Development. In: Wohlin, C. (ed.) XP 2012. LNBIP, vol. 111, pp. 47–61. Springer, Heidelberg (2012)
20. Lavie, D., Stettner, U., Tushman, M.L.: Exploration and Exploitation Within and Across Organizations. The Academy of Management Annals 4, 109–155 (2010)
21. Hoegl, M., Parboteeah, K.P.: Creativity in Innovative Projects: How Teamwork Matters. Journal of Engineering and Technology Management 24, 148–166 (2007)
22. Baker, T., Nelson, R.: Creating Something from Nothing: Resource Construction through Entrepreneurial Bricolage. Administrative Science Quarterly 50, 329–366 (2005)
23. Bechky, B.A., Okhuysen, G.A.: Expecting the unexpected? How SWAT Officers and Film Crews handle Surprises. Academy of Management Journal 54, 239–261 (2011)
24. Boehm, B.W., Abts, C., Brown, W., Chulani, S., Clark, B.K., Horowitz, E., Madachy, R., Reifer, D.J., Steece, B.: Software Cost Estimation with COCOMO II. Prentice Hall, Upper Saddle River (2000)
25. Racheva, Z., Daneva, M., Buglione, L.: Supporting the Dynamic Reprioritization of Requirements in Agile Development of Software Products. In: Proceedings of the Second International Workshop on Software Product Management, IWSPM (2008)

Key Challenges of Improving Agile Teamwork

Nils Brede Moe

SINTEF, Strindveien 4,
NO-7465 Trondheim, Norway
nils.b.moe@sintef.no

Abstract. Inspect and adapt is essential to succeed with agile software development. Our objective was to understand the challenges of software process improvement in agile software development teams. We designed a multiple case study consisting of five projects in three software product companies that applied Scrum. We collected data in semi-structured interviews. We found that long-term quality was often in conflict with short-term progress, specialization hinders self-management, process related problems are difficult to solve and there are major organizational barriers to self-management. The main conclusion drawn from this work is that software process improvement challenges in agile software development are the problems of increasing redundancy to create conditions for the team to self-manage, to learn how to learn, and to improving agile software development as a large long-term organizational change project.

Keywords: Agile software development, multiple case study, software process improvement, single-loop and double-loop learning, learning to learn, retrospective, self-management, team.

1 Introduction

Agile software development is characterized by repeated cycles of thought-action-reflection that foster an environment of learning and adaptation [1]. In Agile development, the empowered self-managing team should base work coordination on face-to-face communication, and is responsible for improving the software development process through frequent reflection. This has been stated in three of the twelve principles of the Agile Manifesto[1]:

- The most efficient and effective method of conveying information to and within a development team is face-to-face conversation.
- At regular intervals the team reflects on how to become more effective, then tunes and adjusts its behavior accordingly.
- The best architectures, requirements, and designs emerge from self-organizing teams.

---

[1] http://agilemanifesto.org

H. Baumeister and B. Weber (Eds.): XP 2013, LNBIP 149, pp. 76–90, 2013.

Agile software development comprises a number of practices and methods [2-4]. Which practices and methods to choose depend on the type and size of the project and the company culture. Also, the various agile software development methods (e.g. Extreme Programming and Scrum) support different part of the life cycle and differ to a large degree in the way they cover project management [5]. Therefore several agile methods and practices are often combined in a project. In other words, software companies need to learn how to improve and change their agile development processes. One can argue that commitment to learning rather than a commitment to any particular agile method is more important to have success with agile software development.

While inspection and adapting is the core of agile software development, there are only a few studies focusing on software process improvement (SPI) and agile development. One such study is the work by Ringstad et al [6] who conclude that that process improvement, although a central concept in agile development is hard to achieve. In the study by Salo and Abrahamsson [7], the authors found that a large portion of the of the agreed improvement actions remained undone. Salo and Abrahamsson argue that there is a need for new SPI mechanisms for agile software development. Further, a study by Qumer and Henderson-Sellers [8] suggests a framework which can be used to create, modify, and tailor situation-specific agile software processes. The model includes among others an agility measurement model and an agile adoption and improvement model. However, this framework was only explored in a limited way.

It's one thing to describe models for how to improve the development process in industry projects running; it's quite another to enable such teams to improve the work processes in practice. Therefore, this study focus on the main barriers and challenges we have seen in empirical studies on the team and organizational level when improving the software development process in agile teams. We have therefore identified the following research question:

What are the software process improvement challenges in agile software development?

To investigate this research question we conducted a case study of SPI in three companies doing agile software development. The main contribution of this paper is that the teams need to increase redundancy for enabling self-management, which is a prerequisite for the teams to improve. Also the teams need to learn how to learn, and to perceive improving agile software development as a large long-term organizational change project.

The remainder of this paper is organized as follows: The next section outlines the background and relevant literature on process improvement in agile software development and organizational learning. Section 3 describes the research methods used, Section 4 reports our results, Section 5 discusses the findings, and Section 6 concludes.

2   Background

As information technology's role in the modern economy grows in importance, society makes exponentially greater demands on the diversity and quality of the software being produced. Time-to-market can spell the difference between a successful product release and bankruptcy. Software process improvement (SPI) is a primary approach to improving software quality and reliability, employee and client satisfaction, and return on investment [9].

In this section we first present background information on software process improvement in an agile context, and then SPI and organizational learning.

2.1   SPI in Agile Software Development

In software development there is a long tradition of work on software processes [9, 10]. Software process improvement (SPI) is about making things better – as opposed to fire fighting or handling crises. It is a way to look at how software developers can do their work better. If software developers only concentrate on solving a problem or correcting a fault, they risk not finding the underlying causes. In the worst case, their actions can make things worse. In addition to identifying problems, the result of SPI should be to identify underlying causes of the problem, define, implement, and evaluate the results of the actions, and finally to carry out possible changes in the rest of the organization. When engaging in process improvement, the goal is to learn about what happened in a process, and to use that knowledge to improve the process as well as the resulting services and products. The improvement work need to be continuous [11].

Agile software development addresses the improvement and management of software development practices on the team-level and within ongoing projects, and seek to move ownership and responsibility from the organizational-level to the team-level [12]. Further, in agile development, processes are practices which evolve dynamically within the team as it adapts to the particular circumstances [13]. Salo and Abrahamsson [7] argue that the SPI in an agile environment is concerned with constant reflection and therefore continuous improvement. The primary focus is on the immediate use of the experiences of developers in improving the ongoing project.

Aaen et al [14] describe SPI in the agile mindset as decentralized with an emphasis on project and team level standardization of processes. Key to this approach is the support for adaptive SPI practices. Learning takes place within the project through continuous sense-and-response cycles, which identify current weaknesses, initiate new efforts, and implement their results as the project evolves and delivers its outcomes.

The agile team is also supposed to be self-managing and empowered, which means from a socio-technical perspective that the team members are responsible for managing, monitoring, and improving their own processes [15]. Therefore, SPI in agile software development can be classified as a bottom-up approach.

2.2   Organizational Learning and SPI

One of the most important driving forces for software process improvement is that the software developers actually learn how to improve their activities [16-18]. SPI can be seen as an organizational change mechanism. The learning process when conducting SPI demands group learning [16], because software development is a highly collaborative activity carried out within teams, projects, departments, and companies; it always concerns a group of people. Agile software development supports group learning through frequent feedback sessions involving the whole development team.

In their theory of learning, Argyris and Schön [19] distinguish between what they call single and double-loop learning in organizations. Single-loop learning is to change practice as problems arise in order to avoid the same problem in the future. For example, management often engages in single-loop learning by monitoring development costs, software quality, sales, client satisfaction, and other indicators of performance to ensure that the organizational activities remain within established limits, keeping the organization "on course". In single-loop learning, if outcomes of actions are not met, the actions are changed slightly to achieve the desired results. It is a feedback loop from observed effects to making some changes or refinements that in turn influence the effects, see Figure 1.

Double-loop learning, on the other hand, is when time is taken to understand the factors that influence the effects, and the nature of this influence, called the governing values [19]. It is about using the problems being experienced to understand their underlying causes, and then to take some action to remedy these causes. One example is what happens when a software error is corrected. Correcting the error itself can be seen as single loop learning, but if something is done with whatever caused the error to be introduced, that is considered double-loop learning. The changes based on this type of understanding will be more thorough. One example is the introduction of the self-managing agile team, which requires that operating norms and rules are allowed to change (double-loop learning) along with transformation in the wider environment [20]. When focus is on single-loop learning, norms and values remain unchanged [21]. Single-loop learning is nevertheless predominant in most organizations [19].

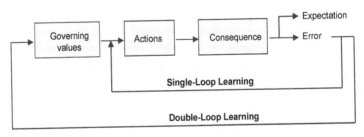

Fig. 1. Single and double-loop learning [19]

To sum up, in single-loop learning a specific problem is solved, while in double-loop learning, a set of governing values (goals and constraints) is questioned, which may impact many future problems. Single-loop learning is about asking "are we doing things right?", while double-loop learning is about asking "are we doing the right things?".

3   Research Method

Since the goal of this research is to explore and provide insight into the phenomenon of SPI in agile software development, it is important to study software development teams in practice. Therefore, we chose a multiple case study. Case studies are especially useful for such exploratory research where an in-depth understanding of a phenomenon in its context is desired [22]. Because variations in culture across software organizations can have important implications for SPI outcomes [23] we designed a multiple case study based on the assumption that the cases from different companies will produce contradictionary results.

3.1   Study Context

As part of on action research program, the author of this paper designed a Scrum training program together with the three companies under study. On the first day of the agile training the participants were introduced to Scrum by an experienced Scrum trainer. The second day focused on tailoring agile practices to the projects, which were later included in this study. After introducing agile software development in the companies, the teamwork and the agile development processes were regularly evaluated, and improvement measures were suggested. Five teams were observed (see Table 1) over three years. In addition to the initial training program, the Scrum masters were given extra training and coaching.

Table 1. Teams and data collection sources

	No. of developers	Team no	Team size	Project length	No. of interviews
MidSoft	16	1	6	11 months	12
		2	6	12 months	12
NorSoft	60	3	7	20 months	13
EastSoft	150	4	8	30 months	11
		5	7	30 months	11

This particular study was initially part of a multiple case study on barriers to self-management in software teams [24]. While the multiple case study (ibid) identified barriers to self-management, this study focuses on the phenomena of software process improvement. We relied on interviews in this study. A brief description of each company will now be given.

3.1.1 NorSoft
This company is one of the leading producers of receiving stations for data from meteorological and earth observation satellites. The company works with large development projects, both as a prime contractor and a subcontractor. Clients range

from universities to companies such as Lockheed Martin and Alcatel, and government institutions such as the European Space Agency and the Norwegian Meteorological Institute. Most of the software systems developed at NorSoft run on Unix and the remainder - on Linux operating system.

The company has approximately 60 employees. The staff is stable and highly skilled, many with Master's degrees in computer science, mathematics, or physics, and it has what can be described as an engineering culture.

3.1.2   EastSoft

EastSoft has approximately 150 employees in three organizational units. About 80% of the employees have a Master's or a Doctoral degree. Most of the people working in the software development department have been trained as engineers (2/3 of the staff) rather than professional software developers (1/3 of the staff) but the proportion of software developers is increasing. The company aims to hire highly skilled staff. Most of the projects relied on the .NET framework in Visual Studio using C#. EastSoft produces specialized software for the engineering domain. The company sells mass-market software, but also writes client specific software on a contract basis. In addition to Norway, the company conducts software development in its offices in China, Eastern Europe, and the UK. All developers and project managers in the projects investigated were located at the company's headquarters in Oslo, Norway.

3.1.3   MidSoft

This company was established in 1996. It has three regional divisions and one separate ICT division. The ICT division consists of a consulting department, an IT management department, and a development department. In addition to software development projects for outside clients, the ICT division develops and maintains a series of off-the-shelf software products, which are developed in-house. During the study, the development department had about 16 employees, divided into a Java and a .NET group.

The company develops a software system for archiving, planning, and coordination, with a combination of textual user interfaces and map functionality. The clients are from all over Norway; one important client was the local government of a Norwegian city's.

3.2   Data Analysis

All material from the transcribed interviews where imported into NVivo, and has been read and coded several times. Coding was done by assigning interesting expressions of opinions in the text to a specific category with other similar expressions. In this way, concepts were identified and their properties and dimensions were discovered in the data. Events, happenings, objects, and actions/interactions, which were found to be conceptually similar in nature or related in meaning, were grouped under more abstract concepts termed categories. A category represents a phenomenon, that is a problem, an issue, or an event that is defined as being significant to the respondents or to the phenomena observed.

One example is the phrase "the retrospective turned out to be just another nice meeting without really discussing the problems", which was coded into the category "Retrospective do not give value". This expression was then seen as one explanation for why the team stopped doing retrospectives.

4   Results

Because different companies mean different organizational culture we assumed that the cases from different companies would produce contradictionary results. However from analyzing the results we found similar results: that short development cycles provided continuous and rapid loops of iterative learning, to enhance the processes, and to guide the improvement. The self-managing team was responsible for these improvement initiatives. However, all teams under study experienced major SPI challenges, especially related to becoming truly self-managing and to handling problems reported during team reflection (team learning).

Four key SPI challenges emerged from the cases:

- Long-term quality is in conflict with short-term progress
- Specialization hinders self-management
- Process problems are difficult to solve
- There are major organizational barriers to self-management

4.1   Key Challenge 1: Long-Term Quality Is in Conflict with Short-Term Progress

Short iterations in agile software development are about creating the most business value for the client (immediate value creation). However, this often seemed to be in conflict with the need for long-term quality, which was especially evident when observing the tension between keeping the time schedule and meeting the quality requirements.

While short iterations and frequent testing made it possible to fix defects continually, several teams were not strict about the "done" criteria - what does it mean that a component or a feature is finished? Teams stopped performing thorough testing at the end of iterations in order to be able to deliver all planned features. The main reason for too little testing was that the team felt they needed to show progress, i.e. to deliver what was decided upon in the planning meeting (team 2). Some Scrum masters and team members even tried to give the impression that the team was better than it actually was. The desire to keep the time schedule in some of the teams hindered the recognition of serious problems with, for instance, a third party component, testing, integration, or performance (team 1). As a consequence, all teams experienced quality problems

Another challenge was that it seemed difficult to prioritize other quality related processes (e.g. refactoring and code review) that would improve the quality in the long run, when these activities would reduce the pace of producing new features.

Furthermore, it seemed difficult to prioritize architectural work and design. One product owner felt that the team was so busy implementing features that no one was taking care of the biggest concern, which was to build architecture to last for ten years (team 4). The team, on the other hand, interpreted the feedback from the product owner during the feedback meetings as a critique to how fast they developed new features. As a result the team tried to speed up even more. Four years later the whole architecture had to be rebuild.

All teams discussed the conflicts related to the challenges above in the retrospectives and daily meetings. Still, they found it difficult to give priority to quality improvement activities when planning and conducting the sprint. The reason was that keeping the schedule and delivering features according to the plan was seen as more important by the team.

4.2   Key Challenge 2: Specialization Hinders Self-management

The team members of a self-managing agile team are responsible for managing, monitoring and improving their own processes. Therefore, the ability of the teams to self-manage was essential for the ability to identify problems, problem solving, and subsequently to determine how SPI was progressing in the companies. However, problems regarding self-management occurred in all teams, and were challenging throughout all projects. Reasons were team members not being genuinely committing to the team plan, as well as missing shared leadership and shared decision-making in the team. Specialization is identified as the main reason for this, and the results supporting this finding are outlined below.

Because of specialization, it was usually prescribed who should do what in the project. Hence, developers mostly worked independently on particular modules according to their specific knowledge, and they were seldom involved in the work of other developers. As a consequence a team member focused on his or her own work, and less on the team processes.

Another effect of specialization was lack of team commitment resulting in team members giving higher priority to individual goals, even though the team goals should be the priority in a self-managing team. A number of the respondents explained that because of specialization, they found it difficult to commit to work they were not involved in, and consequently it was problematic for them to take part in decisions regarding work of others. This made shared decision-making hard; an individual and decentralized decision-making process resulted in difficulties aligning process improvement decisions on the team-level because team members did not know what others were doing.

Finally, because of specialization the teams developed unrealistic plans. The planning meeting is where the team is expected to do shared planning and decision-making. However, the meetings often ended up with only a few people talking and the rest listening. Some people even fell asleep. The poorly managed planning meetings resulted in unrealistic plans with too many tasks, which again affected the quality of the software being developed. As described earlier, some teams pretended to be more effective than they really were. As a consequence, a new iteration often started by completing what was officially done in the previous iteration. The effect was that the plans became even more unrealistic (everyone knew this), and consequently the team members focused even more on their own goals and individual plans and less on improving the team processes.

4.3   Key Challenge 3: Process Problems Are Difficult to Solve

In Scrum, the retrospective meeting is the most important meeting for discussing and suggesting how to solve process related problems. However, because of highly specialized developers and the problems this caused for self-management in the teams, improvement work was challenging and improvement measures were often motivated by individual needs (e.g. solving technical problems, getting new development infrastructure) instead of what the whole team needed.

Through various Scrum meetings, there was a high focus on reporting problems. However, all companies seemed to have difficulties solving their process related problems. The two main reasons, why process related problems were difficult to solve, were related to difficulties with team reflection in the retrospective meeting and the lack of process related problems being reported. These two main reasons will now be described.

There were several signs of problems with the team reflection. As an example, team 1 reported the same problems in several consecutive retrospectives (e.g. lack of backup, problems not being reported, and lack of feedback), but no measures were taken to address the *cause* of the problems. When process issues were discussed, teams often ended up talking about the symptoms and not the cause of the problems. In addition, teams usually discussed whether they were doing things right according to the Scrum theory, but they seldom discussed whether they were doing the right things. One example was the conflict between the need for quality and the need for short-term progress. When a team experienced problems with the product quality, the team discussed how to improve the testing process and the testing framework. The real problem however was found in the interviews, when several developers explained that short-term progress was seen as more important by the team than the quality.

For problems to be solved, first they have to be identified. However, some process problems were not reported or talked about. This became evident when comparing data from observations of daily work and interviews with observations from retrospectives and daily meetings. Team members mostly reported problems related to technology (e.g. development tools, bugs, and integration of third party components). They seldom talked about important process problems such as why the backlog was never completed, why the sprint plan often ended up being unrealistic, why meetings often became unproductive, why some developers were mostly silent in the planning meetings, or why some developers often ended up working on other issues than originally planned.

To understand why problems were not solved it is therefore important to understand why problems were not reported. One reason was that some of the team members perceived the problems as personal and wanted to solve these problems themselves. Another reason was that some felt that there was too little trust within the team and between the team and the product owner; hence, they did not feel confident reporting problems. In team 1 the developers started reporting fewer problems because they did not trust the Scrum master to handle the problems correctly. They felt he was overreacting to problems stated in the daily meetings.

Another team experienced relationship problems with the product owner, since he never gave clear priority to the features for the next iteration. The Scrum master explained that the team newer confronted the product owner regarding this issue. A third reason for not reporting problems was that when the problems were not handled, the team members stopped reporting them. This was seen in team 4, where the team stopped conducting retrospectives for a long period because they felt this type of meeting did not give any value.

4.4   Key Challenge 4: There Are Major Organizational Barriers to Self-management

The implementation of self-managing teams is difficult, if not impossible, if there are critical barriers at the organizational level. Misalignment between team structure and organizational structure can be counterproductive, and attempts to implement self-managing teams can cause frustration for both developers and management. Two important barriers to self-management on the organizational level were identified.

First, shared resources were a challenge because when developers worked on two or more projects in parallel, and different team goals or needs were in conflict, it threatened at least one of the self-managing teams. In addition, some developers had to stop suddenly what they were doing, and support projects they had worked on earlier, without even being formally allocated to such projects. Developers explained that if they got involved in a project, he or she felt bound to it forever. The reason for this was that parts of the organization expected developers to work even if no resources were provided. This was a part of the company culture. When team members knew they would always lose resources during an iteration, it did not make sense for them to commit to the team plane or trying to improve the developing process.

Second, a self-managing team needs generalists —members with multiple skills who can perform each other's jobs as needs arise. However, all companies relied on specialization, and company incentives often supported this culture. An example was found in EastSoft, where one of the most prestigious roles was a chief architect. In the project studied, the chief architect participated in important decision meetings with the management; the management trusted him, and he had much influence on future strategy of their products. Becoming a chief architect was seen as positive both from an individual and the company perspective. Because the chief architect was the one solely responsible for the architecture, other team members were rarely involved in the decision-making. In NorSoft, developers were found protecting their knowledge, that is defending their code by not letting others work on it. If the code was important, then the developers became important to the company. Three years before introducing Scrum, NorSoft had to let some developers go, but not any of the "important" specialists. Therefore, letting others work on your code was considered a risk that could result in a loss of job or position in the company. It was understood that the development process could be improved, because being the only one working on important parts of the code was stressful during hectic periods and delayed the team as a whole.

5   Discussion

The previous chapter described four key findings from studying SPI in three agile companies. To summarize the results briefly: Problems were reported frequently, which made agile software development a strong infrastructure for SPI, but process related problems were difficult to solve. This was caused by problems related to learning and self-management. The self-managing team is the one responsible for SPI on the project level. However, this requires that the team is really able to self-manage; as a team they need to take important decisions about what to improve and how to do it. For a team to self-manage the team autonomy must be strong and the team needs to adopt double-loop learning and learn to learn. In addition, the team must be able to affect managerial decisions, which influence the ability to improve the team's internal processes. This section will discuss the results in light of the research question.

5.1   Creating Conditions for Self-management

Individual goals were found to be more important than team goals, which reduced the team autonomy and the possibility to self-manage. Interaction between group members became difficult and, therefore, threatened collaboration, cooperation, and subsequently the teamwork and the possibility to improve the work process. The observed effects are in agreement with the findings of Kraut and Streeter in their survey on coordination in software development [25]. One explanation why team members did not reduce their individual autonomy was that it was seen as beneficial by the developers. While the organizations seldom debated this problem of high individual autonomy, they frequently experienced and discussed its symptoms. Examples of symptoms were team members making their own individual plans, not reporting problems, taking decisions without informing others, known as decision-hijacking [26], and team members taking decisions based on expert power, known as technocracy [20].

Through frequent planning, daily, and retrospective meetings, team level autonomy increased, which enabled the team to self-manage. Team members experienced this as a positive change; however, at the same time they saw it as rigid control of each team member. This is in agreement with Barker [27], who pointed out that self-managing teams may end up controlling group members more rigidly than with traditional management styles. It can be argued that it caused resistance against change because the need for reducing the individual autonomy was not seen as an immediate improvement by the individuals. Resistance against change also made it difficult for the team to improve their development processes. Hence, this was a challenge for software process improvement in the agile teams.

Teams were also hindered from affecting managerial decisions, which influenced the ability to improve the team's internal processes. Management outside the team did not always respect the team's efforts for improvement, which caused the teams to experience symbolic self-management. Symbolic self-management is a well-known obstacle to true self-management [28]. There seem to be two reasons why management outside the team did not respect or support improvement measures suggested by the team.

First, management did not agree with or understand the reason for the problems reported, because management activities and processes had changed little since the adoption of agile software development in the organization. Examples of the areas with the greatest need for organizational changes were management of resources across teams and handling support. Changing the organizational culture at project level was probably also seen as a threat because it conflicted with existing and established habits of the management. The effect of such threats is confirmed by the argument of van Solingen et al. [16] explaining why SPI and organizational learning are difficult, and Schneider et al [29] who found that management might end up blocking emerging process change when they do not understand the implication of change.

Second, top management was not involved in the process improvement discussion in the Scrum meetings, although it is a prerequisite for becoming a well-functioning SPI organization [11, 30]. Salo and Abrahamsson [31] found that without support from the organizational level, a majority of improvement measures agreed upon within project teams cannot be implemented. One example of an organizational SPI issue not addressed at the organizational level was the need for building redundancy, to make developers cooperate more, and to make the team flexible and adaptable to changing conditions. However, building redundancy requires additional resources, which should be the responsibility of the organization [32]. However, the top management did not see the specialization as a problem, and then did not allocate resources for handling this problem.

5.2   Learning to Learn

Although the teams frequently reported problems, they experienced difficulties making the necessary changes to solve them. It can be argued that when an organization only suggests improvement measures without being able to implement them, only a potential for improvement exist. The main reason was that team members either did not manage or were not willing to discuss the underlying cause of problems. Some developers wanted to avoid interpersonal conflict, and some found it more important to conform to other group members, which is an indication of a lack of openness in the team. As a result the teams experienced ineffective decision-making when discussing the need for improvement. This is in agreement with the findings of McAvoy and Butler [21] on reasons for ineffective decision-making in agile teams. The effect of lack of openness on SPI is also in agreement with van

Sollingen et al [16], who argue that openness and the ability to discuss the underlying problems is one of the most important prerequisites for software process improvement and organizational learning. Because the teams were not able to create a climate for openness and change the way decisions were made, they did not improve the way of reflecting and learning together. In other words, they did not learn to learn. Learning to learn is also known as deutero-learning [19].

A team has learned to learn when it is questioning if we are doing things right (single-loop learning), if we are doing the right things (double-loop learning), and if we make these decisions, when answering "are we doing the right things?" correctly. The teams did mostly single-loop learning by focusing on improving existing agile practices. There were two explanations for this. First, several proponents of agile development claim universal applicability of agile methods, which results in teams focusing on doing things according to the book, and not on questioning if they were doing the right things. Second, some teams tried to give the impression that they were doing better than they actually were. The desire to keep the schedule hindered the recognition of serious problems with the code quality. Impression management [20] is a face-saving process where team members seek to protect themselves from management. This generates shared norms and patterns of group-thinking, which prevent people from addressing key issues.

From an organizational learning perspective, it can be claimed that engaging mostly in single-loop learning was a challenge to SPI, because this stopped the teams from questioning if they were doing the right things, and start learning to learn. Moreover, after several SPI problems were not solved, team members stopped reporting them, which again affected the ability to improve and to become self-managing. For a team to become self-managing it needs to change the operating norms and rules within the team, as well as in the wider environment.

6   Conclusions and Further Work

Software process improvement in agile software development is planned, executed, and evaluated by the empowered self-managing team. The team's ability to implement self-management, i.e. shared leadership, shared decision-making, and high team autonomy, was therefore a key SPI challenge, while specialization was the main obstacle to achieving this. Process problems were identified but often not solved, therefore only the potential for improvement existed. Software process improvement from an organizational learning perspective was particularly challenging because it became evident that the organizations had problems to engage in double-loop learning and to learn how to learn. Making SPI work in agile software development required a change in skills, procedures, structure, strategy, and culture, which required changes on the individual, project, and organizational level.

The main conclusion drawn from this work is that SPI challenges in agile software development are the problems of increasing redundancy to create conditions for the team to self-manage, to learn how to learn, and to perceive improving agile software development as a large long-term organizational change project.

Acknowledgments. This work was supported by the Research Council of Norway through grant 193236/I40. We appreciate the input received from managers and project participants of the investigated company. I am grateful to Torgeir Dingsøyr who gave me valuable feedback.

References

1. Nerur, S., Mahapatra, R., Mangalaraj, G.: Challenges of migrating to agile methodologies. Communications of the ACM 48(5), 72–78 (2005)
2. Erickson, J., Lyytinen, K., Siau, K.: Agile Modeling, Agile Software Development, and Extreme Programming: The State of Research. Journal of Database Management 16(4), 88–100 (2005)
3. Cohen, D., Lindvall, M., Costa, P.: An Introduction to Agile Methods. In: Zelkowitz, M.V. (ed.) Advances in Computers. Advances in Software Engineering. Elsevier, Amsterdam (2004)
4. Abrahamsson, P., et al.: Agile software development methods - Review and analysis. VTT Electronics. VTT Publications (2002)
5. Abrahamsson, P., et al.: New directions on agile methods: a comparative analysis (2003)
6. Ringstad, M.A., Dingsøyr, T., Moe, N.B.: Agile Process Improvement: Diagnosis and Planning to Improve Teamwork. In: O'Connor, R.V., Pries-Heje, J., Messnarz, R. (eds.) EuroSPI 2011. CCIS, vol. 172, pp. 167–178. Springer, Heidelberg (2011)
7. Salo, O., Abrahamsson, P.: An iterative improvement process for agile software development. Software Process: Improvement and Practice 12(1), 81–100 (2007)
8. Qumer, A., Henderson-Sellers, B.: A framework to support the evaluation, adoption and improvement of agile methods in practice. Journal of Systems and Software 81(11), 1899–1919 (2008)
9. Mathiassen, L., Ngwenyama, O.K., Aaen, I.: Managing change in software process improvement. IEEE Software 22(6), 84–91 (2005)
10. Conradi, R., Fuggetta, A.: Improving Software Process Improvement. IEEE Software 19(4), 92–99 (2002)
11. Aaen, I., et al.: A conceptual map of software process improvement. Scand. J. Inf. Syst. 13, 123–146 (2001)
12. Lycett, M., et al.: Migrating agile methods to standardized development practice. Computer 36(6), 79–85 (2003)
13. Aaen, I.: Essence: Facilitating Agile Innovation. In: Abrahamsson, P., Baskerville, R., Conboy, K., Fitzgerald, B., Morgan, L., Wang, X. (eds.) XP 2008. LNBIP, vol. 9, pp. 1–10. Springer, Heidelberg (2008)
14. Aaen, I., Börjesson, A., Mathiassen, L.: Navigating Software Process Improvement Projects. In: Baskerville, R.L., Mathiassen, L., Pries-Heje, J., DeGross, J.I. (eds.) Business Agility and Information Technology Diffusion. IFIP, pp. 53–71. Springer, Boston (2005)
15. Trist, E.: The evolution of socio-technical systems: a conceptual framework and an action research program, in Occasional paper No 2 1981, Ontario Quality of Working Life Centre, Toronto, Ontario
16. van Solingen, R., et al.: From process improvement to people improvement: enabling learning in software development. Information and Software Technology 42(14), 965–971 (2000)
17. Børjesson, A., Mathiassen, L.: Successful process implementation. IEEE Software 21(4), 36–44 (2004)

18. Dybå, T.: Improvisation in Small Software Organizations. IEEE Software 17(5), 82–87 (2000)
19. Argyris, C., Schön, D.A.: On Organizational Learning II: Theory, Method and Practise. Addison Wesley, Reading (1996)
20. Morgan, G.: Images of Organizations, p. 504. SAGE Publications, Thousand Oaks (2006)
21. McAvoy, J., Butler, T.: The role of project management in ineffective decision making within Agile software development projects. European Journal of Information Systems 18(4), 372–383 (2009)
22. Yin, R.K.: Case study research: design and methods, 4th edn. Sage, Thousand Oaks (2008)
23. Muller, S.D., Kraemmergaard, P., Mathiassen, L.: Managing Cultural Variation in Software Process Improvement: A Comparison of Methods for Subculture Assessment. IEEE Transactions on Engineering Management 56(4), 584–599 (2009)
24. Moe, N.B., Dingsøyr, T., Dybå, T.: Overcoming Barriers to Self-Management in Software Teams. IEEE Software 26(6), 20–26 (2009)
25. Kraut, R.E., Streeter, L.A.: Coordination in software development. Communications of the ACM 38(3), 69–81 (1995)
26. Aurum, A., Wohlin, C., Porter, A.: Aligning Software Project Decisions: A Case Study. International Journal of Software Engineering and Knowledge Engineering 16(6), 795–818 (2006)
27. Barker, J.R.: Tightening the Iron Cage - Concertive Control in Self-Managing Teams. Administrative Science Quarterly 38(3), 408–437 (1993)
28. Tata, J., Prasad, S.: Team Self-management, Organizational Structure, and Judgments of Team Effectiveness. Journal of Managerial Issues 16(2), 248–265 (2004)
29. Schneider, K., von Hunnius, J.P., Basili, V.R.: Experience in implementing a learning software organization. IEEE Software 19(3), 46–49 (2002)
30. Dybå, T.: An empirical investigation of the key factors for success in software process improvement. IEEE Transactions on Software Engineering 31(5), 410–424 (2005)
31. Salo, O., Abrahamsson, P.: Integrating agile software development and software process improvement: a longitudinal case study. In: International Symposium on Empirical Software Engineering (ISESE), pp. 187–196. IEEE, Noosa Heads (2005)
32. Fægri, T.E., Dybå, T., Dingsøyr, T.: Introducing knowledge redundancy practice in software development: Experiences with job rotation in support work. Information and Software Technology 52(10), 1118–1132 (2010)

Effects of Negative Testing on TDD: An Industrial Experiment

Adnan Causevic[1], Rakesh Shukla[2],
Sasikumar Punnekkat[1], and Daniel Sundmark[1]

[1] Mälardalen University, Sweden
{adnan.causevic,sasikumar.punnekkat,daniel.sundmark}@mdh.se
[2] Infosys Ltd. India
rakesh_shukla@infosys.com

Abstract. In our recent academic experiments, an existence of positive test bias, that is lack of negative test cases, was identified when a test driven development approach was used. At the same time, when defect detecting ability of individual test cases was calculated, it was noted that the probability of a negative test case to detect a defect was substantially higher than that of a positive test case.

The goal of this study is to investigate the existence of positive test bias in test driven development within an industrial context, and measure defect detecting ability of both positive and negative test cases. An industrial experiment was conducted at Infosys Ltd. India, whose employees voluntarily signed up to participate in the study and were randomly assigned to groups utilizing test driven development, test driven development with negative testing, and test last development. Source code and test cases created by each participant during the study were collected and analysed.

The collected data indicate a statistically significant difference between the number of positive and negative test cases created by industrial participants, confirming the existence of positive test bias. The difference in defect detecting ability of positive and negative test cases is also statistically significant. As a result, similarly to our previous academic study, 29% of all test cases were negative, contributing by revealing as much as 71% of all the defects found by all test cases. With this industrial experiment, we confirmed the existence of a positive test bias in an industrial context, as well as significantly higher defect detecting ability of negative test cases.

Keywords: Test-driven Development, Industrial Experiment, Quality of Testing.

1 Introduction

Performing efficient and effective software testing often comes with many challenges. Increased complexity of software systems, the need for a specific domain knowledge or the lack of testing experience are just a few obstacles a tester is

H. Baumeister and B. Weber (Eds.): XP 2013, LNBIP 149, pp. 91–105, 2013.

faced with in day to day activities. Today, with the presence of Agile methods, the quality of the software product becomes everyone's responsibility, not just the quality assurance or the testing department. A potential problem here is that not every member of the team has the appropriate expertise and sufficient training in quality assurance methods.

Test driven development (TDD) is one example of how developers can focus on the quality of software by writing executable and automated test scripts before writing the actual code. TDD was introduced as part of the eXtreme Programming (XP) methodology [1]. By writing test cases before the code, developers use tests to guide them in the correct implementation of the required functionality. In the literature, TDD is also referred as a test-first approach [2].

TDD was identified, in our industrial survey [3], as a preferred but not often used practice in industry. An interpretation of this finding could be that "respondents would like to use TDD to a significantly higher extent than they actually do". One reason for this preference towards TDD, could be that academic research results often highlight improvements in the code quality when TDD is utilized [4–8]. In our further investigations, a systematic literature review [9] was performed for the purpose of identifying any obstacles for a full scale adoption of TDD in an industrial context. Developer's inability to write efficient and effective automated test cases is considered to be one of the limiting factors. During the autumn semester in 2011, an academic experiment was conducted with master students with the intention of comparing testing efficiency and effectiveness of agile (test-first) and traditional (test-last) developers. This experiment [10] allowed us to investigate various software testing quality metrics in test-driven development by using created test cases, thus investigating the significance of a previously identified limiting factor.

Although we could not find any differences in the quality metrics for testing among the test-first and the test-last group of developers, we did notice that both groups created a much higher number of positive test cases compared to the negative ones. This effect, also known as positive test bias [11, 12], was present for both the test-first and test-last group. Interestingly, when measuring defect detecting ability of test cases, negative test cases detected much more defects compared to the positive ones. But since this was a limited study in an academic context, a larger study in an industrial context was needed to confirm the external validity of our findings and to verify if such an effect exists in the industry and to what extent, when compared to the academic results. Additionally, we want to investigate how test-driven development could utilize creation of negative tests while still "driving" the development. In this paper we present the results of such an industrial experiment.

2   Related Work

Empirical studies, performed for the purpose of investigating potential benefits of TDD focus mainly on the differences in the quality of the produced code. This was one of the finding we noticed in our systematic literature review [9], where we listed 48 empirical studies that had effects of TDD as the focus of the investigation. In most cases, TDD was in the primary focus of the investigation, but in some studies TDD was used together with a different practice, e.g. pair-programming.

However, one study was identified with the focus on quality attributes of *test cases* when a test-first approach was used. Madeyski [13] investigated how usage of TDD can impact branch coverage and mutation score indicators. In his experiment, 22 students were divided in two groups: the test-first and the test-last, with the task of developing a web based conference paper submission system. This experiment shows no statistically significant differences in branch coverage and mutation score indicators, between the test-first and the test-last groups. To the best of our knowledge, after performing our systematic review, we noticed one additional study [14] with the focus on developer's testing ability when following test driven development approach. This was an industrial observational experiment where developers performed programming tasks in their own offices without the control of researchers. Once developers submitted their code and test cases, researchers performed mutation testing to identify complementary test cases to the ones created during TDD process. Those unit tests, created by researchers, were still able to find several software faults in the submitted code.

In our previous academic study [10] we measured the code coverage and the mutation score indicators in a very similar way as it was done by Madeyski in his study. In accordance with the results of Madeyski, we were not able to notice any differences between the experiment groups. For the experiment presented in this paper, we have opted not to measure and analyse those attributes. The reason is that both those indicators are considered as an internal quality attributes of a test suite, while we are more interested in measuring the actual effectiveness of a test cases with respect to the defect detection. Specially, this is useful to distinguish what effect positive and negative test cases have on the overall testing effort. This is why our study design enforces programming interface for all participants, allowing us to execute the test cases of one participant on the code of all other participants.

Having results from our previous studies pointing out that experiment participants have a very small focus on "negative" test cases (existence of a positive test bias), the experiment performed in this study has a built-in mechanism of differentiating whether a particular test case is of a positive or negative type. More detailed explanation of what exactly constitute a negative test case, how we measure defect detecting efficiency and other concepts introduced in this study are presented in the following section.

3   Methodology and Study Design

Before going into the details of the experiment design, its execution and the analysis of the collected data, we would like to present to the reader several concepts which are defining the methodology used this study.

Negative Testing

By the term *negative test case*, we refer to a test case that was created for the purpose of exercising a program in a way that was not explicitly specified in the requirement. On the other hand, a *positive test case* exercises a program behaviour as it is specified in the requirement.

For example, a specification might state: "*... numbers are accepted as an input to the program ...* ", and testing such a program with any numerical input is considered as positive testing. For the same program, if testing is performed by providing a *character* input, that can be called negative testing.

Even in the case of an implicit specification, for example: "*... only numbers are accepted as an input to the program ...* ", testing using *character* inputs can still be considered negative testing, unless it is explicitly stated in the specification how the program should behave upon receiving character inputs.

Quality of Testing

Quality of software has been an active research area for the past few decades and several software measures ranging from simple lines of code to various complexity measures can be found in the literature to evaluate and improve the software quality from process or product perspectives [15]. However there had been no consensus on the universal applicability of any specific software quality metric and their usage had been more context specific and based on the intended objectives.

For our study we are primarily interested in formulating measures that can help in evaluating and improving the quality of testing, a topic which so far has not received much research attention. Obviously quality of testing is strongly related to the ability of test cases in finding defects in the code. However, in the context of new development paradigms like TDD, test cases are created by developers more as a safety net of the implemented functionality. They are capable of detecting wrong changes on the current software implementation, but they are not primarily focussing on finding defects. As a result the final set of test cases that accompany a software solution developed using TDD will show only its correctness but no defects in the same. In order to realistically measure the quality of testing we need to essentially have access to an *ideal test suite* which is capable of finding all the defects. Our approach here will be to approximate such an *ideal test suite* by combining all the test suites developed by several individual developers working on the same problem. Given such a set of multiple implementations and associated test suites, we are then able to cross-compare the ability of test cases to find defects.

Defect Detecting Ability

Defect detecting ability represents a total number of defects a particular test case can find in all the implementations of the same problem created by different developers. This number could be also calculated for all test cases created by a single developer, but more interestingly in the context of this study is to calculate how many defects are detected by negative and positive test cases.

Additionally, considering the differences in the expertise levels of the developers, we would like to give a higher quality value to a test case that is capable of finding defects in an implementation of high quality. Hence the evaluation of the quality of test cases will be much more meaningful if we jointly address it together with the quality of code in which we apply them.

Quality of Code (Q_{code})

Main reason why we need to calculate quality of code attribute is to support calculation of *Quality of Tests* attribute. Quality of the code for every developer (i) is calculated using next formula:

$$Q_{code}(i) = 1 - \frac{N_{FTC}(i)}{N_{TC}}$$

where, N_{TC} is a total number of test cases created by all developers and $N_{FTC}(i)$ represent total number of failing test cases on the code of a developer (i) by executing all test cases from all developers. Once we calculated *Quality of Code* value for each developer, we can now reward test cases who are able to detect defects in the underlying code.

Quality of Tests (Q_{tests})

Quality of test cases for a developer (i) is calculated as a sum of the quality of each test case (j) from a set of test cases (n) of that developer (i):

$$Q_{tests}(i) = \sum_{j=1}^{n} Q_{TC}(i.j)$$

To calculate the quality of an individual test case (j) of a developer (i) we need to know on which developers' code this test case is failing ($m \in M$). Sum of the *Quality of Code* values (Q_{code}) of those developers will define the quality of a particular test case (j):

$$Q_{TC}(i.j) = \sum_{k=1}^{m} Q_{code}(k)$$

Once this calculation is done for every developer, we can have a much better understanding of how much each and every test case contribute to the overall quality of testing. In the context of this study, it is interesting to observe how much negative and positive test cases contribute to the quality of testing.

3.1 Study Design

The design of this experiment originates from the academic study elaborated in [16]. However, to accommodate all challenges with performing such an experiment in industrial context (professional developers in an industrial settings), some modifications to the academic study design had to be done.

This experiment was setup with several goals in mind. As the main goal, we wanted to investigate if the effect of a positive test bias could be identified in an industrial setting regardless if the *test last* approach or TDD was used. We wanted to be able to examine the existence of such an effect by calculating the effectiveness of the provided tests. As an additional goal, in case the positive test bias effect existed, we wanted to investigate if it is possible to eliminate such an effect by providing participants with the support for the negative tests. Based on these goals, the following research questions were defined:

RQ1: *Does the effect of positive test bias exists in an industrial context?*
RQ2: *Is the defect detecting ability of negative test cases the same as the positive ones?*
RQ3: *Is the quality of negative test cases the same as that of positive test cases?*
RQ4: *Is there a difference in the quality of produced tests based on the usage of a specific development practice?*

In order to perform statistical testing, with respect to the stated research questions, following null and alternate hypotheses were formulated:

$\mathbf{H^1_0}$ There is no difference between the total number of positive and negative test cases created by experiment participants.
$\mathbf{H^1_a}$ There is a difference between the total number of positive and negative test cases created by experiment participants.
$\mathbf{H^2_0}$ There is no difference between the number of failing assertions detected by positive and negative test cases.
$\mathbf{H^2_a}$ There is a difference between the number of failing assertions detected by positive and negative test cases.
$\mathbf{H^3_0}$ There is no difference between the quality of positive and negative test cases.
$\mathbf{H^3_a}$ There is a difference between the quality of positive and negative test cases.
$\mathbf{H^4_0}$ There is no difference in the quality of testing based on the usage of a specific development practice.
$\mathbf{H^4_a}$ There is a difference in the quality of testing based on the usage of a specific development practice.

4   Experiment Design

The experiment was performed within Infosys Ltd.[1] India in September 2012, as part of the Infosys InStep[2] internship program. Participants of this experiment are Infosys employees spread around several development centres in India and even some employees participating from the Infosys client's (on-site) locations. The set of participant locations include: Bangalore, Beaverton, Brussels, Chennai, Hyderabad, Mangalore, Melbourne, Mysore, Pune, Trivandrum.

Since the participants of the experiment were not located at one single place, we have opted for a semi-controlled version of the experiment design, compared to the previous fully controlled academic study. This way, participants did not have to be physically present at the same time in the same room to perform their experiments under a supervisor in a controlled environment. Additionally, participants could decide when it was most convenient for them to work on the experiment task, based on their current project related duties, deliverables or deadlines.

At first, the researchers needed to create training materials for each group of participants: (i) Test Last (TL); (ii) TDD; and (iii) TDD with the Support for Negative Testing (TDD+). Upon receiving the list of the experiment participants, the researchers randomly divided them into the three previously mentioned groups. The number of participants in each group was kept as equal as possible. Using the Microsoft SharePoint[3] infrastructure, the training material was distributed by creating a SharePoint Workspace folder for each individual participant. In order for participants to access their SharePoint Workspaces, the researchers sent an invitation email to each participant. Each participant worked individually on an implementation of a defined problem in Java using the Eclipse [17] integrated development environment (IDE). Test cases were written using the jUnit [18] testing framework. The implementation was enforced with the provided programming interface. Upon completing their tasks, the participants of the experiment updated their SharePoint Workspace with their solution to the problem.

The *Bowling Game Score Calculator* problem was used for the experiment. The specification was based on the Bowling Game Kata (i.e., the problem also used by Kollanus and Isomöttönen to explain TDD [19]). From our experience, on average, 3 hours are needed to fully implement the problem and usually around 10 test cases are created during implementation when following TDD approach. Detailed information about the problem and instructions are provided on the first author's webpage[4].

Participants assigned to the TDD group were instructed to use TDD steps to develop software solution. Instructions for TDD were given as prescribed by Flohr and Schneider [20]. Participants assigned to the TDD+ group were

---

[1] http://www.infosys.com

[2] http://www.infosys.com/instep

[3] http://sharepoint.microsoft.com

[4] http://www.mrtc.mdh.se/~acc01/infosys-experiment

instructed to use the same TDD steps with the addition to the very first step. Basically, they were instructed to follow TDD, but also to occasionally write a negative test case based on the input space, domain knowledge, etc. (but not explicitly stated in the requirements). Participants assigned to the *Test Last* (TL) group were instructed to use traditional (test-last) approach for software development and they were considered as a control group for this experiment.

It was expected that some participants may not be familiar with the usage of the jUnit testing framework and/or Eclipse IDE. To avoid such problems, video tutorials were created for each group of participants. Additionally, participants were given an Eclipse project code skeleton which included one simple test case. Specific details of the study, i.e. instruction material, video tutorials and code skeleton, can be found at `http://www.mrtc.mdh.se/ acc01/ infosys-experiment`.

The participants were instructed, upon finalizing their software implementation, to save the source code together with the test cases in their individual and predefined SharePoint Workspace. Additionally, participants had to complete a simple questionnaire stating their opinions on the quality of the provided solution.

5   Execution

The first author of this paper stayed at Infosys development center in Bangalore, India, from 3rd to 28th of September 2012. During the first week of internship it was decided that the experiment will be executed from 10th till 21st of September, 2012. First week was used to prepare training video material, instructions and survey questions for the experiment.

A list of over 100 email addresses of Infosys employees was previously obtained by the second author, who directly promoted this experiment among employees of Infosys. Those employees were randomly distributed in three groups: TL, TDD and TDD+.

Participants were informed that their enrolment in this experiment would support the current research activities within Infosys, but the exact details of the experiment, as well as the goal of the experiment, were not shared with them. Additionally, participants were explained that their source code and test cases would be analysed anonymously and this activity will not be used in any way for the internal employee evaluation.

For each participant, a SharePoint Workspace was created with the dedicated training material and instructions placed in it. As an alternative files could be obtained from Internet. In particular, Eclipse IDE should be obtained as well as an experiment instruction document. Video tutorials were also hosted outside of Infosys intranet and the link was provided to participants. In some cases, Microsoft Office Communicator was used to transfer the required files.

Participation in the experiment was not time-boxed and subjects were given an opportunity to work on their implementations until they have enough confidence in the quality of the submitted solution.

Since one way of measuring the quality of test cases was using a total number of failing assertions, a Java code skeleton was created and provided to subjects to enforce usage of the same programming interface which would ease the process of executing the test cases of a subject X on the code of a subject Y.

Upon finishing their development task, participants uploaded software solution to their dedicated SharePoint Workspace or sent their solutions by email to the first author.

Table 1 present the number of solutions submitted for the experiment analysis by participants of the experiment.

Table 1. Distribution of solutions per groups

Group	Submitted	Removed	Analysed
TL	19	8	11
TDD	21	10	11
TDD+	20	9	11
Total	60	27	33

Once the submitted solutions were individually inspected (code was visually reviewed and tests were executed), several submitted solutions had to be removed before the analysis. Reasons for removal are listed below:

Incomplete solutions
Manually looking at the code it was possible to identify that some provided solutions were not completed. We can only assume they were submitted as such due to external deadlines.

Own failing test cases
Number of solutions had test cases which were failing on their own code. This was usually a sign of an uncompleted solution.

Small number of test cases (≤ 3)
In case a submitted solution did not have a minimum of 3 test cases (average was 13,8), such would be removed from the analysis.

Wrong test cases
It is very important not to have a false positives in the test cases. In case a test case is expecting a wrong result, the same was removed from the test suite, but if most of the test cases are wrong, then the complete solution was removed from analysis.

Different programming interface
Some solutions used a different programming interface which prevented executing other participants test cases on its code, or executing its test cases on other participants code.

6 Analysis

This section provides the analysis of the collected data. The analysis was performed using the R software environment for statistical computing [21]. Aggregated data and the analysis script for R are provided on the first author's webpage[5].

Positive Test Bias
One of the first thing we wanted to investigate with this experiment is the existence of a positive test bias within our participants as defined in the research question **RQ1**. We used the **Wilcoxon** signed rank test for paired nonparametric data in order to test the $\mathbf{H^1_0}$ null hypothesis with $\alpha = 0.05$. With a **p-value of 0.00000731** we can reject the null hypothesis and confirm that a difference between the created number of positive and negative test cases is significantly different for our industrial participants.

Defect Detecting Ability
As previously discussed, it is important to compare defect detecting ability of both positive and negative test cases. By doing that we can explore further how lack of negative tests could potentially affect the overall testing effectiveness as defined in research question **RQ2**. Again, the **Wilcoxon** signed rank test for paired nonparametric data was used in order to test the $\mathbf{H^2_0}$ null hypotheses with $\alpha = 0.05$. We can reject the stated hypothesis since the **p-value is 0.00000302**, confirming that there is a significant difference in the efficiency of positive and negative test cases.

Quality of Test Cases
By calculating the quality of tests, as defined in section 3, we are able to compare quality of negative and positive test cases and investigate if there are any differences between them. This additional analysis is important because even if we are detecting more defects with one type of test cases (negative in this case), we need to make sure that those defects are not detected, for example, only in the code of a lower quality. With this analysis we are addressing research question **RQ3**.**Wilcoxon** signed rank test for paired nonparametric data was once again used in order to test the $\mathbf{H^3_0}$ null hypotheses with $\alpha = 0.05$. We can reject the stated hypothesis as well, since there is a significant difference (**p-value is 0.00000277**) in the quality of positive and negative test cases.

Quality of Testing
As an additional goal of this study, we wanted to cross-compare the quality of tests created by our participants, regardless of the development approach they were using, thus addressing the research question **RQ4**. The **Mann-Whitney**

---

[5] http://www.mrtc.mdh.se/~acc01/infosys-experiment

nonparametric test was used in order to test the $\mathbf{H}^4{}_0$ null hypotheses with $\alpha = 0.05$. We can not reject stated hypothesis (**p-value is 0.4102955**), leading to the conclusion that there is no statistically significant difference in the quality of tests produced by participants using TDD and TL.

7   Interpretation

In this section we discuss the results of our experiment, implications they can have on further research, and potential threats to their validity.

7.1   Evaluation of Results and Implications

Our previous academic experiment [16] was performed with a limited number of participants and although we could see some trends, it was difficult to evaluate statistical significance of the collected data. However, the industrial experiment presented in this study enabled us to perform hypothesis testing using statistical methods on the data we collected.

With the industrial experiment data we can confirm the following hypothesis:

$\mathbf{H}^1{}_0$ There is a difference between the total number of positive and negative test cases created by experiment participants.

$\mathbf{H}^2{}_0$ There is a difference between the number of failing assertions detected by positive and negative test cases.

$\mathbf{H}^3{}_0$ There is a difference between the quality of positive and negative test cases.

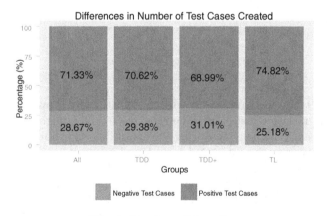

Fig. 1. Number of Test Cases

When looking at the actual differences in the number of created positive and negative test cases, as shown in Figure 1, we can notice that a very similar 70%-30% ratio exists for all groups individually as well as for all participants test cases combined together. Although this may sound like a problem itself, there

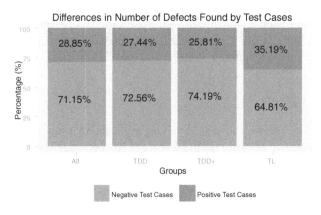

Fig. 2. Defects found by Test Cases

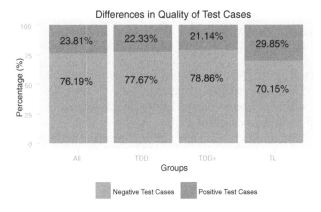

Fig. 3. Quality of Test Cases

is no actually (to the best of our knowledge) scientifically proven optimal ratio of positive and negative test cases. The ratio of 70%-30% might work just fine. This is why we emphasize on measuring the defect detection ability of test cases.

Figure 2 represents the ratio of defects found by positive and negative test cases. There are two interesting observation with this figure: (i) the ratio seems to be the opposite (30%-70%) and (ii) the data presented in this graph is not normalised. When we combine those two observations, we can see that with less than 30% of test cases in our test suite (negative test cases), we are discovering as much as 70% of all the defects detected by a complete test suite.

As a final step in confirming significance of the effectiveness of negative test cases, Figure 3 presents the ratio to what extent positive and negative test cases are contributing to the overall *Quality of Tests* score for individual groups and for all participants together. As we defined in section 3 of this paper, *Quality of Tests* measurement was needed since every defect that was detected by a test case was considered of equal importance, which may not represent a realistic situation. By rewarding test cases who are failing on the code of high quality, we could differentiate between the *raw* number of defects detected and the actual quality they bring into the overall testing effort.

The ratio of quality between positive and negative test cases goes beyond of 30%-70%, confirming that negative test cases are detecting more number of defects, but are also detecting defects on the code of a higher quality, resulting in finding defects that are not commonly discovered by positive test cases.

7.2 Threats to Validity - Reservations

The major advantage of this experiment, compared to our previous academic efforts, is the usage of a large number of industrial developers instead of a small number of master students as the experiment subjects. However, setting up an experimental study in an industrial environment brings many challenges for researchers. Inability to have a full control of the experiment represent the major threat to the validity of this study, which was due to the nature of distributed work at our industrial partner. Additional threat to the validity of this study is the usage of a small scale object of investigation. In our experience from previous academic experiments, on average around 3 hours is needed to fully complete the experiment task. Considering project related duties, deadlines and other responsibilities of our industrial participants, we decided that this task should be convenient for this experiment as well. Furthermore, because of several day to day activities of our industrial participants, experiment was not executed in one day but rather kept open for two weeks which could represent another potential threat to the validity of this study. Another possible validity threat could be the lack of a domain knowledge of the object for most of the experiment subjects.

Internal validity of the study was addressed by using statistical tests to perform hypothesis testing, as well as by providing the data as part of this publication, in an aggregated form. Additionally, by providing sufficient information about the experiment design as well as training and instruction materials, we are addressing reliability threats related to the replication of this study.

8   Conclusions and Future Work

Test driven development, by definition, is a development methodology and not a test design technique. Test cases are considered only as an artefact of the development activity and as such, in their nature, tests have to "drive" the development in the positive sense. This is one of the reason we focused our research activities on the analysis of test cases created using TDD approach and their efficiency in terms of defect detection. By identifying specific testing knowledge, complementary to the testing skills of a TDD developer, we would enable developers to achieve higher quality of software products, eventually leading to a higher adoption of TDD in industry.

Based on our academic results from previous experiments as well as results from this industrial study, it is evident that positive test bias (i.e. lack of negative test cases) is present when test driven development approach is being followed. On average, in our studies, around 70% of test cases where positive while 30% where negative. However, this effect was not only constrained to TDD since test last or traditional developers experienced the same problem as well.

When measuring defect detecting effectiveness and quality of test cases, an opposite ratio was present. Effectiveness and quality of negative test cases were above 70% while positive test cases contributed only by 30%. These results made evident what importance negative test cases have as part of a test suite. The challenge is how to intuitively create them without disturbing the "driving" of the development when following TDD. This problem was approached with TDD+ group of participants in this experiment (test driven development group with the support for negative testing). Essentially, we instructed this group to optionally write a negative test case when they consider it convenient. But, based on our results, this did not create any differences. Our reasoning for this could be again the effect of positive thinking that TDD requires, as well as a general problem of when to consider convenient to write a negative test case. Currently, we are investigating the possibility of extending test-driven development with particular test design technique, to facilitate consideration of unspecified requirements during the development to a higher extent and thus minimise the impact of a potentially inherent effect of a positive test bias in TDD.

Acknowledgments. This work was supported by the Infosys InStep[6] internship program and the SYNOPSIS project at Mälardalen University.

References

1. Beck, K.: Extreme programming explained: embrace change. Addison-Wesley Longman Publishing Co., Inc., Boston (2000)
2. Koskela, L.: Test driven: practical tdd and acceptance tdd for java developers. Manning Publications Co., Greenwich (2007)
3. Causevic, A., Sundmark, D., Punnekkat, S.: An industrial survey on contemporary aspects of software testing. In: Proceedings of the 3rd International Conference on Software Testing, Verification and Validation (ICST), pp. 393–401 (2010)
4. George, B., Williams, L.: A structured experiment of test-driven development. Information and Software Technology 46(5), 337–342 (2003)
5. Erdogmus, H., Morisio, M., Torchiano, M.: On the effectiveness of the test-first approach to programming. IEEE Transactions on Software Engineering 31, 226–237 (2005)
6. Janzen, D.S., Saiedian, H.: On the influence of test-driven development on software design. In: Conference on Software Engineering Education and Training, pp. 141–148 (2006)
7. Gupta, A., Jalote, P.: An experimental evaluation of the effectiveness and efficiency of the test driven development. In: Proceedings of the First International Symposium on Empirical Software Engineering and Measurement, ESEM 2007, pp. 285–294. IEEE Computer Society, Washington, DC (2007)

---

[6] http://www.infosys.com/instep

8. Vu, J.H., Frojd, N., Shenkel-Therolf, C., Janzen, D.S.: Evaluating test-driven development in an industry-sponsored capstone project. In: Proceedings of the 2009 Sixth International Conference on Information Technology: New Generations, pp. 229–234. IEEE Computer Society, Washington, DC (2009)

9. Causevic, A., Sundmark, D., Punnekkat, S.: Factors limiting industrial adoption of test driven development: A systematic review. In: 2011 IEEE Fourth International Conference on Software Testing, Verification and Validation (ICST), pp. 337–346 (March 2011)

10. Causevic, A., Punnekkat, S., Sundmark, D.: Quality of testing in test driven development. In: 2012 Eight International Conference on the Quality of Information and Communications Technology (QUATIC) (September 2012)

11. Teasley, B.E., Leventhal, L.M., Mynatt, C.R., Rohlman, D.S.: Why Software Testing Is Sometimes Ineffective: Two Applied Studies of Positive Test Strategy. Journal of Applied Psychology 79(1), 142–155 (1994)

12. Leventhal, L.M., Teasley, B., Rohlman, D.S., Instone, K.: Positive Test Bias in Software Testing Among Professionals: A Review. In: Bass, L.J., Unger, C., Gornostaev, J. (eds.) EWHCI 1993. LNCS, vol. 753, pp. 210–218. Springer, Heidelberg (1993)

13. Madeyski, L.: The impact of test-first programming on branch coverage and mutation score indicator of unit tests: An experiment. Inf. Softw. Technol. 52, 169–184 (2010)

14. Shelton, W., Li, N., Ammann, P., Offutt, J.: Adding criteria-based tests to test driven development. In: Proceedings of the 2012 IEEE Fifth International Conference on Software Testing, Verification and Validation, ICST 2012, pp. 878–886. IEEE Computer Society, Washington, DC (2012)

15. Fenton, N.E., Pfleeger, S.L.: Software Metrics: A Rigorous and Practical Approach, 2nd edn. PWS Publishing Co., Boston (1998)

16. Causevic, A., Sundmark, D., Punnekkat, S.: Test case quality in test driven development: A study design and a pilot experiment. In: 16th International Conference on Evaluation Assessment in Software Engineering (EASE 2012), pp. 223–227 (May 2012)

17. Eclipse, http://www.eclipse.org

18. jUnit Framework, http://www.junit.org

19. Kollanus, S., Isomöttönen, V.: Understanding tdd in academic environment: experiences from two experiments. In: Proceedings of the 8th International Conference on Computing Education Research, Koli 2008, pp. 25–31. ACM, New York (2008)

20. Flohr, T., Schneider, T.: Lessons learned from an XP experiment with students: Test-first needs more teachings. In: Münch, J., Vierimaa, M. (eds.) PROFES 2006. LNCS, vol. 4034, pp. 305–318. Springer, Heidelberg (2006)

21. R Core Team: R: A Language and Environment for Statistical Computing. R Foundation for Statistical Computing, Vienna, Austria (2012) ISBN 3-900051-07-0

Investigating the Impact of Experience and Solo/Pair Programming on Coding Efficiency: Results and Experiences from Coding Contests

Dietmar Winkler[1], Martin Kitzler[2], Christoph Steindl[2], and Stefan Biffl[1]

[1] Christian Doppler Laboratory for Software Engineering Integration
for Flexible Automation Systems, Vienna University of Technology, Institute of Software
Technology and Interactive Systems, Favoritenstrasse 9-11/188, 1040 Vienna, Austria
{dietmar.winkler,stefan.biffl}@tuwien.ac.at
[2] Catalysts GmbH; Huemerstraße 23, 4020 Linz, Austria
{martin.kitzler,christoph.steindl}@catalysts.cc

Abstract. Developing working software is a key goal of software development. Beyond software processes, following traditional or agile approaches, coding strategies, i.e., solo and pair programming, are important aspects for constructing high quality software code. In addition developer experience has a critical impact on coding efficiency and code quality. Pair programming aims at increasing coding efficiency, code quality, and supports learning of development team members. Several controlled experiments have been conducted to investigate benefits of different development strategies, learning effects, and the impact on code quality in academia and industry. Nevertheless, reported study limitations and various results in different contexts require more studies to fully understand the effects of experience and programming strategies. Coding contests can be promising approaches to (a) involve different participant groups, e.g., junior and senior programmers and professionals, and (b) can represent a well-defined foundation for planning and executing large-scale empirical studies. In this paper we present coding contests as a promising strategy for conducting empirical studies with heterogeneous groups of participants and report on a set of findings from past coding contests. Main results are (a) that the concept of coding contests is a promising way for supporting empirical research and (b) the results partly confirm previous studies that report on the benefits of pair programming and development experience.

Keywords: Coding Contests, Large Scale Controlled Experiments, Solo Programming, Pair Programming, Developer Experience.

1   Introduction

The main goal of software development practices is the construction of high-quality software products. Software processes, e.g., traditional or more flexible agile processes, aim at providing a basic project structure to plan and monitor the overall

H. Baumeister and B. Weber (Eds.): XP 2013, LNBIP 149, pp. 106–120, 2013.

project progress [14]. In addition, constructive practices (e.g., pair programming) are required to deliver pieces of software code and analytic practices (e.g., reviews, inspections, and testing) enable efficient testing of constructed software components. Previous studies focused on comparing pair programming and analytic methods, e.g., peer reviews [9] or software inspection [13], and suggest a combination of constructive and analytic approaches [17] to bundle individual benefits. Test-driven development (TDD) is a well-known and well-established software engineering practice for software development [3] including four steps: (a) select the most valuable requirement from a prioritized backlog, (b) develop tests (test-first approach), (c) construct required code fragments to make test case runs successful, and (d) refactoring of constructed software code afterwards. Thus, test case definition and code construction are tightly intertwined. Typically, test driven development is a key practice in agile development processes, e.g., in Scrum or eXtreme Programming.

An important question is whether individuals perform better than teams (e.g., pairs) working on the same piece of software in terms of a fast delivery of software components at a high level of quality. Some empirical studies (e.g., [8][10][15][16]) reported on benefits on programming performance in various courses in academic environment. Arisholm *et al.* report on an evaluation of pair programming with focus on complexity and programmer experience, also involving industry people [2]. They came to the conclusion that there are mainly benefits for junior programmers rather than intermediates and senior programmers. In addition programming in pairs enables knowledge transfer, training and a common understanding of the product [5][11].

Typically planning and executing controlled experiments require a high effort for preparation and execution. Many studies focus on student experiments rather than involving industry people, who must be hired and paid [18]. As a consequence readers might claim the relevance of the studies for industry because of background knowledge and experience of participants. Thus a key question is how we can include a higher number of professionals in controlled experiments to increase external validity of the aspects under investigation. From the authors perspective coding contests, i.e., some kind of quiz or challenge, can motivate juniors, seniors and professionals to solve challenging tasks in controlled environments as a foundation for conducting empirical studies with heterogeneous groups of participants.

In this paper we (a) present the concept of coding contests and (b) report on a set of findings from a past coding contest, conducted by Catalysts in Vienna, Austria, and Cluj, Romania, in the fall of 2012, to investigate the impact of programming strategies, i.e., solo and pair programming, and developer experience on coding performance. Thus, the remainder of this paper is structured as follows: Section 2 summarizes related work on studies in the area of solo and pair programming and coding challenges as a vehicle for empirical studies. Section 3 highlights the research issues. We present the concept of coding contests and the study design in Section 4 and our initial findings in Section 5. Finally, Section 6 summarizes, concludes and identifies future work.

2   Related Work

This section summarizes related work on programming in teams, i.e., pair programming (Section 2.1) and coding challenges and contests (Section 2.2).

2.1   Solo Programming and Programming in Teams

In contrast to solo programming, where every developer works on his own, pair programming is an established agile software development practice, typically included in an agile software development process like eXtreme Programming and Scrum. Basically, pair programming includes two engineers sharing a common environment and working at the same piece of software. Pair Programming includes two roles, (a) a driver, who implements upcoming tasks, e.g. based on the TDD approach, and (b) an observer, who supports the driver in his implementation task and conduct implicit quality assurance activities (e.g., inspection and continuous reviews). These roles may change frequently. This approach aims at increasing software productivity at a higher level of software quality [15].

Several studies have been published investigating the effects of pair programming in comparison to solo programming in different contexts, e.g., Hulkko *et al.* [6] reported on a study from four software development projects in industry and concluded that pair programming did not provide as extensive quality benefits and productivity increase as claimed in literature. Parrish *et al.* [12] also reported that two-person teams working independently are more productive than working concurrently. Dyba *et al.* [4] investigated effectiveness, project duration, and quality and came to the conclusion that expected benefits strongly depend on developer expertise and complexity of tasks and there is a need for additional studies to get a deeper insight in performance measures of pair programming.

2.2   Empirical Studies and Coding Contests

Basically empirical studies and experiments represent an important foundation to evaluate processes, methods, and products to get evidence on tool application and/or human based activities [7]. Nevertheless, it is often difficult to recruit a sufficient (and large) number of participants to enable empirical evidence with respect to the topic under investigation. Many empirical studies involve students as participants who might be comparable to juniors rather than professionals in an industry context. On the other hand professionals in industry typically do not participate in experiments because of resource limitations and cost. Thus, studies typically focus on pilot evaluations, student experiments, and small-scale prototype applications. Thus, there might be strong limitations regarding the validity of results which should be addressed appropriately.

To overcome these limitations and to motivate participants from academia as well as from industry, challenges and contests can be promising options for carrying out empirical studies. Coding contests exist for more than 30 years like the *"ACM International Collegiate Programming Contest"* [1] which was held for the first time in 1977. Up to now the number of different contests as well as the number of participants is increasing. Usually contests focus on solving as much of the given tasks as fast and as efficiently as possible. These tasks typically focus on algorithmically problems and the developers should have a fundamental knowledge on algorithms, data structures, and mathematics.

ACM's *International Collegiate Programming Contest* (ICPC[1]) and the *International Olympiad in Informatics* (IOI[2]) are providing a platform to identify the best coders in a group of universities or countries. Motivation for the participants is to earn medals (IOI) for themselves or achieve the highest ranking within their organization, e.g., within their university (ICPC). Participation at ICPC is limited to 3 students per university, IOI participants are at most three juniors (aged below 20 years) from every participating country. Thus, the target group of candidate participants is limited. Challenges and contests are also excellent platforms for recruiting purposes and are sometimes addressed by companies. For instance *Google CodeJam*[3] attracts a wide range of people because of very high price money and the opportunity to get hired by the company. *Challenge24*[4] is designed for three-person teams (similar to ICPC) with 24 hours continuous duration and well-known for innovative tasks. *TopCoder*[5] is a crowd-sourcing contest where developers can submit solutions for a defined problem. The results are used to identify the best overall solution, which can be used by companies and/or governmental organizations.

The Catalysts Coding Contest (CCC[6]) offers a moderate prize money and allows participants to choose whether they prefer working on their own or in teams. All participants work on a set of consecutive tasks with increasing complexity within a level-based structure. This level-based structure (the levels have to be solved in sequence) enables a direct comparison of the performance of all participants/teams per level. In addition there are no restrictions that hinder participating. Another benefit is the availability of (anonymous) results on an open data server for further investigations available for academia and industry. Thus the CCC is a promising approach for conducting large-scale empirical studies.

3   Research Questions and Variables

This section presents the initial research questions and the variables used in the coding contest.

---

[1] International Collegiate Programming Contest: http://icpc.baylor.edu/

[2] International Olympiad in Informatics: http://www.ioinformatics.org/

[3] Google Code Jam: http://code.google.com/codejam/

[4] Challenge24: http://ch24.org/

[5] TopCoder: http://www.topcoder.com/

[6] Catalyst Coding Contest (CCC): http://www.catalysts.cc/contest/

3.1   Research Questions

Based on the related work and open issues we identified two important research questions to address (a) coding contests as vehicle for empirical studies and (b) effects of construction software code in teams on time, experience, and team size.

RQ 1. How can we apply coding contests to support controlled experiments? The basic setting of coding contests can help designing and executing controlled experiments easily. In addition our assumption is that coding contests can address and motivate different groups of participants, i.e., junior developers, senior developers, and professionals. The distribution of different skill levels enable comparing the effects based on experiences and skills in a common environment and could enable easy replication and knowledge generation on the investigated research issues.

RQ 2. What are the effects of constructing software code in teams? We apply a level-based concept of the coding contest to address two aspects, (a) time effects on software construction per level and (b) defects per level considering participant experience and team-size, i.e., solo and pair programming. Further we derived four hypotheses:

- H1.0. High experienced participants (professionals) perform similar than less experienced participants (juniors) in terms of required time per level. The alternative hypothesis H1.1 is that experienced participants perform better.

- H2.0: High experienced participants and less experiences participants deliver a similar number of defects per level. The alternative hypothesis H2.1 is that more experience participants deliver fewer defects.

- H3.0: Individuals perform similar than pairs in terms of required time per level. The alternative hypothesis H3.1 is that pairs perform better, i.e., requires less time to complete a level.

- H4.0: Individuals and pairs deliver a similar number of defects per level. The alternative hypothesis H4.1 is that pairs deliver fewer defects per level.

3.2   Variables

According to Wohlin *et al.* [18] we defined a set of variables: *Independent variables* include the contest level concept, task descriptions, and a pre-defined set of test-cases per level. *Dependent variables* are the duration of working time (per level), the number of defects found during test runs, participant experience, and team size.

4   Study and Coding Contest Design

This section summarizes the experiment process, i.e., coding contest setting (Section 4.1), participants (Section 4.2), study material (Section 4.3), data collection and analysis process (Section 4.4). Finally we present some limitations and important threats to validity and illustrate how we addressed them (Section 4.5).

4.1   Experiment Process and Coding Contest Setting

Coding contests are promising approaches for conducting large-scale empirical studies in controlled environments involving a heterogeneous group of participants. Basically the coding contest is structured in four steps (see Fig. 1): (1) *Contest Preparation* includes setup of the material (see Section 4.3), contest advertisements, and organizational issues; (2) *Registration of Participants*, i.e., individuals and teams (pairs); (3) *Contest Execution & Data Collection*; and (4) *Data Analysis and Award Ceremony*.

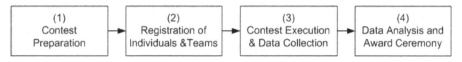

Fig. 1. Coding Contest Process Steps

In contrast to other contests and challenges (see Section 2.2 for some examples) where participants (a) have to select one problem out of a bunch of available problems to be solved and/or (b) restrictions of participation, the CCC is open to all interested people from school, academia, and industry and provides only one problem (after the other) to be solved by all participants. Note that all participants receive similar task-descriptions and have to submit their test results to verify successful task completion. After completing one task the next task will be available to the participants. Every task is assigned to a defined level, which extends the previous level in complexity and/or size. Note that the CCC consists of an overall number of 7 levels, i.e., 7 tasks.

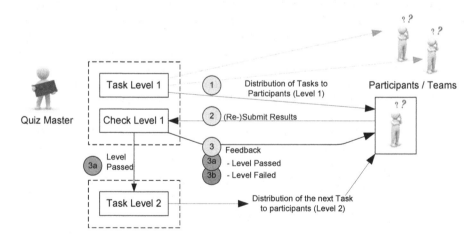

Fig. 2. Study Setting / Level Design of the Coding Contests (Level 1)

Fig. 2 presents an overview of activities at task level 1 and highlights the interaction between the quiz master and the participants. The quiz master, i.e., one of the authors, is responsible for distributing the individual tasks per level to the participants and teams (step 1 in Fig. 2). The participants work on their assigned tasks and submit their results (step 2 in Fig. 2). The results are automatically compared with expected results by a server application *(CatCoder)*. The participants receive a feedback whether the submitted results are correct or not (step 3 in Fig. 2). Note that there is no additional information but just the information whether the results are correct/not correct. Based on the feedback there are two options: (a) the participant continue working on their task assignment in case the feedback has been negative, i.e., some defects have been identified, (step 3b in Fig. 2) and resubmit updated results (step 2 in Fig. 2); (b) the feedback has been positive, i.e., no defects have been found, and the participants passed the level (step 3a in Fig. 2). In parallel the participants increased their level and received a new task assignment related to this next level and continue working on the new assignment. The contest is finished after the participants solved all tasks successfully or the contest time is up (note that there is an upper time limit for the overall contest of 4 hours).

4.2   Participants

The presented empirical study is based on a coding contest carried out in Vienna, Austria, and Cluj, Romania, in the fall of 2012. During the enrollment phase of the contest via Internet individual participants or teams of participants were able to register for the contest. After closing the registration, an overall number of 173 participants had registered for the coding contest. After study completion and an initial check for consistency and availability of collected data, a number of participants have to be excluded from evaluation. An overall number of 51 (about 30% of the 173 registered people) participants were excluded because they did not did not show up after their prior registration, did not provide the required information, i.e., experience level, or did not agree to provide their data for further evaluation. As there was no restriction to programming languages, the participants (122 remaining people) used a wide range of different languages, i.e., Java (28 participants, 23%), C# (27 participants, 22%), C/C++ (40 participants, 33%), and others (27 participants, 22%). To focus on the most prominent (i.e., top three) programming languages we excluded languages, applied by only a small subset of participants, from evaluation. The authors are aware that there might be an impact on the programming language but we did not consider this impact in context of the paper. Finally, the analysis is based on an overall number of 95 participants.

Table 1. Experience-Level and Programming Experience [years]

	Junior	Senior	Professionals	Total
Mean	3.3	5.8	9.8	6.0
Std.Dev	1.43	3.36	5.8	4.27
Min	1	2	5	1
Max	6	15	25	5

At the beginning of the contest the participants were asked to provide data on their experience level based on their current activities, i.e., junior developers (beginners, e.g., up to undergraduate students), senior developers (experienced programmers, typically graduate students) and professionals from industry. In addition we captured data on their software development experience in terms of project participation or working experience in industry. Main reason was to see whether the reported skill level seems to fit to the years of experiences. Table 1 presents the share of experience years of participants and skill classes. As expected, junior developers had on average less working experience compared to senior developers and professionals. Note that seniors (maybe even juniors) could also work in industry and might be considered as "professionals" but we did not investigate this possible overlap in this paper.

4.3   Study Material

Study material includes (a) technical infrastructure and (b) contest material, i.e., task description, requirements and test cases.

Technical infrastructure. Every participant had to bring his own workstation and local software environment. Because programming language and development environment are not restricted, it is the best way for participants to work in their own and well-known development environment. Internet connection is enabled to browse for additional material and to get access to the coding contest environment. The contest environment, e.g., network connectivity and the result server, was provided by Catalysts. After login into the contest environment, a general and encrypted task description can be downloaded by the individual participants. After starting the contest, the task description related to the first level is available for download (password protected). The password for each consecutive level is visible only for individuals or groups that completed the previous level. Note that teams are allowed to work on distributed computers but have to upload the results by using one single account. The results have to be submitted to the control center (i.e., CatCoder) which delivers feedback (correct or incorrect results) to the participants. Note that a level is considered to be completed if all test cases succeed and the results are correct.

Contest Material. The whole task (i.e., general task description) for the contest was to write a lip reading program that calculates the most likely sentence that was formed by a number of input mouth shapes. A mouth shape, in the context of this coding contest, consisted of four pieces: upper lip, lower lip, teeth, and the tongue. Every mouth shape represents one or more letters or syllables of the English alphabet.

- *Level one, two, and three* were easy tasks to provide the baseline for the later levels: Recognize a *letter*, recognize a *word* (out of a dictionary), and recognize a word including *syllables*. Syllables are tricky because they represent two or more letters of the English letters which makes the search for matching words more complex. All possible mouth shapes and which letters/syllables they can represent was provided in the task description and an additional file. The dictionary held 18,609 real English words and was provided in another file inside the task package.

- In *level four*, the task was to calculate the *likelihood* that a particular letter or syllable is followed by another letter of syllables (based on the dictionary).

- This provides the syllable likelihood which is used in *level five*: Since a group of mouth shapes could match many different words, the likelihood for all words has to be calculated and the most likely word will be the result.

- The goal for *level six* was to calculate the likelihood of the words (interpreted out of mouth shapes) inside a sentence. A file with 551,620 words (Collection of Shakespeare texts) provided the baseline.

- In the final level *(level seven)* the teams received only a number of mouth shapes and they had to guess the most likely sentence said. Note that this exercise is based on words inside sentences based on Shakespeare texts.

4.4   Data Collection and Analysis

For analysis purposes, we captured all communication data, i.e., time stamps, number of iterations, and defects per task/level (at least one defect lead to another iteration), and the submitted results (code fragments) for analysis purposes. In this paper we focus on the test results and do not analyze the delivered source code.

Data Collection. Communication data is captured in a log file including submitted results, test cases, timestamp, user name, and test case values. In addition participants are asked to submit their source code in a designated folder structure. Note that source code submission is voluntarily. CatCoder, the server application that hosts the contest, extracts the information of the log file and generates a human-readable spreadsheet presentation including the list of participants ordered by rank. In addition registration data, experience levels, and years of experience (a control value) is available in a database log file for further usage.

Data Analysis. The final result set (i.e., a spreadsheet) holds data of individual participants, experience data, team information (solo or pair programming), and required duration and defects per level. Note that we used the data in an anonymous way by removing confident and private data for evaluation. For evaluation purposes we removed participants who did not provide the requested data or did not permit further data analysis (see Section 4.2 for details). We applied descriptive statistics for data analysis and the t-test at a significance level of 95% for hypothesis testing.

4.5   Limitations and Threats to Validity

Every empirical study has to deal with several threats to validity. We discuss the most important threats and highlight how we addressed them in the study setting: *Conclusion validity.* The study included 95 participants with different backgrounds, i.e., junior and senior developers and professionals. In addition there might be a specific subset of programmers who participate in challenges and contests. Another aspect is that seniors (maybe even juniors) could also work in industry and might be considered as "professionals" but we did not investigate these possible effects in this paper. We applied the t-test at a significance level of 95% for hypothesis testing. To address *internal validity* considerations, the coding contest has a history going back to 2007 and several pilot studies and contests have already been run. Thus the study setup has been proved several times. We avoided communication between the participants but we allowed communication within study teams. We captured the skill level and the years of programming experience prior to the study (during registration). The study duration was limited to 240 minutes (4 hours). *Construct validity* focuses on the relation between theory and observations. The study is based on related work and previous coding contests and addresses efficiency and duration, common variables in empirical studies. *External threats* to validity focus on the participants across different skill levels, i.e., junior and senior developers and professionals. We used a classroom setting to monitor and control study variables, supported by the contest organization team. The contest organization team was responsible for correct contest execution, e.g., they reported whether a pair followed the intended pair programming rules.

5   Results

This section summarizes the initial findings of the coding contest carried out in Vienna, Austria and Cluj, Romania in the fall of 2012.

5.1   Coding Contest Effort and Levels

Table 2 presents the mean effort (Table 2a) of participants based on the last completed (and submitted) task and the individual level achieved (Table 2b). Note that the time stamp is registered on submission time. For example, if the participant successfully completed level 1 and 2 and did not complete level 3; the timestamps for level 1 and 2 are used for calculating the overall working duration; level 2 is the final and highest level. Table 2 presents the results of this analysis step. Regarding the contest effort there is a similar mean overall duration for completing the tasks (2:23 for juniors and 2:11 for professionals). We did not observe any significant differences regarding the mean working duration. It is notable that the standard deviation (SD) for juniors is some higher.

Table 2a. (a) Overall Effort [hh:min]

	Junior	Senior	Prof.	Total
Mean	2:23	2:20	2:11	2:19
SD	1:02	0:56	0:46	0:55
Min	0:37	0:55	0:58	0:37
Max	3:57	3:58	3:33	3:58

Table 2b. (a) Completed Levels

	Junior	Senior	Prof.	Total
Mean	1.8	2.6	2.2	2.3
SD	0.93	1.69	0.67	1.39
Min	1	1	1	1
Max	4	7	3	7

The analysis of the maximum level reached by the participants is quite interesting. Again, as expected juniors (highest level on average: 1.8) completed on average a lower level compared to seniors (highest level on average: 2.6) and professionals (highest level on average 2.2). It was quite surprising that seniors achieved on average a higher level compared to professionals. It is also notable that professionals had the lowest maximum level (maximum level 3) compared to seniors (maximum level 7) and juniors (maximum level 4). This finding is quite surprising and requires a more detailed investigation on the reasons of this effect.

Table 3 presents the results of the analysis of the level-based contest, including the number of participants who completed every level. This number decreases over time, starting from 95 participants and completing with 4 participants who finished the last level (i.e., level 7). It is notable that level 5 and 6 was completed quite fast (less than 20 min on average) by a small number of participants (6 participants completed level 5 and 5 participants completed level 6). Regarding defects delivered in the submitted results, it is notable that level 1 submissions included on average 3.13 defects per participant or team. Nevertheless, the maximum number of defects is 72 at level 1 (an explanation of this high average value). It is also notable that the 5 participants who completed level 6 did not deliver any defect.

Table 3. Overall Effort and Defects per Level

	Level 1	Level 2	Level 3	Level 4	Level 5	Level 6	Level 7
Total	95	68	28	11	6	5	4
Effort mean	1:03	1:06	1:06	0:48	0:20	0:13	0:51
Effort SD	0:42	0:39	0:38	0:23	0:10	0:05	0:21
Min	0:14	0:11	0:12	0:16	0:07	0:08	0:28
Max	3:46	2:49	2:35	1:35	0:32	0:19	1:16
Defects mean	3.13	1.6	2.18	1.18	1.83	0	1.75
Defect SD	8.87	2.59	2.83	1.78	1.94	0	2.06
Min	0	0	0	0	0	0	0
Max	72	12	11	5	5	0	4

5.2   Developer Experience

Table 4 presents the analysis results of the individual experience groups, i.e., Juniors, Seniors, and Professionals, and the individual levels (level 1-7) of the coding contest.

Table 4. Effort and Defects per Level and Experience Level

		Level 1	Level 2	Level 3	Level 4	Level 5	Level 6	Level 7
Juniors		24	13	4	2	0	0	0
Effort	mean	1:17	1:32*[1]	1:05	1:09*[2]	-	-	-
	SD	0:50	0:53	0:28	0:03	-	-	-
	Min	0:29	0:21	0:26	1:07	-	-	-
	Max	3:45	2:49	1:30	1:11	-	-	-
Defects	mean	2.9	1.31	1	1	-	-	-
	SD	5.58	2.06	1.41	1.41	-	-	-
	Min	0	0	0	0	-	-	-
	Max	19	7	3	2	-	-	-

Table 4. (*continued*)

		Level 1	Level 2	Level 3	Level 4	Level 5	Level 6	Level 7
Seniors		51	38	18	9	6	5	4
Effort	mean	**0:59**	**0:56**[*1]	**1:11**	**0:43**[*2]	**0:20**	**0:13**	**0:51**
	SD	0:41	0:31	0:35	0:23	0:10	0:05	0:21
	Min	0:13	0:11	0:22	0:16	0:07	0:08	0:28
	Max	3:34	2:17	2:14	1:35	0:32	0:19	1:16
Defects	mean	**4.08**[*3]	**1.89**	**2.56**	**1.22**	**1.83**	**0**	**1.75**
	SD	11.36	3.1	2.43	1.92	1.94	0	2.06
	Min	0	0	0	0	0	0	0
	Max	72	12	6	5	5	0	4
Professionals		20	17	6	0	0	0	0
Effort	mean	**0:57**	**1:09**	**0:50**	-	-	-	-
	Effort SD	0:31	0:33	0:53	-	-	-	-
	Min	0:25	0:22	0:12	-	-	-	-
	Max	2:09	2:10	2:35	-	-	-	-
Defects	mean	**1.0**[*3]	**1.18**	**1.83**	-	-	-	-
	Defect SD	2.27	1.51	4.49	-	-	-	-
	Min	0	0	11	-	-	-	-
	Max	8	5	6	-	-	-	-

Note that Juniors did not complete any levels above 4 and Professionals did not complete levels above 3. We applied a t-test to test effort and delivered defects per group of participants. Between Juniors and Seniors there was a significant difference regarding the duration required to complete level 2[*1] and level 4[*2]. In both cases the Seniors were significantly faster. Between Seniors and Professional there was a slight significant (93%) difference at the level 1 defects[*3]. We did not observe any additional significant differences.

5.3   Development and Programming Approach

Table 5 presents the analysis results of the development and programming approach, i.e., solo and pair programming and the individual levels of the coding contest.

Table 5. Effort and Defects per Level and Solo/Pair Programming Approach

		Level 1	Level 2	Level 3	Level 4	Level 5	Level 6	Level 7
Solo Programmer		53	40	19	8	5	4	3
Effort	mean	**1:00**	**1:00**	**0:59**	**0:50**	**0:21**	**0:13**	**0:59**
	SD	0:40	0:37	0:36	0:25	0:10	0:06	0:17
	Min	0:14	0:10	0:12	0:16	0:07	0:08	0:43
	Max	3:34	2:32	2:14	1:35	0:32	0:19	1:16
Defects	mean	**3.23**	**1.7**	**1.79**	**1:62**	**2.2**	**0**	**2.33**
	SD	10.61	2.93	2.23	1.92	1.92	0	2.08
	Min	0	0	0	0	0	0	0
	Max	72	12	6	5	5	0	4

Table 5. (*continued*)

Pairs		42	28	9	3	1	1	1
Effort	mean	**1:06**	**1:14**	**1:20**	**0:44**	**0:13**	**0:14**	**0:28**
	SD	0:45	0:39	0:42	0:20	0	0	0
	Min	0:16	0:12	0:26	0:28	0:13	0:14	0:28
	Max	3:46	2:49	2:35	1:07	0:13	0:14	0:28
Defects	mean	**3**	**1.46**	**3**	**0**	**0**	**0**	**0**
	SD	6.14	2.06	3.84	0	0	0	0
	Min	0	0	0	0	0	0	0
	Max	27	7	11	0	0	0	0

We did not observe any significant differences between the two groups. The number of participants who completes more than four levels was too low executing statistical tests. There was only one pair that completed 7 compared to three single programmers on the other hand.

5.4   Final Scoring and Ranking

Based on the summarized results we calculated the overall score of the top-10 performers (see Table 6 for details). It has to be mentioned that the "best participant" was a pair programming team, follow by seven solo programmers and concluded by two pairs. No Professional made it into the top 10; only two Junior reached rank 8 and 10. Seniors were the dominating group. A reason for this could be that younger programmers can handle the stress easier and deliver faster results while the older Professionals who spend much time to create a solid solution. Another reason could be that professionals who are experts on frameworks and architecture are unfamiliar with programming from the scratch but they prefer starting from a sound code base.

Table 6. Top-10 Score of the Coding Contest

Rank	Levels Compl	Total Defects	Program. Appr	Exp. Level	Years of Exp.
1	7	0	Pair	Senior	7
2	7	7	Solo	Senior	15
3	7	9	Solo	Senior	10
4	7	10	Solo	Senior	7
5	6	12	Solo	Senior	7
6	5	23	Solo	Senior	6
7	4	13	Solo	Senior	6
8	4	6	Solo	Junior	3
9	4	13	Pair	Senior	6
10	4	4	Pair	Junior	4

6   Discussion, Conclusion and Future Work

Experiences and/or benefits of software development practice, i.e., solo and pair programming, depend on several factors, as indicated in the related work section, e.g., complexity of the product and experience of developers. While pair programming works well in an educational environment, there are controversial results in industry projects. Nevertheless, additional studies are necessary to fully understand the effect of programming practice in different contexts. Coding contests are a promising option to (a) recruit and motivate a large number of participants at different background and experience levels (e.g., juniors, seniors, and professionals) and (b) enable an easy execution of controlled experiments.

RQ1 focuses on the question how coding contests can support controlled experiments. The coding contest setting presented in this paper attracted people from different areas, i.e., from university and industry, and enable including a heterogeneous group of participants. In addition the basic technical environment and the classroom setting enable the control of relevant parameters and variables important for a controlled experiment. Thus, we conclude that coding contests fits well to requirements given by controlled experiments.

RQ2 focuses on the investigation of experience and team-structure (solo vs. pair programming) and the effects on code construction. We applied the level-based concept of coding contests to evaluate a set of hypothesis:

- H1 states that professionals perform similar than juniors without considering the team approach (H1.0). The results showed that juniors required more time on average to solve their tasks and complete on average fewer levels compared to professionals. A surprising finding was that the maximum reached level for juniors was higher than for professionals. We did not observe any significant differences. Based on the findings H1.0 cannot be rejected and H1.1 must be rejected.

- H2 assumed that professionals deliver similar defects on average compared to juniors. The results showed that professionals delivered fewer defect compared to juniors at the first 2 levels and more at the third level. Note that professionals did not reach level 4+. Another interesting finding was that the seniors delivered most defects at every level, but – in contrast to professionals (maximum level 3) and juniors (maximum level 4) – 4 seniors completed the contest with level 7, i.e., the final level. H2.0 is not supported by the findings.

- H3 focuses on team effects, i.e., how solo programmers perform in contrast to pair programmers. The results showed on average a higher effort for completing level 1-3 and similar or less effort for level 4-7. This finding indicates benefits for pair programmers regarding more complex tasks. Note that the winner of the contest is a pair programming team and there are 3 pair programming teams in the top 10 but there are 7 solo programmers in the top score. However, hypothesis is not supported by the results and, thus, rejected.

- H4 assumes that pairs promise delivering higher product quality, i.e., fewer defects. The results support this assumption for all levels, except level 3. Note that pair programming teams did not deliver any defect regarding the contest levels 4-7, but there was only one pair programming team who completed level 5 to 7. Thus, this hypothesis must be rejected.

The results presented in the paper showed initial results of the coding contest, conducted in the fall of 2012. Thus, future work will include additional and in-depth analysis of the initial findings, including the investigation of the effects of different programming languages, different locations, and in-depth analysis of source code and test cases with respect to code and test case quality. The team from Catalysts has already conducted several contests in the past (starting in 2007) and is also planning upcoming coding contests in the future. Thus, future work will also include the analysis of results in a series of contests, in terms of replication and/or the introduction of new measures, related to upcoming research challenges for consideration in future contests .

References

[1] Amraii, S.A.: Observations on teamwork strategies in the ACM international collegiate programming contest. Magazine Crossroads 14(1) (2007)
[2] Arisholm, E., Gallis, H., Dyba, T., Sjoberg, D.I.K.: Evaluating Pair Programming with Respect to System Complexity and Programmer Expertise. IEEE TSE 33(2) (2007)
[3] Beck, K.: Test Driven Development by Example. Addison-Wesley Longman (2002)
[4] Dyba, T., Arisholm, E., Sjoberg, D.I.K., Hannay, J.E., Shull, F.: Are two heads better than one? On the Effectiveness of Pair Programming. IEEE Software 24(6) (2007)
[5] Cockburn A., Williams L.: The costs and the benefits of pair programming. In: XP
[6] Hulkko, H., Abrahamsson, P.: A Multiple Case Study on the Impact of Pair Programming on Product Quality. In: Proceedings of ICSE, pp. 495–504 (2005)
[7] Juristo, N., Moreno, A.M.: Basics in Software Engineering Experimentation. Springer (2010)
[8] McDowell, C., Werner, L., Bullock, H., Fernald, J.: The Effects of Pair Programming on Performance in an introductory programming course. In: Proc. of the 33rd SIGCSE Techn. Symp. on Computer Science Education, pp. 38–42 (2002)
[9] Müller, M.: Two controlled experiments concerning the comparison of pair programming to peer reviews. Journal of Systems and Software 78, 166–179 (2005)
[10] Nawrocki, K., Wojciechowski, A.: Experimental Evaluation of Pair Programming. In: Proc. of the 12th European Software Control and Metrics Conf., pp. 269–276 (2001)
[11] Padberg, F., Müller, M.: Analyzing the Cost and Benefit of Pair Programming. In: Proc. of the Int. Symposium on Software Metrics, pp. 166–177 (2003)
[12] Parrish, A., Smith, R., Hale, D., Hale, J.: A field study of developer pairs: Productivity impacts and implications. IEEE Software 21(2), 76–79 (2004)
[13] Phongpaibul, M., Boehm, B.: An empirical comparison between pair development and software inspection in Thailand. In: Proc. of ISESE, pp. 85–94 (2006)
[14] Sommerville, I.: Software Engineering, 9th edn. Addison-Wesley Longman (2010)
[15] Williams, L., Kessler, R.R., Cunningham, W., Jeffries, R.: Strengthening the case for pair programming. IEEE Software, 19–25 (2000)
[16] Williams, L., McDowell, C., Nagappan, N., Fernald, J., Werner, L.: Building Pair Programming Knowledge through a Family of Experiments. In: Proc. of ISESE (2003)
[17] Winkler, D., Varvaroi, R., Goluch, G., Biffl, S.: An Empirical Study On Integrating Analytical Quality Assurance Into Pair Programming. Short Paper, ISESE (2006)
[18] Wohlin, C., Runeson, P., Höst, M., Ohlsson, M.C., Regnell, B., Wesslen, A.: Experimentation in Software Engineering. Springer (2012)

Visualizing and Managing Technical Debt in Agile Development: An Experience Report

Paulo Sérgio Medeiros dos Santos[1], Amanda Varella[2], Cristine Ribeiro Dantas[2], and Daniel Beltrão Borges[2]

[1] Federal University of Rio de Janeiro, System Engineering and Computer Science Department, Cidade Universitária – Centro de Tecnologia.
Rio de Janeiro, Brazil
pasemes@cos.ufrj.br
[2] Petrobras, Exploitation and Production Business Solutions, Centro
20031-912 Rio de Janeiro, Brazil
{amanda.varella,cristine.dantas,
daniel.borges}@petrobras.com.br

Abstract. This paper reports the experience of an architecture team of a software development department with 25 agile teams in supporting technical decisions regarding technical practices. The main motivation to use technical debt metaphor was its acknowledged potential in driving software development and maintenance decisions, especially those long term maintenance tradeoffs which are usually less visible to developers and decision makers in general. We propose the use of a "technical debt board" with main technical debt categories to manage and visualize the high-level debt, combined with tools to measure it at low-level (software metrics and other kind of static analysis). We have found that our approach improved the teams' awareness about the technical debt, stimulated a beneficial competition between teams towards the debt payment and enhanced the communication regarding technical decisions.

Keywords: technical debt, software quality, visualization, agile practices.

1 Introduction

One of the main tenets that make agile methods effective is the right balance between the importance given to the people developing the software and the engineering practices dedicated to keep its quality. In establishing this balance, agile teams can leverage from the embodied tacit knowledge in the team and the technical readiness for change of the software product [1] to attain its primary objective: deliver value.

However, this equilibrium can be hard to achieve. And, if not consciously monitored, it seems that it can be more easily inclined towards the people or management side. The following aspects help explain this situation. First, the agile development de-emphasis to long-term planning in favor of short-term adaptiveness, although it represents a strength in a rapidly changing development environment, can create a temptation to neglect best practices that are essential to long-term success [2]. Second, most major agile methods such as Scrum and Crystal are more focused in the

H. Baumeister and B. Weber (Eds.): XP 2013, LNBIP 149, pp. 121–134, 2013.

managerial aspects of software development than in providing engineering guidance [3] – one important exception is Extreme Programming. Last, the engineering practices commonly used in agile methods require highly qualified professionals [4] which must be able to deal with the lack of upfront design and investment in the life cycle architecture [1, 5] besides, these professionals must be capable of realizing automated testing and continuous integration [6].

In fact, all these aspects are implicitly present in the agile manifesto (http://agilemanifesto.org/). We cite four principles directly related to this discussion: (i) the continuous delivery of valuable software to the client, (ii) continuous attention to technical excellence and good design enhances agility, (iii) simplicity – the art of maximizing the amount of work not done – is essential and (iv) welcome changing requirements, even late in development. Combining the ideas of these principles, we have the following challenge: how to balance quality, simplicity, agility and welcome change in delivering value to the client?

Thus, although delivering value is the ultimate objective of agile methods, delivering it as fast as possible without an adequate attention to the engineering practices can represent a problem. In 1992 Ward Cunningham created a metaphor to a code that is written in a fast and "dirty" way or, more technically, code that is produced taking shortcuts that fall short of best practices. He called this metaphor Technical Debt [7]. Like a financial debt, the technical debt incurs interest payments, which come in the form of the extra effort that has to be done in future development because of inappropriate design choices [8]. This includes all aspects of software development including its documentation, test cases and source code.

There are many reasons to get into technical debt – not all bad, especially when it is taken in a conscious manner. In addition, technical debt is not limited to practices and techniques associated with the code design itself. More broadly, technical debt can be characterized by aspects associated with the development of the software product as a whole [9], including: lack of automated tests, unnecessary coupled code, duplicated code, infrastructure related issues like flawed automatic building, lack of continuous integration and automated deployment.

Although the issues related with the technical debt are in the surface technical, this type of issues cannot always be objectively addressed. It is not possible to pay the technical debt simply saying to the developers: you must write automated tests, don't couple your code, don't duplicate your code or refactor your code. When dealing with this kind of situation, cultural factors must also be managed in order to make developers capable of dealing with tension between engineering best practices and other factors such as ship date and skills of engineers that are available.

This paper reports an experience of how a software development department of a big oil company located in Brazil dealt with a scenario similar to the one described above. In an advanced stage of agile adoption, the department was facing a condition where the managerial aspects were already fairly consolidated with the introduction of Scrum, but the engineering practices were lagging behind in terms of maturity. We describe how we have used the technical debt metaphor to stimulate software developers to bring the managerial/engineering equilibrium to an optimal state where the value delivery is maximized in long-term.

2   Background

As an oil and gas company, Petrobras (http://www.petrobras.com.br) develops software in areas which demands increasingly innovative solutions in short time intervals. The company started officially with Scrum in March of 2009, using its lightweight framework to create collaborative self-organizing teams that could effectively deliver products. After the first team had adopted Scrum with a relative success, the manager noticed that the framework could be used in other teams, and thus he invested in training and coaching so that the teams could also have the opportunity to try the methodology. At that time, only the software development department for E&P, whose software helps to Exploit and Produce oil and gas, had management endorsement in adopting scrum and agile practices that would let teams deliver better products faster. About one year and half later, all teams in the department were using Scrum as its software development process. The developers and the stakeholders in general noticed expressive gains with the adoption of Scrum. The results had varied from the skill of the team leadership in agile methodologies, customer participation, level of collaboration between team members, technical expertise among other factors.

The architecture team of the software development department for E&P was composed of four employees, whose responsibility was to help teams and offer support for resolution of problems related to agile methods and architecture. At that time, it had to work with 25 teams which had autonomy regarding its technical decisions. In fact, autonomy was one of the main managerial concerns when adopting agile methods.

After Scrum adoption, there was active debate, training and architectural meetings about whether Agile engineering practices should also be adopted in parallel with managerial practices; in hindsight, it would have accelerated the benefits had they been adopted. But the constraints of time and budget, decisions made by non-technical staff, and the bureaucracy in areas such as infrastructure and database, led to the postponement of those efforts initially. Moreover, the infrastructure area had only build and continuous integration (CI) tools available. And, unfortunately, these tools were not taken seriously by the teams. The automated deployment was relatively new and was postponed because of fear of implementing it in immature phase. Other tools and monitoring mechanisms were not used by the teams even so the architecture team was aware of its possible benefits.

Despite all initiatives in training and supporting in agile practices such as configuration management, automated tests and code analysis, teams, represented by 25 focal points in architectural meetings, did not show much interest in adopting many agile practices – particularly technical practices. Delivering the product on the date agreed with the customer and maintaining the legacy code were the most urgent issues. Analyzing retrospectively it seems that the main cause for this situation was that debt was getting accrued unconsciously. Serving the client was a much more visible and imperative goal. This can be one explanation for the ineffectiveness of prior attempts in introducing technical practices. Be it by the means of specialized training or by the support of the architecture team.

With these not so effective attempts to promote continuous improvement with teams, the architecture team sought a way to motivate them to experiment agile practices without a top-down "forced adoption". The technical debt metaphor, described in next section, was the basis for the approach.

3   Related Works and the State of the Practice

Technical debt has been a central theme among researchers and practitioners in the last years as an alternative perspective for software development and maintenance decisions. It offers a real world metaphor which is naturally understandable by most software stakeholders and serves as tool to evaluate the tradeoffs between proposed enhancements, corrective maintenance and technical/non-functional improvements. Besides that appeal, what seems to be the most significant contribution of the technical debt prism is that it brings to the light the long term maintenance tradeoffs which are usually less visible to developers and decision makers in general.

It is possible to identify three main effort directions in the technical literature and informal sources (blogs) related to technical debt.

The first are those [10, 11, 12, 13] seeking to identify the main properties of technical debt and conceptualize the main sources of its accumulation. This includes interviews with practitioners to see how they interpret technical debt and how it manifests in their daily activities [10, 13]. In addition, it also includes discussions about technical debt characteristics, such as described in [11] and [12]: visibility (to make it visible for daily decisions), value (to estimate its size and help deciding when it should be paid) and intentionality (unintentional, when it is a result of low quality work and intentional, for tactical (short-term) and strategic (long-term) reasons).

The second group [14, 15, 16, 19] is linked to how the debt can be managed and deciding when it should paid. There are many approaches to do that. In [14] four of them are cited, including the simple cost-benefit analysis, where the cost of paying the interest versus principal is analyzed, and the portfolio-based, where technical debt items are treated as assets that composes a portfolio managed to maximize the return of investment or minimize the investment risk. Both [15] and [16] are cost-benefit approaches and [19] proposes a portfolio-based approach. Valuing and making technical debt visible are the basic inputs for these approaches. And, in fact, these two properties are directly related to each other as it only possible to manifest something that can be observable (in this case, valued). Examples of technical debt measurement ranges from the use of rough estimates [15, 19] to the more precise quantitative data based on source code metrics [16].

The use of source code or, generally, "low-level" software metrics to estimate a value for technical debt forms the third main active area. In [17], automatic static analysis is empirically evaluated as mean to quantify the values of technical debt at code level. And in [18] the relative technical debt value associated with three code smells (data class, duplicated code and god class) is investigated.

Despite the effort on identifying means of how technical debt can be measured (and visualized), it seems that only low level aspects are being focused on. The use of static analysis tools and source code metrics are self-explanatory examples. And even on those works that describe how it can be estimated qualitatively, the attention is turned to software products and not to software practices. For instance, examples of technical debt items in [15] are: architectural design violations, test skipped, outdated documentation and design debt.

Given the context aforementioned, especially regarding the role of the architecture team serving various teams in parallel and the fact that the teams have autonomy in its technical decisions, there was a need for the technical debt estimation and visualization in a "macro-level", i.e., not only associated with source code aspects but with technical practices involving the product in general. This would give the opportunity to see the actual state of the department and indicate the "roadmap" for future interaction with the development teams.

The actions involved in introducing this kind of visualization and the management activities based on that visualization are described in next section.

4   Actions

Given the challenge in addressing the issues caused by the technical debt, the architecture team started to discuss some initiatives that could help the area: (i) recognize that the lack of attention paid to the technical debt was a problem (teams and management), (ii) visualize the existing technical debt, (iii) quantifying the amount of technical debt, (iv) create mechanisms of feedback to see the technical debt rising or decreasing and (v) take actions to correct implementations that lead to technical debt.

It is important to mention that these actions were not planned upfront, but they emerged according to the feedback that the architecture team was having in trying to implement the technical debt awareness in the department.

4.1   Recognize That the Lack of Attention Paid to the Technical Debt Was a Problem

The first step the architecture team had to take was to make sure every developer knew the concept of technical debt. As in the pair "reckless x inadvertent" in Martin Fowler's [8] quadrant of technical debt, most of the team members did not know the exact meaning of technical debt. The architecture team then started to do a series of presentations about the theme. What is technical debt; what is its size; why do we accumulate technical debt and how do we pay it; and how to benefit from technical debt were topics presented to the audience.

The architecture team had also the challenge to speak to different audiences. More technical presentations were made to the teams, but to the upper level management, another language was needed, so everyone could understand the topic by their own point of view.

At that time, many teams were already struggling with problems of poor architecture, rework, delays, and poor quality. All of these issues where impacting the relationship with their clients.

4.2   Visualize the Existing Technical Debt

The software development department was already having some initial Kanban [21] implementations. As one of the main principles of Kanban is visualization, these ideas were permeating the minds of the group, and many initiatives of change management were taking visualization into account.

The architecture team modeled a board, where the lines corresponds to teams and the columns are the categories and subcategories of technical debt, based on the work of Chris Sterling [9] as illustrated in Figure 1.

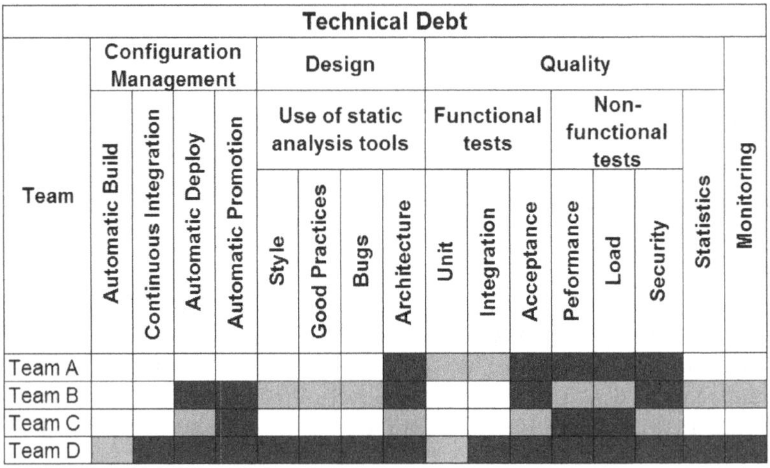

Team	Technical Debt													
	Configuration Management				Design							Quality		
					Use of static analysis tools				Functional tests			Non-functional tests		
	Automatic Build	Continuous Integration	Automatic Deploy	Automatic Promotion	Style	Good Practices	Bugs	Architecture	Unit	Integration	Acceptance	Performance	Load	Security	Statistics	Monitoring
Team A																
Team B																
Team C																
Team D																

Fig. 1. Technical debt categories

In each cell, formed by the pair team x technical debt category, the maturity of the team was evaluated according to predefined criteria. Examples of these criteria are displayed in Table 1. For full description please see Appendix A. Notice that in the real board shown in Figure 2, we used the colors red, yellow and green to show the compliance level of each criterion. So, we kept the reference to these colors in the text even though Figure 1 uses a gray scale (white = green, yellow = light gray and red = dark gray).

The criteria just provided a direction of what kind of practices would be focused, but not give directives on how it could be achieved. This was the moment where the architecture team could offer its support. In addition, the criteria were not a rigid target. For instance, for unit tests, the ideal coverage level was dependent on the system architecture, technologies involved (e.g., programming language and frameworks), the criticality of the application and other factors. All of this was subject of discussion between the development teams and the architecture team. And that was one of the biggest benefits on bringing the debt visible.

The architecture team, in its internal conversations, was concerned that this approach could make the teams feel compelled to follow the orientations. This was not the objective, on the contrary the objective was to make teams aware of the

Table 1. Criteria examples for technical debt assessment

	Continuous Integration	**Unit Tests**
Red	There is no job in the CI Tool.	There are no Unit Tests.
Yellow	There is a job scheduled in the CI Tool.	There are some Unit Tests.
Green	There is a job scheduled in the CI Tool and the team is committed to keep the build working (compiling and with unit tests passing).	There are Unit tests in a level that the team is comfortable with.

problem and take their own actions to amend their technical difficulties. And if the teams were not capable of addressing the problem, the architecture team should be consulted for support. Thus, this initiative was first presented to the teams' focal points and it was explained that the main objective was not to constrain anyone, but to allow the visualization of their actual state regarding the technical debt and have the possibility to monitor their own progress. The proposal was presented in a very objective way, focusing on the engineering issues. The focal points did not offer resistance. Actually, many of them thought that the initiative was a good opportunity to improve their overall work (even with their own "problems" exposed).

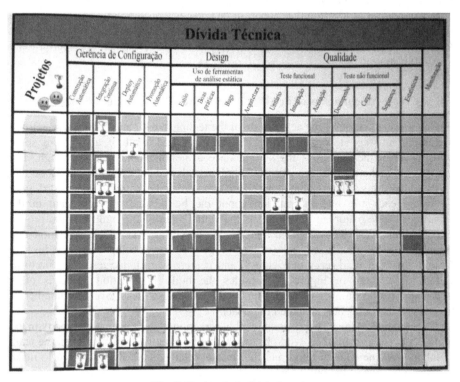

Fig. 2. Real technical debt board

After the design of the technical debt board, each team was invited to a rapid meeting in front of the board, where all team members talked about the status of each criterion, translating it to the respective color. During these meeting the teams could also conclude that some categories were not relevant or applicable for their systems. This meeting should happen every month, so that the progress of each category could be updated. At the end of the meeting, the team members agreed which of the categories would be the aim for the next meeting or, to put it another way, where they would invest their efforts in reducing the technical debt. The real board is presented in Figure 2. Blank cells represent categories not relevant or applicable. Team names from in the first column were removed from the figure.

4.3   Quantifying the Amount of Technical Debt

To measure the technical debt at source code level, the architecture team has made use of the tool Sonar (http://www.sonarsource.org/) [20]. Sonar has a plugin that allows estimating how much effort would be required to fix each debt of the project. Sonar considers as debts: cohesion and complexity metrics, duplications, lack of comments, coding rules violation, potential bugs and no unit tests or useless ones. The details of its formula can be found in [20]. The important aspect is that an estimative is calculated, and Sonar shows the results financially and the effort in man days necessary to take the debt to zero (the daily rate of the developer in the context of the project must be informed).

It is important to mention that Sonar, in fact, use many other tools internally to analyze the source code – each one for different aspects of the analysis. It works as an aggregator to display results of other tools such as PMD, Findbugs, Cobertura and Checkstyle among others.

4.4   Create Mechanisms of Feedback to See the Technical Debt Evolution

Having a visualization of the actual state of the technical debt and having it quantified was important step. However, having the debt quantified in a tool, and making some adjustments in the course of the system once a month would not be enough. The teams could make the debt rise during a whole month without even knowing about it.

To address this situation, the architecture team created a virtual tiled board (Figure 3), where each tile had information about the build state of each team in the department. The major information was the actual state of the build and the project name (which was removed from figure). If everything was ok (compilation and automated tests), the tile is green (white in Figure 3), if the compilation was broken, the tile turns red (dark gray in Figure 3) and if there were failed tests, the tile turns yellow (light gray in Figure 3). Besides the build information, there is other information: total number of tests, number of failed tests, test coverage, number of lines and technical debt (calculated in Sonar).

The virtual tiled board was placed in a big screen in a place where everybody in the room could see it from their workplaces. The main objective was that when the team members saw their failed build and that instant feedback would lead them to make corrective actions so the build could go green again.

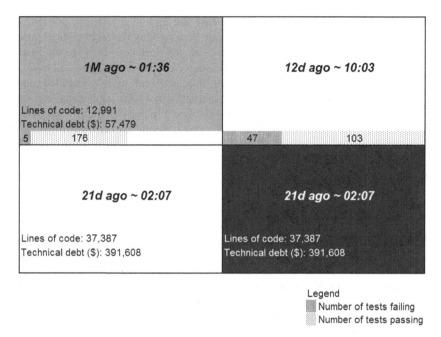

Fig. 3. Some of the virtual tiled board cells in detail (project names were removed from it)

4.5   Take Actions to Correct Implementations That Lead to Technical Debt Rising

As the mechanisms of feedback were implemented, the teams had instant information about what should be done to lower the levels of technical debt. With this information, they could prioritize which categories they would try to improve in the next month. If the team had some difficulties addressing any of the categories, they could call upon the architecture team support. In the following months after the board implementation, the architecture team kept making presentations about each category and how to deal with them.

5   Lessons Learned

In general terms, we think that the aforementioned actions can lead to small changes that over time will add up to significant positive change for teams and organizations. The main evidence for that, in our experience, is summarized below.

5.1   Make Visible. Don't Dictate.

The line between being firm about the value of implementing Agile practices and sensitive to the freedom and independence of teams is a difficult one to take right. With the board exposed, the approach was to encourage teams to self-evaluate theirs technical debt, instead of someone, in our case the architecture team, pointing out problems. As a result, the teams showed initiative on seeking the architecture team for help with issues related to technical debt, as for instance, how to implement automated deployment or how to improve the source code testability for unit tests.

From the moment the debts were inserted, interest began to be contracted, and at some future time it may have to be paid. Making them visible and managing them, allowed strategic decision making to choose the best time to pay them – once it was possible to see how it was accumulating and its possible impacts/costs throughout the software development lifecycle.

Visualization was a powerful way to simplify complexity, expose the reality and, consequently, motivate teams to improve.

5.2   Improved Communication

Again, visibility was a key enabler to improve communication among development teams, architecture team and upper management. It turned the discussions around technical issues focused and oriented much efforts towards a common (visible) goal. The meetings around the board is now a regular practice in the department and in many situations development teams have opportunity to discuss about (the once unfamiliar) techniques to deal with their debt.

Another important benefit of the afore-described approach was establishing the basic concepts and tools around the technical debt theme which, again, facilitated the discussions. Developers are now more aware of the main factors that can contribute to the technical debt accumulation, are more open to discuss about it and know how to measure and address (technical practices) it.

5.3   Debts Paid at a Rate Higher than Expected

Besides the mentioned benefits, it was observed that debts were paid at a rate higher than expected. We interpreted this as a result of the competition among teams. In addition, we have noticed that this was stimulated by the introduction of gamification elements. Gamification [23] is the application of game elements and digital game design techniques to non-game problems, such as business and social impact challenges. It is used in applications and processes to improve user engagement, timeliness, and learning.

To apply gamification elements in our context items such as trophies exposed at the board of technical debt motivated teams to improve quality and pay debts. Every improvement made at the board, earned the team a trophy (the board in Figure 2 has some attached to it). This made visible how teams were evolving and kept the motivation for sustaining the progress.

We have calculated a raw estimative of how the technical debt payment progressed in the first year. To measure this progress, we kept the technical debt evolution history in a spread sheet, but only for the first thirteen projects (i.e., the first technical debt board) – this data was not made public. The progress was measured in the following manner. Supposing that the red/yellow/green represents an interval scale, the difference between red/yellow and yellow/green is one unit – for a max of 416 "units of debt" representing the worst situation of all projects "in red" in a board with thirteen projects. Considering the initial state of the board, the projects had 327 units of debt. From this initial state in 06-17-2011 to almost one year after in 05-14-2012, the projects already had 226 units. This constituted a progress of 30% which was above our initial expectations considering past experiences in fomenting technical improvements. It represented a great (visible) achievement in our department. It is interesting to notice, in addition, that this progress was not homogeneous among teams. Some teams evolved faster than others. And that, in our view, was one of the factors that stimulated competition.

The virtual tiled board also played an interesting role in bringing additional gamification elements to the technical debt management as teams immediately started to react to the red or yellow colors for broken builds. This was a result of an emerging social commitment of being seen different among their peers who kept their build green. The build status changes minutes after the source code check-in/commit by the team and this rapid feedback loop caused a strong change in the culture of the team members who after just a couple of weeks were already treating the build status with a high priority. This improved the perception of the teams in keeping their main/trunk branch closer to a deployable state as possible.

Thus, in addition to visibility, gamification was a powerful mechanism to motivate teams in monitor their technical debt.

6   Final Remarks

After Scrum adoption, the most visible symptoms of dysfunction in our software development department were related to agile engineering practices, where teams were accumulating a huge amount of technical debt. This paper showed how an architecture team at Petrobras has managed the technical debt in an agile context, seeking to reduce the high costs generated by debt issued. Working the change management iteratively, getting feedback for new actions, the intense use of visualization, the application of concrete measurements, and working together with the teams in a collaborative, not imposing manner, all that in context had proved to be powerful tools to obtain the desired results.

Another important contribution of this paper was proposing an approach for addressing the technical debt at a high-level. The proposed approach, besides the use of tools to estimate technical debt based on low-level source code metrics and reports, involves people to analyze the main contributing technical debt factors and plans the appropriate time to deal with it. In this manner, the board as a visual instrument has demonstrated to be useful in our context.

References

1. Boehm, B.: Get ready for agile methods, with care. Computer 35, 64–69 (2002)
2. Dinakar, K.: Agile development: overcoming a short-term focus in implementing best practices. In: Proceedings of the 24th ACM SIGPLAN Conference Companion on Object Oriented Programming Systems Languages and Applications, pp. 579–588. ACM, New York (2009)

3. Abrahamsson, P., Warsta, J., Siponen, M.T., Ronkainen, J.: New directions on agile methods: a comparative analysis. In: Proceedings of the 25th International Conference on Software Engineering, pp. 244–254 (2003)

4. Merisalo-Rantanen, H., Tuunanen, T., Rossi, M.: Is Extreme Programming Just Old Wine in New Bottles. Journal of Database Management 16, 41–61 (2005)

5. Mishra, D., Mishra, A.: Complex software project development: agile methods adoption. Journal of Software Maintenance and Evolution: Research and Practice 23, 549–564 (2011)

6. Svensson, H., Host, M.: Introducing an Agile Process in a Software Maintenance and Evolution Organization. In: 9th European Conference on Software Maintenance and Reengineering, CSMR 2005, pp. 256–264 (2005)

7. Cunningham, W.: The WyCash portfolio management system. SIGPLAN OOPS Mess. 4, 29–30 (1992)

8. Fowler, M.: Technical Debt (2009),
   http://martinfowler.com/bliki/TechnicalDebt.html

9. Sterling, C.: Managing Software Debt: Building for Inevitable Change. Addison-Wesley Professional (2010)

10. Lim, E., Taksande, N., Seaman, C.: A Balancing Act: What Software Practitioners Have to Say about Technical Debt. IEEE Software 29, 22–27 (2012)

11. Brown, N., Cai, Y., Guo, Y., Kazman, R., Kim, M., Kruchten, P., Lim, E., MacCormack, A., Nord, R., Ozkaya, I., Sangwan, R., Seaman, C., Sullivan, K., Zazworka, N.: Managing technical debt in software-reliant systems. In: Proceedings of the FSE/SDP Workshop on Future of Software Engineering Research, pp. 47–52. ACM, New York (2010)

12. McConnell, S.: Technical Debt,
    http://forums.construx.com/blogs/stevemcc/archive/
    2007/11/01/technical-debt-2.aspx (2007)

13. Klinger, T., Tarr, P., Wagstrom, P., Williams, C.: An enterprise perspective on technical debt. In: Proceedings of the 2nd Workshop on Managing Technical Debt, pp. 35–38. ACM, New York (2011)

14. Seaman, C., Guo, Y., Izurieta, C., Cai, Y., Zazworka, N., Shull, F., Vetro, A.: Using technical debt data in decision making: Potential decision approaches. In: 2012 Third International Workshop on Managing Technical Debt (MTD), pp. 45–48 (2012)

15. Seaman, C., Guo, Y.: Measuring and Monitoring Technical Debt. In: Zelkowitz, M. (ed.) Advances in Computers. Academic Press (2011)

16. Zazworka, N., Seaman, C., Shull, F.: Prioritizing design debt investment opportunities. In: Proceedings of the 2nd Workshop on Managing Technical Debt, pp. 39–42. ACM, New York (2011)

17. Vetrò, A.: Using automatic static analysis to identify technical debt. In: Proceedings of the 2012 International Conference on Software Engineering, pp. 1613–1615. IEEE Press, Piscataway (2012)

18. Fontana, F.A., Ferme, V., Spinelli, S.: Investigating the impact of code smells debt on quality code evaluation. In: 2012 Third International Workshop on Managing Technical Debt (MTD), pp. 15–22 (2012)

19. Guo, Y., Seaman, C.: A portfolio approach to technical debt management. In: Proceedings of the 2nd Workshop on Managing Technical Debt, pp. 31–34. ACM, New York (2011)

20. Gaudin, O.: Evaluate your technical debt with Sonar (2009),
    http://www.sonarsource.org/
    evaluate-your-technical-debt-with-sonar/

21. Anderson, D.: Kanban: Successful Evolutionary Change for Your Technology Business. Blue Hole Press (April 7, 2010)
22. Gaillot, E.: What is Coding Dojo (2012), http://codingdojo.org/cgi-bin/wiki.pl?WhatIsCodingDojo
23. Werbach, K.: Gamification, University of Pennsylvania (2012), https://www.coursera.org/course/gamification

Appendix A - Technical Debt Criteria

	Red	Yellow	Green
Automatic Construction	No build tool used	Build tool is used but build is dependent on local configuration	Build tool is used and build is not dependent on local configuration
Continuous Integration	There is no job in the CI Tool	There is a job scheduled in the CI Tool	There is a job scheduled in the CI Tool and the team is committed to keep the build working
Automatic Deployment	Deployment is manual	Deployment is an automated process using a build tool command	Deployment is an automated process using the CI Tool
Continuous Delivery	Release to staging environments is manual	Release is an automated process for validated artifacts using a build tool command	Release is an automated process using a build pipeline
Style Good Practices Bugs	No static analysis tool used	Static analysis tool is configured with static rules	Static analysis tool is configured and the team is committed to keep high levels of rules compliance
Architecture	No architecture analysis tool used	Architecture analysis tool is configured with architectural (dependency) rules	Architecture analysis tool is configured and the team is committed to keep high levels of rules compliance
Tests: Unit/ Integration/ Acceptance/ Performance/ Load/ Security	No Tests	Some Tests	There are tests in a level that the team is comfortable with

Statistics	No statistics on the code quality	Statistic on the code quality are collected	Statistic on the code quality are collected and the team is committed to keep high levels of quality
Monitoring	No monitoring	The monitoring tool is configured to alert the team when the application is not responding	The monitoring tool is configured to alert the team when the application or any of its dependences are not responding

How Are Agile Methods and Practices Deployed in Video Game Development? A Survey into Finnish Game Studios

Jussi Koutonen and Mauri Leppänen

Department of Computer Science and Information Systems
P.O. Box 35 (Agora), FI-40014 University of Jyväskylä, Finland
jussi.koutonen@sysdrone.fi, mauri.leppanen@jyu.fi

Abstract. Agile methods and practices are largely deployed in software engineering. Game development shares many features that have given rise to the emergence of agility in software engineering. There is, however, a lack of understanding of the extent to which agile methods and practices are actually deployed in video game development and with which impacts. This paper reports on a survey into Finnish game studios. It shows that Scrum and, to a lesser degree, XP and Kanban are frequently used in the game studios. The most positive impacts of agility concern communication, quality of video games, and finding fun and implementable features earlier.

Keywords: video game development, Scrum, XP, Kanban, agile practices.

1   Introduction

The game industry is increasingly expanding. In 2007 the software portion of video game revenue was $9.5 billion, exceeding that of movies industry [38]. According to the forecast by PricewaterhouseCoopers [45], total global spending on video games will expand to $83.0 billion in 2016, growing at a 7.2 percent compound annual rate. The growth is expected to be rapid especially in the segment of online and wireless games with smartphones and tablets.

Game industry faces, however, a number of challenges. Players' expectations of getting "wow" and flow reactions in terms of visual appearance, script, sound world and technological novelty are growing. The games have to offer better and better player experience and co-experience [9]. Developing groundbreaking video games is very demanding [13]. The projects involve people with various expertise, making envisioning, communication, coordination and control most complicated [27, 36, 44]. Development budgets of high profile games are approaching the ones of Hollywood movies. Furthermore, game industry is a very competitive and risky field [42]. A publisher accepts a great risk in investing tens of millions for a development project without knowing whether the game is a success or not. It is estimated that only the top 5% of products make a profit. Industry employment is also fairly volatile, similar to other artistic industries [12].

H. Baumeister and B. Weber (Eds.): XP 2013, LNBIP 149, pp. 135–149, 2013.
© Springer-Verlag Berlin Heidelberg 2013

Game development has been traditionally based on the waterfall model or some of its variants [12, 50]. Due to its inspirational and unpredictable nature [56], many teams favor iterative processes including prototypes [44, 36]. An iterative process enables testing ideas in earlier phases and making rapid changes if necessary. This way a game's features emerge while the developers continually play-test to aspire a fun, entertaining and compelling game. An iterative and incremental way of working is inherent in agile methods [3], such as Scrum [54], XP (eXtreme Programming) [11], Lean [43] and Kanban [5, 32].

Although there is a large array of studies on games and their development, most of them discuss some specific issues, e.g. details of game mechanics or game experience. There are only some studies on game development methods and processes (e.g. [12, 57, 49, 50]). Yet fewer are those studies [27, 39, 40, 55, 56] that address agile game development. In particular, understanding of agile methods in use and their impacts on game development is yet to be achieved.

The research problem of our study is: To which extent game studios deploy agile methods and practices, and how they impact on game development? We accomplished the study as a survey targeted to Finnish game studios. The game industry has grown in Finland perhaps faster than in most countries. The total revenue of the Finnish game industry was estimated to be 335 million euro in 2011 [18]. Most of the studios are small, but there also are some large and successful studios, such as Rovio Entertainment (http://www.rovio.com/en/) whose product Angry Birds has become a worldwide phenomenon. The game has been downloaded more than 1 billion times (summer 2012). Another flourishing studio is Supercell with its Clash of Clans.

The remainder of the paper is organized into six sections. In Section 2 we shortly discuss video games and game development. In Section 3 the agile approach and agile methods and their use in software engineering are outlined. Section 4 provides a literature review of agile game development. In Section 5 we describe our research method and process, and Section 6 reports on the results of the survey. The paper ends with a summary and conclusion.

2   Video Games and Game Development

A *video game* is a game played by electronically manipulating images produced by a computer program on a monitor or other display (Oxford Dictionary). There is a large variety of game genres categorized by e.g. gameplay interaction, purpose, platform, and publisher [6, 63]. Every game has its rules. In addition to specific rules, game rules produce emergent properties such as player experience or playability that are quite difficult to predict or design. Player experience is different from that obtained from other home entertainments [52]. Looking at TV or films, reading books and listening music are passive entertainments which contain no interaction, whereas playing games a person can affect future events with his/her actions. Games can be fun in many respects [24]: sensation, fantasy, narrative, challenge, fellowship, discovery, expression, and submission.

Developing games is a complex endeavor [22, 13, 42] due to e.g. multiple disciplines, a large number of roles, divergent ambitions, conflicts of interests [21], and difficulties in anticipating what kind game will have a success in rapidly changing markets. These entail problems in schedules (cf. crunch time), coordination, team building, testing, and product family engineering [42, 19, 22, 39, 26]. Game development is particularly difficult for innovative, completely new kinds of games [33].

Game development is often compared to software engineering [42, 39, 36], and indeed, its outcome is software and to produce it similar phases have to go through. However, video games also resemble films in terms of creativity and aethestic components. Crawford [17] argues that game design is an art, science, a craft, or any combination of the three. There is one unique aspect that seems to separate the video game from traditional software: the requirement to be fun [35]. This requirement, unlike many others in software engineering, has no metric that can be applied. What is fun for one audience may not be for another. However, fun must be supported by and validated at each stage of the development process. To do this, games must be developed in a highly iterative manner.

There exists no single game development process model, which could act as a standard for the industry [37, 15]. Studios have different semi-formal or formal procedures [8] and philosophies [37]. However some commonalities exist. Development of a commercial game is usually divided into multiple phases which are defined by milestones [48, 49, 50]. Contracts between publishers and developers are typically based on these milestones [21]. Earlier the development process was based on the waterfall model or some of its variants [50, 12]. Nowadays, many teams use iterative processes including prototypes [44, 36], and some of them have adopted agile methods and practices [27, 39, 40].

There are some generic models that synthesize features of multiple methods of game development. Van de Weerd [61] used a formal method comparison approach to construct a reference method to give an overview of the phases, activities, steps and deliverables in the game development process. Manninen et al. [36] propose game development to consist of six major phases: concept, pre-production, production, quality assurance, release & launch, and post-release. Typical for game development is that the process is iterative [34, 56].

3   Agile Development

Software engineering has radically changed since the new millennium. The *agile approach* emerged to provide new values, principles and practices [3], particularly for situations characterized by e.g., hard to predefine and volatile requirements, first-to-market thinking, release orientation, dependence on good people, and negotiable quality [7, 14, 16]. The values emphasize individuals and interactions over processes and tools, working software over comprehensive documentation, customer collaboration over contract negotiation, and responding to change over following a plan [3]. These have led to incremental, iterative and adaptive development.

Agility is a highly multifaceted concept with different meanings [16, 1, 25]. Conboy [16] develops a definition and formative taxonomy of agility, based on a literature review of agility across a number of disciplines. The definition goes as follow: agility means "the continual readiness of an ISD method to rapidly or inherently create change, proactively or reactively embrace change, and learn from change while contributing to perceived customer value (economy, quality, and simplicity), through its collective components and relationships with its environment." [16, p. 340).

Agility is believed to reduce time-to-market, help coping with rapidly changing requirements and priorities, lower defect rates, improve product quality and process productivity, increase customer-value, as well as reach sustainable pace and balanced workload, thus improving developers' motivation and morale.

There is a large array of agile methods and principles, such as Scrum, eXtreme Programming (XP), DSDM, FDD, Kanban and Lean. The most used methods are Scrum, XP, and their combination and variants [58]. In the following, we shortly outline Scrum, XP and Kanban.

Scrum is "a framework within which people can address complex adaptive problems" [54]. In the literature, it is often said to be an agile method. Scrum has been built on three "pillars" (transparency, inspection, and adaptation), three main roles (development team, product owner, Scrum master), five events (sprint, sprint planning meeting, daily scrum, sprint review, and sprint retrospective), and three main artifacts (product backlog, sprint backlog, increment) [54]. Although the Scrum Guide [54] does not explicitly define a process, it is commonly associated with some kind of process model (see e.g. [2]).

XP (eXtreme Programming) is "a lightweight methodology for small to medium-size teams developing software in the face of vague or rapidly changing requirements" [10]. It provides a large set of practices that are divided into 13 primary practices and 11 corollary practices [11], meaning that the latter ones should be implemented after the primary practices have been taken into use. The set of XP practices include e.g., sitting together, cross-functional team, informative work space, stories, pair programming, quarterly cycle, ten-minutes build, continuous integration, and test-first programming.

Kanban has been derived from Lean thinking [62,43, 5]. In the simplest form, it is based on three principles [32]: visualize the workflow, limit WIP (work in progress), and measure the lead time. The first principle guides to split the work into pieces, write each item on a card and put on a kanban board. The second principle means that explicit limits are assigned to how many items may be in progress at each workflow state. The third principle tells to optimize the process to make lead times as small and predictable as possible.

In software engineering, the adoption of agile methods has already bridged the "crossed chasm" [59, 20, 4]. According to the latest survey [58] more than 80% of respondents said their organizations have adopted agile development practices. Scrum and Scrum/XP variants continue to make up more than two-thirds of the methods being used. Kanban and Scrumban were used in 6 % of the organizations.

4   Agile Game Development

There is a myriad of academic publications on agile software development, but only a few of them address agile game development. Here, we first quote Keith [27] and Musil et al. [39] to describe how they see the usage of agile values, principles and practices in game development. After that, we describe some empirical studies [40, 41, 56, 55] on how agile methods and practices are used in game development.

Clinton Keith [27] states that the values of the Agile Manifesto, with minor changes, are applicable for game development. He applies Scrum practices and presents four game development stages: concept, pre-production, production and post-production. In concept stage, ideas are generated, possibly prototyped, on a regular basis in time-boxed sprints. In pre-production stage, teams explore what is fun and how they are going to build assets to support it during production. They also create levels and other assets that represent production quality. In production stage, teams focus on creating an eight- to twelve-hour experience using the core mechanics and processes discovered during pre-production. This stage focuses on efficiency and incremental improvements. In post-production stage, teams polish the game experience, with the content brought to shippable quality. After that, the game is submitted to hardware testing.

Keith [27] criticizes some Scrum practices. Especially, the use of the sprint backlog in production stage causes problems in practice. That is why, he suggests Lean principles, in particular kanban, for production stage. From XP, suitable practices are informative working space, pair programming, continuous integration, test-driven development, user stories and short releases [27].

Musil et al. [39] propose a game development process, which is composed of three phases: pre-production, production and project closure. The main tasks of pre-production are to identify possible software project candidates, as well as to carry out requirement analysis, risk assessment and general project requirements like financing. Production receives the complete project package from pre-production and creates a sellable product with the given time, money and quality. The overall production workflow is based on Scrum, whereby it is separated into the three process time lines: vision loop, sprint loop, and validation loop. Project closure covers the distribution of the final game as well as retrospective analysis (post mortems), processing of created tools and integration of lessons-learned into the company's knowledge base.

Musil et al. [40] conducted a web-survey in the Austrian game industry (20 game studios) to identify the state of the practice and possible future trends regarding process and method support. Nine process methods were provided for the selection grouped into flexible (Scrum, XP, Agile/Lean), traditional (RUP, Crystal Clear, PSP/TSP) and unstructured methods (others). 23% of the respondents did not use any software process, but developed games ad-hoc. 77% of the studios applied flexible methods, and 61,5 % Scrum.

Petrillo and Pimenta [41] investigated how Agile principles and practices were adopted in game development, by gathering evidences through a postmortem analysis of 20 game development projects. 13 agile practices of Scrum, XP and Agile modeling methods were identified, including qualified team, belief in the success of the project, creativity stimulus, focus on the product, version control, using simple tools, and programming good practices. As can be seen, the list also contains general practices, not only agile practices.

Stacey and Nandhakumar [56] studied three computer game studios and recognized similarities between game development and agile development: getting feedback is equally important value although feedback in game development comes mostly from in-house, not from customers, and a fluid communication is an important value in agile development, as well as in game development. They noticed that the studios did not deploy agile methods as such but rather some of agile practices. Schofield [55] discusses the use of five XP practices (test-driven development, pair programming, continuous design, real customer involvement and energized work) in game development. He states that XP encourages the designer to steer the game during development and make more changes in the game design. XP practices focus development energy into delivering results quickly and keeping the project flexible.

5   Research Method and Process

Our research objective was to find out to which extent Finnish game studios deploy agile methods and practices and how their usage impacts on game development. From alternative research methods (e.g., case study, action research, and postmortem analysis) we selected survey [29] because data collected from a large population enables better generalization. To make the threshold of answering lower, we used an unsupervised survey [28] in which participants completed and submitted an online questionnaire through web browser and answers were recorded anonymously.

We took several steps to ensure that enough people return the survey with meaningful information [29]. First, we wanted to select respondents that are knowledgeable, willing and motivated to answer the questions. We used the language that is close to the one the practitioners use in their work. We presented questions in simple and unambiguous sentences to avoid misunderstandings and in a well-structured form to increase the clarity. The persons were also promised a copy of the research report for their reflection and benchmarking.

The population of the survey contained all the Finnish game studios with five or more employees. The size limit was based on an assumption that work in very small studios is not well organized and may apply more or less ad hoc ways of working. To find respondents, we contacted two professional associations, the Finnish Game Developers (http://www.pelinkehittajat.fi/) and Neogames (http://www.hermia.fi/neogames/). Using their lists of the member studios we asked each studio to name a knowledgeable person. This way we found 45 suitable studios, from which 37 gave direct contact information. We sent the invitation letter to them in July 2011, and got answers from 20 companies.

The questionnaire addresses four themes: background information, game development process, deployment of agile methods and practices, and experiences. *Background theme* concerns the general information about the game studios (no. of employees, age), their products (no. of game platforms and game genres), and development projects (size, no. of concurrent projects). These are relevant for analyzing impacts on the ways of developing games and applying agile methods and practices. *In Game development process theme* we were keen to learn which development tasks are accomplished and in which phases. These questions are based on a general phase structure derived from Keith [27] and Manninen et al. [36]. Unfortunately, we are not able here to report on the answers to these questions due to the space available.

Agile methods and practices theme was defined first to reveal which agile methods (Scrum, XP, Kanban, other) are used in each of the phases. Second, we wanted to find out which of nine Scrum practices, nine XP practices and three Kanban principles are deployed in the studios. Finally, in *Experience theme* we examined experiences the game studios had got from applying agile methods and practices. The questions were presented in the form of statements derived from Petrillo et al. [42], Musil et al. [40], and Keith [27].

The questionnaire was edited through several iterations, including pre-testing by four persons. After receiving the answers we followed the recommendations by Kitchenham [31]: the number of the answers for each question was checked (four respondents did not answer the questions about the use of agile methods and practices), for closed questions the distributions were calculated, and the answers to open questions were used to clarify the interpretation of the structured data.

The quality of a research study should be assessed in terms of reliability and validity. *Reliability* "is concerned with how well we can reproduce the survey data" [30]. "If another researcher later on conducted the same study, the results should be the same" [51]. We enhanced the repeatability of the survey by using the structured, web-based and pre-tested questionnaire, thus minimizing a researcher's effect on respondents.

Validity is concerned with "how well the instrument measures what it is supposed to measure" [30]. *External validity* is concerned with the extent to which it is possible to generalize the research results [51]. External validity is dependent on the size of the sample in relation to the population and its representativeness. We got a rather reliable estimate of the number of the Finnish game studios suitable to our study (N=45), and received answers from 20 studios. The response rate (44%) can be considered to be fairly good for making generalizations with regard to this population. In other countries, the sizes, funding principles and labor markets of the game studios, as well as the diffusion stage of agile methods in general can differ from those in Finland. Without knowing the contextual factors, generalization should be considered with care. On the other hand, the Austrian survey [40] shows that in corresponding circumstances the use of agile methods can be similar. *Internal validity* can be assessed in terms of several types of validity. Here, we consider *content validity* that is a subjective assessment of how appropriate the instrument seems to persons with the knowledge of the subject matter [30]. In order to address the subject matter in a proper way, the themes and questions were strongly based on relevant literature on game development and agile approach. The questionnaire was pre-tested by four persons.

6   Results

6.1   Background Information of the Game Studios

Based on the answers, the game studios were rather young: seven (35 %) studios had been on the markets for 0-2 years, eight (40 %) studios for 3-5 years and three studios for 5-10 years. Only one studio was over 10 year old. They were also rather small; half of the studios had 15 or less employees, five (25%) studios had 16-50 employees, and only two (10%) studios had more than 50 employees. The most common game platforms were PC (70%) and mobile devices (65%). Nine (45 %) companies concentrated on one platform, while the others made games for 2-6 platforms. The most common game genres were Casual (70%), Action-adventure (30%), Platformer (30%), Adventure (25%), and Strategy (20%). Other genres included Simulation, Music, Racing, Serious and Role-playing games. Eight (40%) companies developed games of three or more genres.

Game development projects normally took less than one year. In seven (35%) companies, projects took less than half a year in average, in six (30%) companies ½-1 year, and in six companies for 1-2 years. In one company the projects took in average more than 3 years. The size of the project team was commonly 1-5 persons (35 %) or 6-15 (60%) persons. In one company, the size of the project team was 16-30 persons.

The last question of this theme concerned the number of concurrent projects. Five (25 %) companies had only one project at a time, six (30%) companies two projects, three (15%) companies three projects, four (20%) companies four projects and two (10%) companies five or more projects.

6.2   Agile Methods Used in the Game Studios

In the third part of the questionnaire, the respondents were asked about agile methods (Scrum, XP, Lean, Kanban, other) they are using in the game development phases (concept definition, pre-production, production, post-development, other phase). Scrum was the most common method: more than 50% of the companies deployed Scrum in production, pre-production and post-production phases, and more than 30% also in concept definition phase. The second common method (25%) was "Other method". Lean was deployed in about 10 % of the studio in all the phases except post-production. Kanban was used only by one studio (in concept definition phase). Surprisingly, XP was not mentioned in this context. A likely reason for this is that XP was not recognized as a method but a set of practices. This is line in the finding of Stacey et al (2008) that game studios did not deploy agile methods as such but rather some of agile practices. Another explanation is that the studios using a customized mix of Scrum and XP answered "Other method". Young studios did not use agile methods so largely as older ones, perhaps due to their more ad-hoc like processes. Three respondents explained their "Other method" answer saying that they use customized Scrum or other agile method. One answer to the open question elaborates that for concept definition they select a method case-by-case; sometimes Scrum, sometimes a "one-man innovation process".

6.3 Agile Practices Used in Game Studios

The questions of this part addressed the use of nine Scrum, nine XP and three Kanban practices in the game development phases, with the following options: "in all the phases", "in concept definition", "in pre-production", "in production", "in post-production", "not used" and "do not know". Four respondents did not answer to the questions about the Scrum practices, and eight respondents did not answer to the questions about the XP and Kanban practices.

Scrum practices were most commonly used in the game studios (see Table 1). Yet, for each of the Scrum practices 25 - 44 % of the respondents said they do not use it. Daily Scrum and Sprints were the most deployed practices in "All phases". Most of the Scrum practices were more often used in pre-production and production phases than in concept definition and post-production phases.

Table 1. The use of Scrum practices in game development phases ([1] = all phases, [2] = concept definition, [3] = pre-production, [4] = production, [5] = post-production, [6] = not used, [7] = do not know) (n = 16)

Scrum practices	[1]	[2]	[3]	[4]	[5]	[6]	[7]
Daily Scrum	5	0	3	4	3	6	0
Sprint	5	2	7	7	4	4	0
Sprint planning meeting 1	2	3	6	7	3	6	0
Sprint planning meeting 2	1	3	5	7	3	6	0
Sprint review meeting	3	1	4	6	4	6	1
Sprint retrospective	1	1	4	5	2	7	1
Sprint burn down chart	0	1	3	6	2	7	1
Product backlog	4	2	7	8	5	4	0
Sprint backlog	4	1	7	8	5	4	0

From the large set of the XP practices [11] we selected those nine that were mentioned in existing literature on game development. The answers showed that XP practices are largely used (see Table 2). The most used XP practices were cross-functional teams, informative work spaces and continuous integration. The most uncommon XP practices were Quarterly cycle and Ten-minutes build. The latter result seems a bit surprising because Continuous integration and Ten-minutes build are commonly used together. Pair programming and Test-first programming were not largely used although they belong to the set of the primary XP practices [11].

Kanban practices were quite slightly used in the game studios. "Limit Work in Progress (WIP)" was deployed in all the phases only by two game studios. Work Visualization was used in all the phases by one company, and another company deployed it in concept definition. No game studio "measures the lead time".

Table 2. The use of XP practices in game development phases ([1] = all phases, [2] = concept definition, [3] = pre-production, [4] = production, [5] = post-production, [6] = not used, [7] = do not know) (n = 12)

XP practices	[1]	[2]	[3]	[4]	[5]	[6]	[7]
Sitting together	4	3	2	1	1	6	0
Cross-functional team	5	2	3	3	2	4	0
Informative work space	4	2	3	3	2	4	2
User stories	2	1	2	2	0	7	1
Pair programming	1	1	2	1	1	7	2
Quarterly cycle	0	0	0	1	0	11	1
Ten-minutes build	0	0	0	0	1	9	2
Continuous integration	3	0	4	4	4	4	0
Test-first programming	2	0	4	1	0	6	3

6.4   Impacts of Agile Methods and Practices to Game Development

Finally, we asked the respondents' opinions about the impacts of agile methods and practices on game development. The questions about potential positive impacts were presented in the form of statements (e.g. Quality of code has improved), to which the respondents could answer: "Agree", "Partly agree", "Partly disagree", "Disagree", or "Do not know". The statements were based on assumptions of, and findings from empirical studies on, impacts of the agile approach on software engineering [53, 11] and game development [27, 40, 42]. They were divided into two groups: those concerning development work, and those involving project management. Four respondents did not answer to these questions. The summary of the answers is presented in Figures 1 and 2.

From Figure 1 we can conclude that all the statements of the impacts got more positive (agree, partly agree) than negative (partly disagree, disagree) answers. The most positive impacts was perceived as regards to communication between the professionals (60%), quality of games (more than 60%), and finding fun (60%) and implementable (60%) features more quickly. Other positive impacts involve such issues as team awareness and problems in game design. Interestingly, improvements in quality of code (30%) and communication between the stakeholders (35%) were not experienced so largely. Some of the issues were considered difficult to assess (cf. Testing games, Quality of code).

From Figure 2 we can see that the opinions are divided more strongly than above. The most positive impact was seen to occur in the easiness of project management (65%), scope management (55%), and sticking to the dead line (50%). Instead, despite the use of agile practices there still existed problems in feature creep and overwork, especially in the later part of the project. Some of the issues on project management were difficult to assess (cf. replacements in the personnel).

In the final question, the respondents were asked to describe potential negative impacts of using agile practices on game development. Examples of the negative impacts reported are:

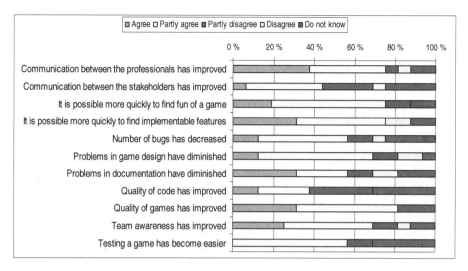

Fig. 1. Positive impacts of agile methods and practices to game development work (n = 16)

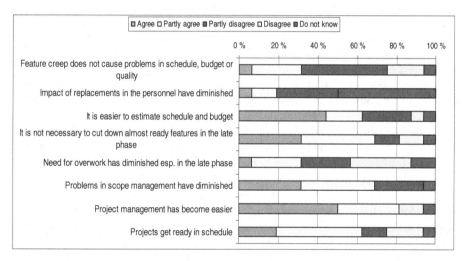

Fig. 2. Positive impacts of agile methods and practices to project management of game development (n = 16)

"Agile methods transfer responsibility to teams and rules of working get an essential role. This does not necessarily suit all the teams."

"Taking the inevitability of changes a bit too much for granted creates a window of opportunity for feature creep"

"At the worst, there exists continuous crunch time if [rules for] sprints are taken too seriously."

7   Discussion and Conclusion

This paper explores the use of agile methods and practices in Finnish game studios. Based on the survey, the Finnish game studios are rather young and small, yet including some fairly large ones (e.g. Rovio Entertaiment, 224 employees in 2011, 500+ in 2012). The game platforms are mostly PC and mobile devices. Development projects in average are small in terms of development time and number of employees. Reasons for that presumably are the industry's rapidly changing and risky nature, funding problems, and small job market. In this regard, the situation resembles the one in Austria [40].

All the studios, except one, deployed agile methods at least in some of the development phases. The most commonly mentioned method was Scrum, as was also the case in the Austrian survey [40]. XP, Lean and Kanban were used in the smaller scale. Some studios applied a mix of several agile methods, but not in the way Keith [27] suggested, i.e. the use of Lean and Kanban in production phase. Instead, agile processes resembled more the one suggested by Musil et al. [39]. No dependences between the use of agile methods, on the one hand, and the size of the studios or the number of the concurrent projects, on the other hand, were found.

At the level of agile practices, the survey showed that Sprint and its related events (Daily Scrum, Sprint planning, Sprint review) and artifacts (Product, Sprint backlog) from Scrum, as well as cross-functional teams, informative work space, and continuous integration from XP were in large use. These findings were as expected when taking into account special features of game development [33, 42, 44]. Compared to a large survey on Agile and Lean usage in Finnish software industry in 2011 [47], agile methods and practices were less frequently used in game development.

The survey indicated that agile methods and practices benefit game development in many ways. An iterative and incremental process enables inventing, designing and testing ideas of a playable game and betters the quality of the game (cf. [55]). Benefits were also perceived as faster recognition of fun and implementable features, and as better communication. The finding that quality code was not improved makes to suspect that continuous integration was not always applied in a proper manner (cf. together with automated testing). Although agility was seen to help scope management, estimation of schedule and budget, and sticking to the schedule, there were still problems as regards overwork and feature creep (cf. [42]).

As the survey included quite a large sample of the game studios in Finland, it provides a good descriptive view to the state of agile game development. However, the study has some limitations. First, the findings can only be generalized into the contexts with situational features similar to Finland. Second, to obtain a deeper insight into the use of agile methods and practices in the game studios, how this use evolves [60], and how it affects the productivity and quality of game development, we need a series of case studies. We should also pay more attention to ways the game studios customize and deploy agile methods and practices to match them to their needs. Despite of these limitations, the study provides interesting information about the current state of agile adoption in game development, which is of value for those who are considering how to improve the productivity and quality of their game development.

References

1. Abbas, N., Gravell, A.M., Wills, G.B.: Historical roots of agile methods: Where did 'Agile Thinking' come from? In: Abrahamsson, P., Baskerville, R., Conboy, K., Fitzgerald, B., Morgan, L., Wang, X. (eds.) XP 2008. LNBIP, vol. 9, pp. 94–103. Springer, Heidelberg (2008)
2. Abrahamsson, P., Salo, O., Ronkainen, J., Warsta, J.: Agile software development methods – Review and analysis, vol. 478. VTT Publications (2002)
3. Agile Alliance: Agile Manifesto (2001), http://agilemanifesto.org/
4. Ambler, S.W.: Surveys Exploring the Current State of Information Technology Practices (2011), http://www.ambysoft.com/surveys (accessed April 2011)
5. Anderson, D.: Kanban – Successful evolutionary change for your technology business. Blue Hole Press (2010)
6. Apperley, T.: Genre and game studies: towards a critical approach to video game genres. Simulation Gaming 37(6), 6–23 (2006)
7. Baskerville, R., Pries-Heje, J.: Short cycle time systems development. Information Systems Journal 14, 237–264 (2004)
8. Bates, B.: Game design, 2nd edn. Thomson Course Technology (2004)
9. Battarbee, K.: Co-experience. Understanding user experience in social interaction. Dissertation thesis, University of Art and Design, Helsinki, Finland (2003)
10. Beck, K.: Extreme programming explained: embrace change. Addison-Wesley (1999)
11. Beck, K., Anders, C.: Extreme programming explained: embrace change, 2nd edn. Addison-Wesley (2004)
12. Bethke, E.: Game development and production. Wordware Publishing, Inc. (2003)
13. Blow, J.: Game Development: Harder Than You Think. Queue 1(10), 28–37 (2004)
14. Boehm, B., Turner, R.: Rebalancing your organization's agility and discipline. In: Maurer, F., Wells, D. (eds.) XP/Agile Universe 2003. LNCS, vol. 2753, pp. 1–8. Springer, Heidelberg (2003)
15. Chandler, H.: The game production handbook, 2nd edn. Infinity Science Press (2009)
16. Conboy, K.: Agility from first principles: reconstructing the concept of agility in information systems development. Information Systems Research 20(3), 329–354 (2009)
17. Crawford, C.: The art of computer game design. McGraw-Hill (1984)
18. FIGMA (2012), http://www.figma.fi/index.php/tiedotteet/113-suomen-pelimyynti-laski-viime-vuonna-pelikehittajat-huikeassa-kasvussa
19. Flynt, J., Salem, O.: Software Engineering for Game Developers, 1st edn. Software Engineering Series. Course Technology PTR (2004)
20. Forrester: From agile development to agile engagement. Forrester Research (May 2009), http://www.forrester.com/research
21. Fullerton, T., Swain, C., Hoffman, S.: Game design workshop: designing, prototyping and playtesting games. CMP Books, San Francisco (2004)
22. Gershenfeld, A., Loparco, M., Barajas, C.: Game plan: the insider's guide to breaking in and succeeding in the computer and video game business. St. Martin's Griffin Press, New York (2003)
23. Gibson, A.: Agile game development and fun. Technical Report, University of Colorado, Department of Computer Science (2007)
http://www.cs.colorado.edu/department/publications/theses/docs/bs/andrea_gibson.pdf

24. Hunicke, R., LeBlanc, M., Zubek, R.: MDA: A formal approach to game design and game research. In: Proc. of the Challenges in Game AI Workshop (2004)
25. Iivari, J., Iivari, N.: The relationship between organizational culture and the deployment of agile methods. Information and Software Technology 53(5), 509–520 (2011)
26. Kanode, C., Haddad, H.: Software engineering challenges in game development. In: 6th Intern. Conf. on Information Technology: New Generations, pp. 260–265 (2009)
27. Keith, C.: Agile game development with Scrum. Addison-Wesley (2010)
28. Kitchenham, B., Pfleeger, S.: Principles of survey research. Part 1: Turning lemons in lemonade. SIGSOFT Software Engineering Notes 26(6), 16–18 (2001)
29. Kitchenham, B., Pfleeger, S.: Principles of survey research. Part 2: Designing a survey. SIGSOFT Software Engineering Notes 27(1), 18–20 (2002)
30. Kitchenham, B., Pfleeger, S.: Principles of survey research. Part 4: questionnaire evaluation. SIGSOFT Software Engineering Notes 27(3), 20–23 (2002)
31. Kitchenham, B., Pfleeger, S.: Principles of survey research. Part 6: Data analysis. SIGSOFT Software Engineering Notes 28(2), 24–27 (2003)
32. Kniberg, H., Skarin, M.: Kanban and Scrum – making the most of both, Enterprise software Development Series, InfoQ (2009)
33. Koivisto, E., Suomela, R.: Using prototypes in early pervasive game development. In: Sandbox Symposium, San Diego (2007)
34. Kreimeier, B.: Game design methods: A 2003 survey (2003), http://www.gamasutra.com/view/feature/2892/game_design_methods_a_2003_survey.php
35. Lewis, C., Whitehead, J.: The Whats and the Whys of games and software engineering. In: Proc. of Workshop on Games and Software Engineering, pp. 1–4 (2011)
36. Manninen, T., Kujanpää, T., Vallius, L., Korva, T., Koskinen, P.: Game production process: A preliminary study. University of Oulu, Finland (2006)
37. McGuire, M., Jenkins, O.: Creating Games: Mechanics, Content, and Technology. A K Peters (2009)
38. Moore, M., Novak, J.: Game industry career guide. Cengage Learning, Delmar (2010)
39. Musil, J., Schweda, A., Winkler, D., Biffl, S.: Improving video game development: Facilitating heterogeneous team collaboration through flexible software processes. In: Riel, A., O'Connor, R., Tichkiewitch, S., Messnarz, R. (eds.) EuroSPI 2010. CCIS, vol. 99, pp. 83–94. Springer, Heidelberg (2010)
40. Musil, J., Schweda, A., Winkler, D., Biffl, S.: A survey on a state of the practice in video game development, Report IFS-QSE 10/04. Institute of Software Technology and Interactive Systems, Vienna (2010)
41. Petrillo, F., Pimenta, M.: Is agility out there? Agile practices in game development. In: Proc. of the ACM Int. Conf. on Design of Communication, pp. 9–15 (2010)
42. Petrillo, F., Pimenta, M., Trindade, F., Dietrich, C.: What went wrong? A survey of problems in game development. ACM Computer in Entertainment 7(1) (2009)
43. Poppendieck, M., Poppendieck, T.: Lean software development – An Agile toolkit. Addison & Wesley (2003)
44. Potanin, R.: Forces in play: the business and culture of videogame production. In: Proc. of the 3rd International Conf. on Fun and Games, pp. 135–143 (2010)
45. PricewaterhouseCoopers: Global entertainment and media outlook 2012-2016; Video games (2012), http://www.pwc.com/gx/en/global-entertainment-media-outlook/segment-insights/video-games.jhtml
46. Rabin, S.: Introduction to game development. Charles River Media (2005)

47. Rodriguez, P., Markkula, J., Oivo, M., Turula, K.: Survey on agile and lean usage in Finnish software industry. In: Proc. of ESEM 2012 Conference, pp. 139–148 (2012)
48. Rollings, A., Morris, D.: Game Architecture and Design. The Coriolis Group (2000)
49. Rouse, R.: Game Design: Theory & Practice. Wordware, Inc. (2000)
50. Rucker, R.: Software engineering and computer games. Addison Wesley (2002)
51. Runeson, P., Höst, M.: Guidelines for conducting and reporting case study research in software engineering. Empirical Software Engineering 14(2), 131–164 (2009)
52. Sanders, E.: Virtuosos of the experience domain. In: IDSA Education Conf. (2001)
53. Schwaber, K., Beedle, M.: Agile software development with Scrum. Prentice-Hall (2002)
54. Schwaber, K., Sutherland, J.: The Scrum guide – The definitive guide to Scrum: The rules of the game (2011), http://www.scrum.org/storage/scrumguides/Scrum_Guide.pdf
55. Schofield, B.: Embracing fun: Why extreme programming is great for game development. Gamasutra: The Art & Business of Making Games (March 2007)
56. Stacey, P., Nandhakumar, S.: Opening up to agile games development. Comm. of the ACM 51(12), 143–146 (2008)
57. Tran, M., Biddle, R.: Collaboration in serious game development: a case study. In: Proc. of the 2008 Conf. on Future Play, pp. 49–56 (2008)
58. VersionOne: State of Agile Survey – The state of Agile Development (2011), http://www.versionone.com/pdf/2011_State_of_Agile_Development_Survey_Results.pdf
59. Vijayasarathy, L., Turk, D.: Agile software development: a survey of early adopters. Journal of Information Technology Management 19(2), 1–8 (2008)
60. Wang, X., Coboy, K., Pikkarainen, M.: Assimilation of agile practices in use. Information Systems Journal 22(6), 435–455 (2012)
61. van de Weerd, I., de Weerd, S., Brinkkemper, S.: Developing a reference method for game production by method comparison. In: Ralyté, J., Brinkkemper, S., Henderson-Sellers, B. (eds.) Situational Method Engineering: Fundamentals and Experiences. IFIP, vol. 244, pp. 313–327. Springer, Boston (2007)
62. Womack, J., Jones, D.: Lean thinking: Banish waste and create wealth in your corporation. Simon & Schuster (1996)
63. Ye, Z.: Genres as a tool for understanding and analyzing user experience in games. In: Proc. of Conf. on Human Factors in Computing Systems, pp. 773–774 (2004)

Inter-organizational Co-development with Scrum: Experiences and Lessons Learned from a Distributed Corporate Development Environment

Raoul Vallon, Stefan Strobl, Mario Bernhart, and Thomas Grechenig

Research Group for Industrial Software, Vienna University of Technology
Vienna, Austria
raoul.vallon@inso.tuwien.ac.at

Abstract. Distributed development within a single organization adds a lot of overhead to every software development process. When a second organization joins for co-development, complexity reaches the next level. This case study investigates an agile approach from a real world project involving two unaffiliated IT organizations that collaborate in a distributed development environment. Adaptations to the regular Scrum process are identified and evaluated over a six-month-long period of time. The evaluation involves a detailed problem root cause analysis and suggestions on what issues to act first. Key lessons learned include that team members of one Scrum team should not be distributed over several sites and that every site should have at least one Scrum master and one product owner.

Keywords: distributed development, agile development, Scrum, software development process, subcontracting, virtual teams.

1 Introduction

Agile development has gained widespread popularity over the last ten years in very different domains (e.g. embedded software projects [1], mobile application development [2] or aerospace [3]). It has been adopted by large companies such as Intel [4], Microsoft [5], Yahoo! [6] or SAP [7] and has thus found its way in multi-team and multi-site corporate environments. Although originally designed for collocated teams, related agile studies have reported the adaption of agile principles to e.g. a distributed Scrum [8], [9] or Extreme Programming (XP) [10] implementation in recent years.

Distributed development challenges one of the core strengths of Scrum: team members need to interact and communicate on a daily basis to form self-organizing teams and meet sprint goals. However, distributed environments complicate communication and coordination [11]. Technical tool support plays a bigger role in the process [12], [13] as well as knowledge management and transfer [14]. Consequently team members need to work harder to synchronize and meet sprint goals.

H. Baumeister and B. Weber (Eds.): XP 2013, LNBIP 149, pp. 150–164, 2013.
© Springer-Verlag Berlin Heidelberg 2013

This case study strives to contribute to this field of research by investigating an agile distributed development approach based on Scrum. The process implementation involves two unaffiliated Austrian IT organizations, which are separated by about 300 kilometers. According to Kajko-Mattsson et al. [15], expected problem fields include communication, customer collaboration, trust, training and technical issues. We will further investigate the adaptations to Scrum and the compromises that need to be made, when two organizations with different corporate cultures join forces to develop software.

We defined the following research question:

RQ: How can agile development be applied to an inter-organizational, multi-site and multi-team development environment and what challenges, if any, emerge in this setting?

The rest of the paper is organized as follows. Section 2 describes the research settings and applied methods. Section 3 provides an observation of strengths and weaknesses in the process implementation. Section 4 conducts a problem root cause analysis. Section 5 discusses results including lessons learned, suggestions for practice and related work. Section 6 provides the conclusion.

2   Research Design

The case study covers a six-month-long period of time including evaluation and presentation of results. The nature of the case study is exploratory according to Yin's research on the application of case studies [16]. As such, it strives to identify problem areas in the field of agile distributed development and serves as a prelude to further follow-up studies. Findings of this exploratory study are put in context with related studies during the discussion of results.

2.1   Research Settings

Two unaffiliated organizations, the main supplier (MS) and the additional supplier (AS), collaborate to develop three software products that share a common codebase. Both suppliers have successfully applied regular Scrum before and chose to implement an adapted version of Scrum to better suit the needs of a distributed development environment. The two organizations develop at their own sites, separated by about 300 kilometers.

The MS is a large company whose IT department is involved in the development of the three software products. It is solely responsible for requirements engineering with all three customers and provides the bigger part of the development staff.

The AS is a medium-sized core software development company and a subcontractor to the MS for the development of the three products. It complements the MS's development with additional staff and know-how but has no contact with customers.

Table 1 shows the distribution of team members over the two suppliers. The MS has one product owner (PO) for each software product and three Scrum masters (SM) serving three teams. The AS does neither have a PO nor a SM on site.

Table 1. Distribution of team members over the two suppliers

Co-Developers	Dev	Test	SM	PO	Sum
Main Supplier (MS)	11	3	3	3	20
Additional Supplier (AS)	8	2	0	0	10
Overall	19	5	3	3	30

2.2   Research Method

The research is divided into three phases.

Observations. One of the authors examined the Scrum implementation in use as an external observer. As such, he took part in various meetings and conducted interviews with members of all roles (product owner, Scrum master, developer, tester). The interviews lasted from 20 to 45 minutes and have been audio-recorded. He took field notes, pictures and collected planning sheets and meeting minutes. He has been granted read-only access to several electronic tools involved such as the issue tracking system. This phase lasted for three months.

Case Analysis. After the observation phase the collected data was analyzed. The authors extracted problems from the following sources: retrospective meetings, interviews, field notes, meeting minutes and the project documentation. Problems were categorized in problem clusters and root causes suggested in a problem root cause analysis. The approach was top-down, i.e. most prominent problem clusters were analysed first according to the authors' evaluation. This phase lasted for two months.

Presentation of Results. The last phase involved a presentation and discussion of results with team members including lessons learned, suggestions for practice and related studies. This was the concluding step in the last month.

3   Observation Phase

The following observations summarize the different aspects of the Scrum implementation applied in the case study including strengths and weaknesses.

Formation of Scrum Teams. Three Scrum teams have been formed across all products and based on logical requirement areas. Figure 1 shows the distribution of team members. The product owner and the Scrum master roles are both on the MS's site. The AS complements the MS with additional developers and testers (QA) but has no official Scrum roles. However, two developers have emerged as unofficial Scrum masters for the AS. They care most for the process implementation and discuss impediments with the MS. One of these unofficial Scrum masters travels to the MS's site once a week for face to face updates and discussions.

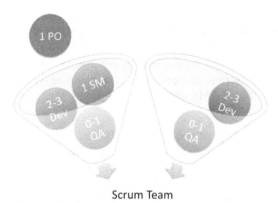

Scrum Team

Fig. 1. Distribution of Scrum team members: the AS joins the MS's Scrum team with developers and QA but has no official Scrum roles

Each Scrum team holds a daily video conference meeting, where respective team members of the MS and AS participate. Additionally a Scrum of Scrums (SoS) meeting is established for inter-team communication, as pictured in figure 2.

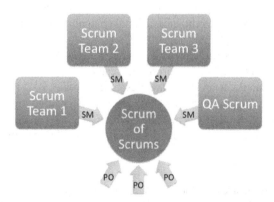

Fig. 2. Scrum of Scrums (SoS) is held at the MS only. Testers of all three Scrum teams form a virtual QA Scrum team and also participate in the SoS.

It is held daily at the MS's site. Since the AS does not have official Scrum roles, the MS handles all inter-team coordination. Testers (QA) are assigned to the three Scrum teams, but hold an additional daily meeting to stay synchronized and also send a representative to the SoS. Product owners also participate to evaluate the progress.

Two-Tiered Planning Process. Planning covers one month, i.e. two sprints. It is a two-tiered process: at first, planning is done at the MS's site with one of the two unofficial Scrum masters of the AS present. The Scrum teams decide, which of the prioritized user stories in the product backlogs they want to implement in the next two sprints.

The second level planning continues at the AS's site: The unofficial Scrum master returns from the MS with pre-estimated (via planning poker [17]) user stories for the AS. Team members volunteer for certain tasks until all tasks are assigned. When a team member accepts a task, it adjusts the original estimation of the MS to his own. One of the unofficial Scrum masters updates a planning spreadsheet during the meeting and shares it with the MS afterwards.

Joint Sprint Review. The sprint review is held after each sprint. It is primarily held at the MS, but the AS joins via video conference. Additionally, one of the AS's Scrum masters is present at the MS's site to represent the AS in person as well. The rest of the AS's team is mainly observing the review, but can raise questions or concerns when necessary. The review consists of feature demonstrations and discussions about different areas of the current product increments and takes about two hours.

Joint Retrospective. The sprint retrospective is held monthly after two sprints with the same setup as the sprint review. The retrospective is divided into six steps (the AS's on-site representative conducts the steps on behalf of his colleagues):

1. Individual evaluation of the last month from good to bad on a 15-part scale. Each team member may put one point on the scale drawn on paper.
2. Evaluation and discussion of the measures taken against impediments since the last retrospective.
3. Every participant writes three remarks (either positive or negative) on paper and puts them on the flipchart, shortly presenting each.
4. The individual remarks from step 3 are clustered to topics.
5. Every participant has three points that can be assigned to one or more of the clustered topics according to his personal weighting.
6. Measures for the top three topics are discussed that will be implemented in the next two sprints.

Product and Sprint Backlog. Each product owner maintains a product backlog on the MS' site for his product. At the time of the observation phase the AS did not have access to the product backlog, but worked with the sprint backlog only (planning spreadsheet from the two-tiered planning process).

Scrum Board. Both the MS and the AS are using paper Scrum boards. Each Scrum team operates one board. Since the two suppliers are based at different locations, six boards would be needed, but the AS currently only uses one general board on his site covering all three teams. The workflow on the board is defined as: *User Stories, TO DOs, In Progress, Review* and *Done*.

The first column *User Stories* contains user stories from the backlog. Sticky notes of the same color are used to break the user stories into smaller tasks that run through the remaining workflow. The column *Review* denotes the tasks being reviewed and tested by a colleague (at any supplier's site). Tasks in *Done* are production-ready. Tasks on the Scrum board are also marked with the issue tracking number of the electronic tool in use. The Scrum boards of both suppliers are synchronized every day during the daily Scrums (for each team).

Burndown Chart. The burndown charts are drawn and updated on paper at the MS's site only (one per team). The AS does not operate one on his own, but the MS includes the AS's tasks in his chart.

Behavior Driven Development. The two suppliers develop software using *behavior driven development (BDD)* [18], which is an extension to *test driven development (TDD)* [19]. The goal is to define the software's behavior in terms of human readable, but executable acceptance criteria [18]:

> **Given** some initial context,
> **When** an event occurs,
> **Then** ensure some outcomes.

These acceptance criteria can be automated to test the correct behavior of the software. They should be understandable to the customer yet precise enough to be executable. BDD also helps provide a common language and reference point for stakeholders, business analysts, developers and testers.

Means of Communication. The main means of communication between the two suppliers are joint meetings via video conference and telephone calls. Individual concerns are discussed in emails, instant messaging and screen sharing sessions.

3.1   Retrospective

In the three retrospective meetings during the observation phase, issues overweighed strengths by far due to the complex development environment. Named strengths were *improved communication and collaboration* in general and *continuous improvement*. Team members identified the following drivers for improvement:

- Willingness and commitment to change and improve
- Good working atmosphere and employee attitude
- Highly motivated people
- Team work

The list of problems taken from retrospective meetings is notably longer. Both team members of the MS and AS reported to suffer from **constant stress in the two-week sprint** due to the following reasons:

- Workload too high in relation to available staff
- Planning delay in general and also between the two suppliers
- Too little time to follow BDD workflow in a two-week sprint

Late planning was reported since inter-organizational planning was frequently not ready until a few days into the sprint iteration. This made it very hard for team members to reach sprint goals. The **BDD workflow** introduced a lot of overhead. Testers constantly struggled to finish automation of BDD scenarios within the Sprint which resulted in broken test cases and thus **bad code quality**. Problems with the speed of **remote access for the AS** arose, which slowed down co-development. Minor issues regarding the **quality of use cases** were also reported.

3.2   Interviews

Three prominent issues have been identified from one on one semi-structured interviews that have been stressed by all interviewees. One of these issues, **overhead of communication and coordination**, addressed the inadequate quality of video conferences, especially with larger groups (joint sprint review/retrospective). A **lack of electronic tool support** has also been criticized, especially by the AS. The AS did not have access to the main paper Scrum boards and burndown charts at the MS's site and progress was synchronized mostly during daily Scrum meetings. **Two-tiered sprint planning** put pressure on team members' commitment since planning took too long and was frequently not ready at the beginning of new sprint iterations.

3.3   Summary

Table 2 provides an overview of observed problems and their weighting by team members during retrospective meetings. After all of the interviews were conducted, each interviewee was asked to select the most prominent problem out of three problems that arose in all interviews. The ranking is also shown in table 2.

Table 2. Observed problems in the case study

Source	Problems	Weighting by team members
Retrospectives	High Stress-Level	30,7%
	Late Planning	25,8%
	BDD Workflow	12,9%
	Code Quality	12,9%
	Remote Access for AS	9,7%
	Use Cases	8,0%
Interviews	Communication and Coordination Overhead	1st
	Lack of Tool-Support	2nd
	Two-Tiered Sprint Planning	3rd

4   Case Analysis

After the observation phase, the data collected was analyzed. Problems were identified and clustered from different sources: retrospective meetings, interviews, field notes, meeting minutes and the project documentation. The result was eight problem clusters with the following top-down prioritization: distributed development, transparency, commitment, planning, estimation, predictability, self-organizing teams and tools. The problem clusters have been analyzed for two months. Table 3 shows the result of the analysis: problem clusters and corresponding identified root causes in the case study.

Table 3. Problem clusters and identified root causes

Problem Clusters	Identified Root Causes
Distributed Development	No Official Scrum Roles at the AS
	Joint Estimation and Planning
	Inter-Company Distribution of Team Members
Transparency	Suppliers not Collocated
	Communication Issues
	Little Documentation
	No Overview over All Teams
Commitment	Commitment Fails with Insufficient Planning
	Commitment Fails with Late Planning
	Commitment Fails with Frequent Changes
	Little Respect for Iterations
Planning	Late Actual Beginning of Sprint
	Little Participation of AS
	Little Information for AS
Estimation	User Story Estimation in Hours
	Pre-estimations by MS
Predictability	No Proper Sprint Velocity
	Further Impediments for Better Predictability
Self-Organizing Teams	Tasks Assigned to Team Members
	Estimations Based on Individuals
	Cross-Team Working Agreements
Tools	Tools Lack Scrum Compatibility
	Limited Remote Access for AS
	Paper Scrum Board and Burndown Chart

Distributed Development. All three Scrum teams are staffed by members of both suppliers, yet all product owners and Scrum masters are on the MS's site. Nevertheless, two of the AS's team members have emerged that do more coordination work than their colleagues. They care more for the Scrum process than others (Scrum master) and travel to the MS to attend meetings and discuss user stories in person (product owner). The team members on the AS's site are 10 people distributed over three different Scrum teams. It is very hard to remain self-organizing and in compliance with the Scrum process, when contact to the remaining team members is hard to establish and no role is officially assigned to look after the process at the AS's site.

This poses a big problem for the AS, as these two to three team members are separated from the rest of the MS-based team. As a result, the AS has formed a virtual team to manage his own resources with a single paper Scrum board covering all three teams. The follow-up planning session is also held for the whole AS's virtual team, including members of all three real Scrum teams.

Transparency is a big issue between the two suppliers due to the physical distance of 300 kilometers. The whole process becomes more complex and less transparent. Low quality video conferences and little available documentation further handicap communication and coordination. There is no high level overview of the progress of all three teams available to everyone since Scrum boards and burndown charts are drawn on paper.

Commitment is hard to achieve with late planning and frequent changes within the sprint iteration. The teams cannot commit to sprint goals when the user stories are not properly and timely specified. As a result, estimations are not reliable.

Planning and Estimation. The MS pre-estimates user stories and uses this estimation as a basis for planning. The AS is thus not adequately involved in the planning process apart from updating the estimations of the MS (for his own user stories only). Planning is often not ready until a few days into the sprint, which causes delays for both suppliers. Estimation is done in hours. This does not represent complexity well because different people need different amounts of time to work on a user story.

Predictability. Sprint velocity cannot be properly measured because the MS runs a paper burndown chart that is based solely on tasks (derived from user stories). The only available ratio is tasks per sprint, which does not represent any complexity because it does not take into account hours (or story points). Further impediments to a better predictability are a varying understanding of the BDD workflow among team members and code quality issues.

Self-organizing Teams. Two developers emerged at the AS's site that do more coordination work and impediment handling than others. The distributed environment complicates coordination between teams and it is hard for the AS to efficiently complement the MS-based teams. Moreover, cross-team working agreements regarding the BDD workflow need to be elaborated and agreed upon to reduce interdependency issues.

Tools. The electronic tools in use all lack Scrum support, which prevents a proper process implementation. There are currently four paper Scrum boards in use, three at the MS's site for each team and a combined one at the AS's. These are cumbersome to synchronize, which slows down the tracking of other teams' progress. The burndown charts are also drawn on paper and only available to the MS.

5   Discussion

The six-month-long case study involved two suppliers MS and AS from unaffiliated organizations, which joined forces to co-develop three software products. The research question was *"How can agile development be applied to an inter-organizational, multi-site and multi-team development environment and what challenges, if any, emerge in this setting?*

The following adaptations to the Scrum process have been made for the case study's setting:

- Two unofficial Scrum master-like roles emerged at the AS that frequently paid visits to the 300-kilometers-away MS to improve the flow of information
- Three Scrum teams have been formed, each consisting of members from both development partners
- Joint daily Scrum/two-week review and monthly retrospective meetings are held via video conference calls
- Scrum of Scrums is held daily at the MS's site without participation of the AS
- Two-tiered planning process (MS first, AS second) in use covering two sprints

The analysis showed that finding a working Scrum implementation is indeed very challenging in an inter-organizational distributed development setting. Eight problem clusters were identified as illustrated in figure 3. The relation between problem clusters may not be as linear in real-world projects, but it serves as an illustration of underlying constraints. It should also be regarded as an impulse on what problems to act first: the suggested approach is bottom-up starting with enabling truly self-organizing teams.

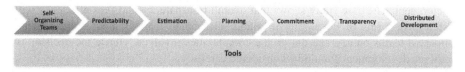

Fig. 3. Proposed identified relation of problem clusters. Problems should be solved bottom-up from self-organizing teams to distributed development.

Self-organizing teams are one of the central components of Scrum and need to be established first. *Predictability* evolves when long-lived self-organizing teams are allowed to work in sprint iterations without outside interference. *Estimation* and *planning* can only be accurate once predictability is reliable. The case study shows that *commitment* cannot be achieved without timely planning. Providing *transparency* is one of Scrum's highest goals, i.e. making impediments visible to everyone. All the precedent problem categories need to be solved before transparency can be achieved.

Distributed development is the central problem in this case study, since the two suppliers are not collocated. Collaboration can only be improved by solving the other problem categories first. Choosing the right *tools* for the specific project setting supports the whole value stream and has even greater impact in distributed development environments as team members need to rely more heavily on electronic means of communication.

The major problem in the Scrum implementation was that the process was focused on the MS. This observation is supported by numerous identified root causes during the problem root cause analysis:

- No official Scrum roles at the AS
- Little participation of AS
- Little information for AS
- Paper Scrum boards and burndown charts
- Pre-estimations by MS
- Limited remote access for AS

Due to these reasons, planning and commitment frequently failed during the observation phase in the case study. During retrospective meetings the general consensus was that communication and coordination between the suppliers is improving, but one on one interviews still disclosed many problems.

The MS is the main contractor in this project environment. Greater involvement of the AS could lead to a more efficient development output. Scrum does not work well in a hierarchical setting as the formation of self-organizing teams is denied and transparency is decreased.

5.1   Lessons Learned

Inter-organizational Co-development Adds Another Layer of Complexity. The case study shows that co-development between unaffiliated organizations adds new complexity and challenges to overcome. The reasons are often organizations varying in size and corporate culture. The introduction of hierarchies has no space in agile development. The case study shows that overall transparency and thus efficiency will decrease. In terms of development output, distributed teams cannot compete with collocated teams on average due to the complexities involved. Hence the decision to distribute development should be considered carefully.

Increased Effort for Self-organizing Teams. Both suppliers have run regular Scrum before. Retrospective meetings and observations showed that the distribution of development across two suppliers complicated software development. The level and willingness of cooperation between team members determines success or failure. In general, it is harder for teams to remain self-organizing as more effort is needed to synchronize with distant team members.

Organizational Change Takes Time. The larger the organization, the harder it is to introduce changes. This could especially be observed with the MS, where changes took long to be realized compared to the AS which is smaller in size. Compromises had to be made to deal with organizational impediments such as the switch to paper boards.

Beware of a Superficial Scrum Adoption. The number one organizational impediment to a successful adoption of agile principles is silver bullet thinking and superficial adoption [20]. The case study showed that although distributed development caused many problems, underneath many "regular" Scrum values have not been met, such as self-organizing teams and the respect for iterations.

5.2   Suggestions for Practice

A lot of coordination and synchronization overhead was introduced by having multi-site Scrum teams. We suggest **forming single-site Scrum teams only.** For this case study's setting an additional Scrum team on the AS's site can be formed including a Scrum master and a product owner instead of having three multi-site teams. The **on-site Scrum master and product owner** also enforce an **equal involvement of all sites** in the distributed Scrum process. Additionally **decent electronic tool support for the Scrum process is essential** in a distributed environment for inter-team coordination.

These measures help increase transparency and improve overall development output. The case study showed that the appreciation of agile core values such as the respect for iterations is of major importance especially in distributed development environments.

5.3   Related Studies

The suggestion to **form single-site Scrum teams** aligns with one of the best practices of the Scrum Alliance: form distributed but isolated Scrum teams that are linked through the Scrum of Scrums [21]. However, Sutherland et al. provides a success story in [21] stating that distributed integrated teams (over two sites) are more efficient than the suggested best practice. Our exploratory study shows many identified problems with the latter approach. Hence, we suggest implementing the Scrum Alliance's best practice, especially if team members are not agile experts. Vax et al. also conclude in [22] that you need the right expertise and team for distributed Scrum.

Penttinen et al. propose guidelines in [23] for three types of subcontracting teams in Scrum: sub-contractor team (team with only sub-contractor members), mixed team (an on-site mixed team) and a virtual team (a multi-site mixed team). In our case study we had three virtual teams. Penttinen et al. also conclude that a virtual team is the most complex option and most of the time a temporary one.

Instead of an **on-site Scrum master or product owner**, Paasivaara et al. mention the possibility of having an "ambassador/rotating guru" in [8], who is sent to other sites for a longer period of time. This measure serves as a compromise between a full on-site Scrum master/product owner and the short-term visits conducted in the case study at hand.

In related publications we can see a growing interest in bringing agile to (globally) distributed software development [24], [25]. One of the conclusions over several case studies reviewed by Hossain et al. in [24] is that Scrum needs to be extended to work in a distributed setting, which has also been shown in our case study.

5.4   Limitations

Since this is a single case study, generalizability of results is limited. One of the authors took the role of an external observer to minimize bias. As such, he was not part of the team and thus was not able to fully capture each detail of daily work.

6   Conclusion

This case study investigated a Scrum-based agile approach to distributed development between two unaffiliated organizations. We identified that the prominent problem was that the developing partners formed an unequal partnership. The MS provided two thirds of the staff involved. The AS joined as a subcontractor with developers and testers but had no Scrum roles on site. Joint retrospective meetings showed that the stress level was very high for both development partners. The main reason was a weak flow of information between the MS and the AS, which resulted in frequent issues with planning and estimations. Although the coordination and communication improved over time, it has still been the main issue in most interviews conducted.

The fact that two unaffiliated organizations joined forces to develop a software product added a new layer of complexity to distributed development. The Scrum adaptations included moving most regular Scrum meetings to video conference ones, but the process implementation was strongly focused on the MS: The Scrum of Scrums was held in person at the MS's site only and the AS did not have any official Scrum roles. The paper Scrum board and burndown charts were also based at the MS's site which decreased transparency for the AS.

We suggest the formation of single-site self-organizing teams instead of multi-site ones. Scrum masters and product owners should be present on all sites to ensure an equal involvement of all developing parties in the process and improve the flow of information. The case study further showed that an extensive electronic tool support is crucial to the self-organization of teams in a distributed development environment.

References

1. Xie, M., Shen, M., Rong, G., Shao, D.: Empirical Studies of Embedded Software Development Using Agile Methods: a Systematic Review. In: 2nd International Workshop on Evidential Assessment of Software Technologies, pp. 21–26. ACM, New York (2012)
2. Scharff, C., Verma, R.: Scrum to Support Mobile Application Development Projects in a Just-in-time Learning Context. In: 2010 ICSE Workshop on Cooperative and Human Aspects of Software Engineering, pp. 25–31. ACM, New York (2010)

3. Vander Leest, S.H., Buter, A.: Escape the waterfall: Agile for aerospace. In: 28th Digital Avionics Systems Conference, pp. 6.D.3-1–6.D.3-16 (2009)
4. Chen, J.Q., Dien, P., Wang, B., Vogel, D.R.: Light-Weight Development Method: A Case Study. In: 2007 International Conference on Service Systems and Service Management, pp. 1–6 (2007)
5. Begel, A., Nagappan, N.: Usage and Perceptions of Agile Software Development in an Industrial Context: An Exploratory Study. In: 1st International Symposium on Empirical Software Engineering and Measurement, pp. 255–264 (2007)
6. Chung, M.-W., Drummond, B.: Agile at Yahoo! From the Trenches. In: 2009 Agile Conference, pp. 113–118. IEEE Computer Society, Washington, DC (2009)
7. Schnitter, J., Mackert, O.: Large-Scale Agile Software Development at SAP AG. In: Maciaszek, L.A., Loucopoulos, P. (eds.) ENASE 2010. CCIS, vol. 230, pp. 209–220. Springer, Heidelberg (2011)
8. Paasivaara, M., Durasiewicz, S., Lassenius, C.: Using Scrum in Distributed Agile Development: A Multiple Case Study. In: 4th International Conference on Global Software Engineering, pp. 195–204 (2009)
9. Bannerman, P.L., Hossain, E., Jeffery, R.: Scrum Practice Mitigation of Global Software Development Coordination Challenges: A Distinctive Advantage? In: 45th Hawaii International Conference on System Science, pp. 5309–5318 (2012)
10. Hildenbrand, T., Geisser, M., Kude, T., Bruch, D., Acker, T.: Agile Methodologies for Distributed Collaborative Development of Enterprise Applications. In: 2008 International Conference on Complex, Intelligent and Software Intensive Systems, pp. 540–545 (2008)
11. Korkala, M., Abrahamsson, P.: Communication in Distributed Agile Development: A Case Study. In: 33rd EUROMICRO Conference on Software Engineering and Advanced Applications, pp. 203–210 (2007)
12. Dullemond, K., van Gameren, B., van Solingen, R.: How Technological Support Can Enable Advantages of Agile Software Development in a GSE Setting. In: 4th International Conference on Global Software Engineering, pp. 143–152 (2009)
13. Niinimäki, T.: Face-to-face, Email and Instant Messaging in Distributed Agile Software Development Project. In: 6th International Conference on Global Software Engineering Workshop, pp. 78–84 (2011)
14. Dorairaj, S., Noble, J., Malik, P.: Knowledge Management in Distributed Agile Software Development. In: 2012 Agile Conference, pp. 63–73 (2012)
15. Kajko-Mattsson, M., Azizyan, G., Magarian, M.K.: Classes of Distributed Agile Development Problems. In: 2010 Agile Conference, pp. 51–58 (2010)
16. Yin, R.K.: Applications of Case Study Research (Applied Social Research Methods). Sage Publications (2011)
17. Grenning, J.: Planning Poker or How to Avoid Analysis Paralysis While Release Planning (2002), http://renaissancesoftware.net/files/articles/PlanningPoker-v1.1.pdf
18. North, D.: Behavior Modification. The evolution of behavior-driven development. Better Software Magazine (March 2006)
19. Beck, K.: Test Driven Development By Example. Addison-Wesley Professional (2003)
20. Larman, C., Vodde, B.: Scaling Lean & Agile Development. Thinking and Organizational Tools for Large-Scale Scrum. Addison-Wesley, Boston (2009)
21. Sutherland, J., Viktorov, A., Blount, J., Puntikov, N.: Distributed Scrum: Agile Project Management with Outsourced Development Teams. In: 40th Hawaii International Conference on System Sciences, p. 274a (2007)
22. Vax, M., Michaud, S.: Distributed Agile: Growing a Practice Together. In: 2008 Agile Conference, pp. 310–314 (2008)

23. Penttinen, M., Mikkonen, T.: Subcontracting for Scrum Teams: Experiences and Guidelines from a Large Development Organization. In: 7th International Conference on Global Software Engineering, pp. 195–199 (2012)
24. Hossain, E., Ali Babar, M., Paik, H.: Using Scrum in Global Software Development: A Systematic Literature Review. In: 4th International Conference on Global Software Engineering, pp. 175–184 (2009)
25. Jalali, S., Wohlin, C.: Agile Practices in Global Software Engineering – A Systematic Map. In: 5th International Conference on Global Software Engineering, pp. 45–54 (2010)

A Metrics Model to Measure the Impact of an Agile Transformation in Large Software Development Organizations

Jeanette Heidenberg[1,2,3], Max Weijola[1,2], Kirsi Mikkonen[3], and Ivan Porres[1,2]

[1] Åbo Akademi University, Department of Information Technologies,
Joukahaisenkatu 3-5 A, 20520 Turku, Finland
Givenname.Surname@abo.fi
[2] Turku Centre for Computer Science, Joukahaisenkatu 3-5 B, 20520 Turku, Finland
[3] Ericsson R&D Center Finland, Hirsalantie 11, 02420 Jorvas, Finland
Givenname.Surname@ericsson.com

Abstract. As the adoption of agile and lean methods continues to grow, measuring the effects of such a transformation can be valuable but challenging due to the many variables influencing the outcome of a software project. In this paper we present a metrics model developed for measuring the effects of an agile and lean transformation on software development organizations. The model was developed iteratively in cooperation with industry partners within the Cloud Software Finland research project. The resulting metrics model is applicable to projects of any size, complexity and scope, using metrics that support agile and lean values. The model can be used to measure both past and ongoing projects, regardless of whether the process model used is plan driven or agile. In order to evaluate the metrics model, the proposed model has been piloted in an industry setting.

Keywords: Metrics, Measurements, SPI, Transformation, Lean, Agile.

1 Introduction

Agile and lean software development methods keep growing in popularity among software companies of all sizes. Recent surveys performed by both academic researchers and IT consultants show agile and lean adoption ranging from 55%, as reported by Rodriguez et.al. [1], to 80%, as reported by VersionOne [2], in companies ranging in size from 11 to over 1000 employees [1].

The benefits of agile and lean deployment has been discussed extensively in the literature [3,4,5,6,7,8]; and so has the drawbacks of plan driven software development [9,6]. The discourse, however, mostly deals with the differences between the two ways of working in qualitative terms. The quantitative impact of agile and lean adoption in software organizations still needs further study [10].

Quantitatively and objectively comparing a development organization before and after an agile transformation is a challenging task. In this article, we use the term agile transformation to denote a sudden, disruptive change in the development process in an organization in order to adopt agile methods. In a large

H. Baumeister and B. Weber (Eds.): XP 2013, LNBIP 149, pp. 165–179, 2013.

scale agile transformation there are many factors affecting the outcome, and measuring the impact of only the transformation while excluding other factors is difficult. Since the transformation is performed in a real industry context, not in a controlled academic environment, there will inevitably be uncontrollable factors such as changes in the economic climate, shift in demand, and changes in the performance of the sales staff [11]. One can also expect uncontrollable factors internal to the software development organization, such as turnover of development staff, to impact the results.

Any transformation of the way of working may require a notable investment from the organization, both in a monetary aspect, as well as in disrupted working routines and possible resistance to change among some of the employees. Cohn [11] mentions phenomena such as waterfallacies and agile phobies as examples of such resistance. The organization may have embarked on the transformation with the goal of increasing the delivered value, and may after the transformation ask itself: *Was the transformation worth the effort?*. For this reason, an organization may look for a way of quantifying the impact of the transformation, despite the challenge of performing such measurements in an industry setting.

Indeed, this need for quantifying the impact of agile and lean transformations arose among the industry partners of the *Cloud Software Finland* research project [12] as a complement to already used qualitative measurements, such as interviews and surveys. It led us to formulate our research question: *"How can the changes of an agile transformation be measured by quantitative objective metrics?"*

In this article, we propose a software process improvement (SPI) metrics model for quantitatively comparing a software development organization before and after an agile and lean transformation. The model was iteratively developed and refined to focus on measuring efficiency, business value and lead-time with a number of industry partners within the *Cloud Software Finland* research project. The metrics proposed in the model are based on a *goal question metrics* (GQM) approach [13] where both the questions and metrics have been chosen and refined with a set of criteria to allow comparison between plan driven and agile. The questions and metrics were also chosen to continuously support the organization's agile transformation and new way of working.

The remainder of this paper is structured as follows. Section 2 gives a short background and we present previous work done in the field. In Section 3 our context and research method are described in more detail, including metrics selection criteria (Section 3.3). The goal for the transformation metrics model is presented in Section 4. Section 5 describes the partial literature survey undertaken to map the current state of agile and lean metrics. Our proposed metrics are described in Section 6. A pilot case and examples of the metrics in the model in an organization is presented in Section 7. The metrics are validated against the selected set of criteria in Section 8. Discussion and conclusion are presented in sections 9 and 10 respectively.

2   Background and Previous Work

Metrics in software development have been the subject of both research and practice for a long time resulting in many proposed best practices. Due to the introduction of agile and lean methods during the early 2000's, new best practices and research have been reported for metrics applied in agile settings [14,15,16,17,18,19].

Hartmann and Dymond suggest that agile metrics should affirm and reinforce lean and agile principles [14], since using inappropriate (plan driven) metrics can not only be inefficient but also threaten an emerging agile culture. Petersen and Wohlin discusses measurements used in lean manufacturing (e.g. Capacity Utilization), which are inappropriate in a software engineering setting due to the creative nature of the work [16]. Dubinsky et al. discusses the benefits of tailoring custom measurements for an organization as a means of communicating what behavior is considered important and therefore measured [15].

The topic of empirically comparing development processes has been identified as relevant by researchers. Mainly the reported findings have supported the deployment of agile methods. In the recent work of Concas et al. [20], software quality metrics were related with certain agile development phases and practices. However, the topic is still in need for further study [19,8], as very few reports on quantitative, empirical studies comparing the situation before and after an agile transformation exist.

One study that compares the effects of moving from a plan driven to an agile approach to software development is the case study by Petersen and Wohlin from 2010 [8]. The focus in the case study was on qualitative data gathered from interviews, with only a few quantitative performance metrics included for support. Our focus, however, is on quantitative data.

Another study comparing a transformation is the recent case study by Sjøberg, Johnsen and Solberg [19] focusing on the effects of a company migrating from Scrum to Kanban. They do use quantitative metrics, focusing on the variables lead time, quality, and productivity. The fact that they are mainly comparing two agile approaches limits the applicability of their research in our setting.

Two studies that we found useful for our work are Petersen's and Wohlin's work on flow [16], in combination with Staron and Meding's work on bottlenecks [18]. The main difference is in the purpose of the research. Their purpose was to continuously improve an agile way of working, by analysing the current way of working in order to find improvement opportunities. Our need for comparing the situation before and after a transformation is slightly different.

3   Research Question, Method and Context

3.1   Context

The need for a metrics model emanated from Finnish software companies collaborating with universities in the *Cloud Software Finland* [12] research project. One of the goals of this project is to support the Finnish software industry in transforming their operations with the help of agile and lean methods. The size of the companies range from fairly large organizations, developing complex embedded software systems to smaller companies providing software development and consultancy services. Furthermore, both the software development processes and cultures of the companies in the project vary to a great extent. Some organizations have completed agile and lean transformations, whereas others are in different stages of transformation. Within this research project, there were already studies ongoing focusing on the qualitative measurement of agile and lean transformations, whereas our work pursues the quantitative aspect of the same transformations.

3.2   Research Question

As agile and lean methods are gaining popularity, we agree with previous work [10,19] that establishing a model for measuring the impact of a transformation is relevant for both researchers and practitioners. With this in mind and in the context described above, we formulate the following research question.

RQ - *How can the changes of an agile transformation be measured by quantitative objective metrics?*

As an answer to this question, we create a metrics model to be used for measuring an agile transformation. In order to ensure that the metrics model is useful for comparing the situation before and after a transformation, we set up the following criteria for selecting the metrics of the model.

- *C1*. The metrics must be applicable to both plan driven and agile projects.
- *C2*. The metrics must support the agile principles (as described in the agile manifesto [21]).
- *C3*. The metrics must be feasible to collect for both past and on going projects.
- *C4*. The metrics must be possible to collect and use in projects of any scope, size and complexity.
- *C5*. The metrics must be objective, i.e. metrics colletion should not require the judgment and interpretation of experts.

3.3   Research Method

The metrics model in this paper has been iteratively developed in a series of workshops with both industry experts and researchers. Much valuable knowledge have also been obtained through literature study and the software research community.

   The metrics model in this paper was developed in five distinct steps. As the first step, in early 2011, the goal for the model was defined and iteratively refined with respect to goal coordinates according to the GQM method [13] as described in Section 4. The second step involved refinement of the goal and probing for candidate metrics during formal and informal workshops (Section 4). When proposals for the goal and questions were available, as the third step a literature survey was undertaken to map the state of the art in agile and lean transformation metrics. The literature survey is described in Section 5, with the goal of discovering metrics already proven useful and relevant in literature. The fourth step consisted of iteratively evaluating the metrics discovered in the literature survey against both the questions in the first and second step, as well as against the selection criteria presented in the research question in Section 3.2. Finally, as the fifth step, when both researchers and industry representatives reached an agreement on the metrics to be included in the model, a pilot evaluation was performed to exemplify the data gathering and visualization of a subset of metrics at Ericsson R&D Center Finland, further described in Section 7.

4   Defining the Goal and Questions for the Transformation Metrics Model

In this section we describe the background to the GQM [13] approach as the foundation to the metrics model. We start with the background leading to the model, followed by an overview of the goal and questions derived from collaboration with industry partners.

4.1   Background and Development of the Model

Based on the needs and state of the industrial partners in the Cloud Software Finland research project a measurement model was jointly developed and iterated using a GQM [13] approach. Our main partner in the early iterations of the metrics model was Ericsson R&D Center Finland and as the model matured and was refined other partners joined the research effort.

In this work we have based our transformation metrics model on agile metrics best practices from literature to support the agile transformation during the measurements, as described in Section 2.

4.2   Goal

The general goal of transforming and improving development operations was identified in a project wide survey in 2011 (see Section 3.1). This goal was further discussed and defined in 2011 within the case company and subsequently iterated to clarify the goal coordinates *issue, object* and *viewpoint* as described by Basili et al. [13]. The beginning stage of defining the measurement goal consisted of a workshop day with open discussions.

From a later workshop, held in a world café [22] format, the GQM *coordinate issues* of the goal, **business value delivery** and **efficiency** were extracted to be of key importance. The workshop participants represented many different roles in the organization, such as: Scrum masters, developers, testers, product owners and line managers. The last coordinate issue, **end-to-end lead time**, was at

the time of the workshop counted as part of efficiency, but was later discovered
to be more important and subsequently separated.

The final GQM goal coordinates are presented below:

Purpose: Improve
Issue: End-to-end lead time, business value delivery and efficiency
Object: The software development process
Viewpoint: From the whole organizations and customer viewpoint

The iterations and refinement of the goal coordinates were finalized during fall
2011 resulting in the following goal:

Goal: *Improve end-to-end lead time, business value delivery and efficiency
for the software development process from the whole organization's and customer's viewpoint.*

When improving the lead time, business value delivery and efficiency, there is a
risk that the quality suffers. In order to ensure that this has not been the case,
we also added quality as an issue to measure.

4.3   Questions

Based on the goal and aforementioned coordinate issues, four questions were
proposed:

Q. 1: *Are we more responsive in the new way of working?*
Q. 2: *Do we have better throughput in the new way of working?*
Q. 3: *Do we have a better workflow distribution in the new way of working?*
Q. 4: *Do we have better product quality in the new way of working?*

4.4   Metrics

The final step in the GQM modeling was to determine the metrics to be used.
This step proved to be the most challenging and time consuming. According to
Basili et. al. [13] one important factor in choosing metrics is to maximize the
use of existing data sources. The use of existing data sources was particularly
important in the research setting since the researchers were separate from the
measured organization and the transformation was already taking place.

As input towards finding the right metrics for each question, the researchers
conducted a literature survey as described in Section 5 and analyzed the results.
From the state of the art in metrics, best practices were extracted. These acted
as a base for selecting and crystallizing the right metrics in the GQM approach
for the current research setting.

The four questions and the eight metrics chosen for inclusion in the metrics
model are described in more detail in Section 6. In the next section, Section 5,
we describe the literature survey undertaken to map the current state of research
in SPI and agile metrics.

5 Literature Survey

A literature survey was performed to map the current status of Software Process Improvement (SPI) evaluation and agile metrics. The literature research was performed by the researchers in October 2011 as an on-line search in the following collections: SpringerLink [23] , IEEE Xplore [24] and ACM Digital Library [25].

The search strings used were: Lead-Time AND Lean, Lead Time AND Lean, Business Value AND Lean, Business-Value AND Lean, Metric AND Lean, Metrics AND Lean, Metrics AND Agile, Metric AND Agile. The search terms were entered in each database manually, which can lead to some inconsistencies due to human error. The titles of the search results were evaluated and the abstracts of relevant publications were further examined. The relevant publications were saved and subjectively ordered by precedence with numbers from 1-3 depending on assessment of the researchers and the number of times the publications appeared in the search results.

After the on-line search phase was finished the abstracts of the saved publications (70 in total) were evaluated a second time and relevant articles were chosen for reading. This method of both systematically and subjectively eliciting relevant articles depended on the research environment where the research questions were not completely finalized from the beginning.

Additionally some research was conducted in on-line journals such as Agile Journal [26] to further broaden the understanding of the topics and related terminology from practitioners and the agile community.

Approximately 20 articles were chosen as relevant for the future work at the end of the literature research. These were studied in detail and annotated, also interesting references were further examined resulting in a big matrix of publications, their goals and metrics. The matrix was discussed by the researchers and candidate metrics were selected for the metrics model.

In addition to the concrete metrics discovered in the literature survey, many proposed best practices for agile measurement have been presented and discussed in literature [14,15,27]. The best practices were a valuable input in the work of creating the metrics model, although not all practices could be satisfied.

Subsequent workshops with industry representatives strengthened the potential use of some metrics, whereas other metrics proved difficult to gather from, e.g., old projects and had to be abandoned for this work. The resulting metrics for each question is presented in Section 6.

6 Proposed Metrics

The metrics for the model were chosen with the selection criteria, described in Section 3.2, in mind. Besides the applicability to both agile and plan driven settings, the availability and objectivity of the data are of importance.

Two metrics were chosen for each of the questions to add redundancy in case some metric would prove to not be possible to collect. The relatively high number of metrics also represents the different organizations that have been collaborating in this work. When applying the model (as described in Section 7), organizations are encouraged to consider how many questions to try to answer and which metrics are possible to collect to answer these questions.

The metrics are defined by a textual description, the measured *attribute* and the actual *metric*, as described by Meneely et al. [28].

6.1   Q. 1: Are We More Responsive in the New Way of Working?

With this question we want to investigate if the response time has improved. This question relates to the *better end-to-end lead time* in the specified goal.

Responsiveness is often regarded as a key factor in software development. As Reinertsen [29] argues, in areas where response time is important, this is the only metric that should be used for improving service. One such important area is support operations where solving bugs and problems quickly is of high value to stakeholders.

Similarly, during development of new features, fast lead-time is important for numerous competitive advantages such as fast feedback loops and reducing the risk of requirements becoming outdated (waste), both examples of where decisions might decay over time [30].

Metric 1 – Customer Service Request (CSR) Turnaround Time. The first metric measures the turnaround for customer service requests. The metric is calculated from a timestamp when the request first comes to the development organization and from a timestamp when the request is resolved.
Attribute: Time
Metric: CSR date solved - CSR date created.

Metric 2 – Cycle-Time per Feature. The second metric measures cycle-time for features selected for development. Quick cycle-time is essential for competitive advantages as noted by Petersen [17]. The metric is calculated from a timestamp when the feature is added to the backlog and timestamp when the feature is ready for delivery. Cycle-time is regarded as a part of the lead-time. This metric also supports metric 4 – *Business value / Work effort*, since shorter cycle-time makes more frequent releases easier.
Attribute: Time
Metric: Feature delivery ready date - Feature added to backlog date.

6.2   Q. 2: Do We Have Better Throughput in the New Way of Working?

Where the first question concerned timeliness, this question aims to investigate whether the total amount of value delivered is greater in the new way of working during similar time periods and projects. The benefits of increased throughput have been discussed widely, including Andersson [31].

Metric 3 – Functionality / Work Effort. With the second question's first metric we want to measure how much functionality (also denoted as product size [27]) that can be delivered in relation to a certain work effort. The proposed metric is the ratio of test points, as described by Dubinsky et al. in [15,27] divided by total time spent on the development measured in person hours. This metric (similarly to metric 1) also supports metric 4, since more functionality can be split into more frequent releases.

Attribute: Throughput

Metric: Test points / Person hours

Metric 4 – Business Value / Work Effort. Business value is measured as more frequent major releases [11] in relation to the work effort (person hours).

Attribute: Throughput

Metric: Number of major releases in a year / Person hours

6.3   Q. 3: Do We Have a Better Workflow Distribution in the New Way of Working?

The third question, concerning *workflow distribution* characterizes the new iterative way of working, as this is one of the goals for an agile transformation. Measuring the workflow helps the organization identify that a change in the way of working has indeed taken place.

Metric 5 – Commit Pulse. Commit pulse measures how continuous integration is within sprints [15,27] by counting the number of check-ins daily. The check-in data can be visualized in a diagram with days on the x-axis and number of commits on the y-axis. The aim is to have an even check-in pulse throughout sprints without high spikes of commits at the end of sprints.

Attribute: Regularity

Metric: Number of days between commits

Metric 6 – Flow. Measuring the flow in an organization supports responsiveness as proposed by Petersen & Wohlin [16], connecting also this metric back to the first questions. Having a continuous smooth flow without bottlenecks allows the development organization to better respond quickly to customer requests.

Attribute: Flow

Metric: Flow diagrams

6.4   Q. 4: Do We Have Better Product Quality in the New Way of Working?

With the three previous questions concerning the improvement of the development process, the final question takes into account the quality aspect of the product developed. Improvements in other areas must not take place at the expense of product quality.

Metric 7 – Number of External Trouble Reports (TR). External trouble reports are defect reports submitted from external users. This metric measures the total number of external trouble reports during a certain time period in a release of software in the old way of working compared to total number of external trouble reports from a similar project and similar time period in the new way of working.

Attribute: Amount

Metric: Number of external TR's originating from a certain release

Metric 8 – Days Open, External Trouble Reports. The final metric measures the average days external trouble reports have been unsolved from creation until solved. This metric is related to *Question 1: Are we more responsive...*, but it also measures the quality of the product. If trouble reports consistently take longer to solve, then it is likely that the defects found are more complicated or that the code base is more difficult to maintain. Both of these are indications that the quality of the product has deteriorated.

Attribute: Time

Metric: TR date solved - TR date created

7   Using the Metrics Model in an Organization

To exemplify the use of the metrics model in an organization, data was gathered and analyzed from the agile and lean transformation Ericsson R&D Center Finland carried out during 2008-2011. Examples of these are displayed in Figure 1 and Figure 2, where Metric 1 and Metric 8 are shown respectively, with data plotted from both before, during and after the transformation. For the baseline, *old Way of Working (WoW)*, a set of features was selected from a typical development project in the plan driven development process from a two year period during 2007-2009. The *new WoW* was represented by a similar set of features from the agile and lean development process from a similar two year period in 2011-2012. Additionally some data was analyzed from the time (in 2010) when the transformation was taking place.

The collection of the data was considered cheap with respect to the amount of time necessary to extract the data by Ericsson R&D Center Finland representatives. The researchers gained access to the raw data files as well as were familiarized with the organization's terminology. Due to confidentiality, only trends can be shown in the metric visualizations, where all scales are linear and start the y-axis from zero.

8   Validation of the Model with Respect to the Criteria

In Section 3.2 we listed five criteria used for selecting the metrics of the proposed model. In this section we explain why we consider these criteria to be fulfilled by the included metrics.

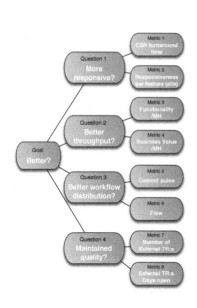

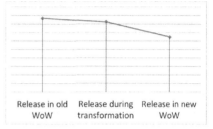

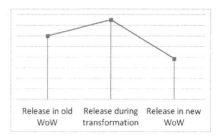

Fig. 1. Metric 1: Average number of days open for CRSs

Fig. 2. Metric 8: TRs average days open

8.1   C1 and C4: Plan Driven and Agile Projects, Independent of Scope, Size and Complexity

With the exception of the workflow distribution metrics (Metrics 5 and 6 – commit pulse and flow), all the selected metrics are such that they measure the development effort from an external point of view. The time and effort for delivering service requests, features, functionality, business value, and trouble reports are measured looking at the point when they enter and exit the development organization. As such they ignore the internal process used to produce the result, and thus render the metrics independent of the internal process model used, i.e. plan driven or agile (C1). As the metrics do not consider the internal workings of the project measured, it is also agnostic to scope, size and complexity (C4).

In contrast, the workflow distribution metrics have the express purpose to illustrate the difference between the two process models, in order to verify that a change in way of working has indeed taken place. Metric 5 (commit pulse) is trivial to collect in any organization using a version control tool for the produced source code, regardless of the process model used. Metric 6 (flow) requires that the organization uses some form of time tracking tool for the development activities, and has continued to do so after the transformation. This may not always be the case.

8.2   C2: Support for Agile Values

As noted by Hartmann and Dymond, the inappropriate use of metrics can threaten an emerging agile and lean culture [14]. For this reason, we were careful to select metrics that support agile values (C2). The core values and principles described by the agile manifesto [21] are centered around responsiveness, early delivery of working software, cooperation and communication, technical excellence, simplicity, self-organization and human interaction. Throughout the selection process, these values have served as a guide.

8.3   C3: Feasible to Collect for Both Past and Ongoing Projects

From a research point of view, it would be ideal to have the opportunity to define what metrics to collect a year before a transformation takes place. In reality, the need to measure a transformation arises at the start of the transformation at the earliest, and sometimes not until the transformation is complete. For this reason, the metrics defined should be feasible to collect after the fact. Any metrics initiative is a trade-off between cost of data collection and metric accuracy. In this case the trade-off becomes more pronounced due to the fact that it can be extremely costly to gather data for past projects. By working closely together with industrial partners and verifying that the data we ask for can be collected, we have achieved a model that is usable for both past and ongoing projects.

8.4   C5: Objective

All the data collected is quantitative and, with the exception of Metric 6 (flow,) requires no interpretation of experts. The entry and exit dates for implemented items as well as the number of items present should all be objective information present in the documentation of the projects measured. The flow metric is a slightly more complex metric that requires plotting and analysis of the plotted curve. This does not compromise the objectivity of the metric, but makes the implications of it slightly more cumbersome to analyze.

9   Discussion and Future Work

The metrics model proposed in this paper is intended to be a practical tool for use in software development organizations undergoing transformation from more traditional ways of working to agile and lean ones. The main challenge lies in the contrast between the old and new; in finding metrics that can be used in and accepted by both worlds. Especially the agile and lean philosophy rules out certain traditional productivity metrics such as lines of code per person hour or capacity utilization. This type of metric can, however, still be found in the agile literature. An example of a metric we chose not to use is churn (number of added, deleted and modified lines of code) per developer as presented by Sjøberg, Johnsen and Solberg [19]. We expected that this type of metric would meet with resistance and even be considered harmful in the agile way of working. Instead, we focused on measuring throughput in terms of the produced functionality and business value.

Another challenge in comparing the old and new way of working of an organization undergoing transformation is the fact that not all measurable changes originate from the transformation itself. In a real world situation, other factors will always impact the measurements. By choosing metrics that measure the operations of the development organizations (such as lead-times and defect reports), rather than metrics that measure the operations of the whole company (such as revenue and customer satisfaction) we hope to have minimized the effect of external factors. Internal factors, however, such as development staff turnover, cannot be factored out. This is a known limitation of this metrics model, which should be taken into account when the model is used. Any organization using the model should analyze and list the internal factors expected to impact the measurements. It is also worth noting that no metric model is immune to manipulation. For this reason, it is crucial that the collection of data be transparent, reproducable and honestly reported in order for the results to be trustworthy

The agile and lean community emphasises produced value as a measurement for productivity. The challenge we faced with this metric is that it is typically not collected in traditional ways of working. In fact, we found through our literature research that it is rarely collected in agile or lean ways of working. One could assume that the business value of a product could easily be extracted in hindsight by looking at the revenue produced for a product. This may work if the product catalog is simple, but proved to be impossible with the complex product portfolio of the software companies in the Cloud project. We have suggested a model for expressing business value for complex products in agile projects [32], but this proved costly to recreate after the fact for plan driven projects. The metric we used for measuring produced business value: the number of major releases, proved to be practical in both worlds, but can be argued to be a bit imprecise. This is an area we would still like to investigate further.

The metrics model developed here was created with the specific needs of our partners in mind. We are currently planning to investigate the general applicability of this model by running a series of case studies in different companies undergoing similar transformations.

10   Conclusions

In this paper we have proposed a metrics model for comparing development in plan driven processes to agile and lean development processes. The metrics model has been piloted with data from Ericsson R&D Center Finland, showing that the data needed for the model is indeed feasible to be collected both for ongoing, agile projects and past, plan driven projects and that the metrics are sensitive to an organizational transformation.

Our intention with the metrics model is twofold: 1) To contribute to current research in the field of comparing the effects of changing software development processes with a metrics model applied in an industry setting. 2) To support organizations by enabling them to show the benefits of agile and lean transformations with the use of quantitative objective data to complement qualitative studies in the field.

Our proposed metrics model consists of eight metrics, combined into pairs, connected to four questions, all aiming for one goal. Both the questions and the goal were iteratively developed during workshops in which both researchers and industry partners participated. The metrics were carefully selected to be compliant with a set of five criteria to maximize their usefulness in measuring agile and lean transformations.

Future work includes first and foremost applying the metrics model in different case companies to further validate the usefulness and applicability of the metrics model.

Acknowledgements. This work was funded by the CLOUD Software Finland project [12]. From Ericsson R&D Center Finland we would like to thank Christian Engblom, Kaisa Kettunen, Leena Pitkäranta, and Outi Väättänen for their help and support. We also wish to thank Marta Olszewska from Åbo Akademi for her participation in the project.

References

1. Rodríguez, P., Markkula, J., Oivo, M., Turula, K.: Survey on agile and lean usage in finnish software industry. In: Proceedings of the ACM-IEEE, ESEM 2012, pp. 139–148. ACM, New York (2012)
2. VersionOne: State of agile survey (2011), `http://versionone.com/pdf/2011_State_of_Agile_Development_Survey_Results.pdf`
3. Ebert, C., Abrahamsson, P., Oza, N.V.: Lean software development. IEEE Software 29(5), 22–25 (2012)
4. Šmite, D., Moe, N., Ågerfalk, P.: Agility Across Time and Space: Implementing Agile Methods in Global Software Projects. Springer (2010)
5. Anderson, D.: Agile Management for Software Engineering: Applying the Theory of Constraints for Business Results. The Coad Series. Prentice Hall (2004)
6. Leffingwell, D.: Scaling Software Agility: Best Practices for Large Enterprises. The Agile Software Development Series. Prentice Hall (2007)
7. Parnell-Klabo, E.: Introducing lean principles with agile practices at a fortune 500 company. In: Proceedings of the Conference on AGILE 2006, pp. 232–242. IEEE Computer Society, Washington, DC (2006)
8. Petersen, K., Wohlin, C.: The effect of moving from a plan-driven to an incremental software development approach with agile practices. Empirical Softw. Engg. 15(6), 654–693 (2010)
9. Royce, W.W.: Managing the development of large software systems: concepts and techniques. In: Proceedings of IEEE WESCON 26 (1970)
10. Dybå, T., Dingsøyr, T.: Empirical studies of agile software development: A systematic review. Inf. Softw. Technol. 50(9-10), 833–859 (2008)
11. Cohn, M.: Succeeding with Agile: Software Development Using Scrum. Addison-Wesley Professional (2009) ISBN 978-0321579362
12. Cloud Software Finland: Cloud software finland, `www.cloudsoftwareprogram.org`
13. Basili, V.R., Caldiera, G., Rombach, H.D.: The goal question metric approach. In: Encyclopedia of Software Engineering. Wiley (1994)

14. Hartmann, D., Dymond, R.: Appropriate Agile Measurement: Using Metrics and Diagnostics to Deliver Business Value. In: AGILE 2006 Conference (Agile 2006). IEEE Computer Society (2006)
15. Dubinsky, Y., Talby, D., Hazzan, O., Keren, A.: Agile Metrics at the Israeli Air Force. In: Proceedings of the Agile Development Conference, ADC 2005, pp. 12–19. IEEE Computer Society, Washington, DC (2005)
16. Petersen, K., Wohlin, C.: Measuring the flow in lean software development. Software: Practice and Experience 41(9), 975–996 (2011)
17. Petersen, K.: An Empirical Study of Lead-Times in Incremental and Agile Software Development. In: Münch, J., Yang, Y., Schäfer, W. (eds.) ICSP 2010. LNCS, vol. 6195, pp. 345–356. Springer, Heidelberg (2010)
18. Staron, M., Meding, W.: Monitoring bottlenecks in agile and lean software development projects – A method and its industrial use. In: Caivano, D., Oivo, M., Baldassarre, M.T., Visaggio, G. (eds.) PROFES 2011. LNCS, vol. 6759, pp. 3–16. Springer, Heidelberg (2011)
19. Sjøberg, D.I., Johnsen, A., Solberg, J.: Quantifying the effect of using kanban versus scrum: A case study. IEEE Software 29, 47–53 (2012)
20. Concas, G., Marchesi, M., Destefanis, G., Tonelli, R.: An empirical study of software metrics for assessing the phases of an agile project. International Journal of Software Engineering and Knowledge Engineering 22(04), 525–548 (2012)
21. Agile Alliance: Agile manifesto, www.agilemanifesto.org/
22. World Cafe: World cafe, http://www.theworldcafe.com/method.html
23. Springer: Springer link, www.springerlink.com/
24. IEEE: IEEEXplore, www.ieeexplore.ieee.org/
25. ACM Digital Library: ACM Digital Library, www.dl.acm.org/
26. Agile Journal: Agile journal, www.agilejournal.com/
27. Hazzan, O., Dubinsky, Y.: Agile software engineering. Undergraduate topics in computer science. Springer, Berlin (2008) ISBN: 978-1-84800-199-2
28. Meneely, A., Smith, B., Williams, L.: Validating software metrics: A spectrum of philosophies. ACM Transactions on Software Engineering and Methodology
29. Reinertsen, D.G.: The Principles of Product Development Flow: Second Generation Lean Product Development. Celeritas Publishing (2009)
30. Cockburn, A.: What engineering has in common with manufacturing and why it matters - ac (September 2006)
31. Andersson, D.: Agile management for software engineering: applying the theory of constraints for business results. Pearson Education Inc. (2004)
32. Heidenberg, J., Weijola, M., Mikkonen, K., Porres, I.: A model for business value in large-scale agile and lean software development. In: Winkler, D., O'Connor, R.V., Messnarz, R. (eds.) EuroSPI 2012. CCIS, vol. 301, pp. 49–60. Springer, Heidelberg (2012)

Perspectives on Productivity and Delays
in Large-Scale Agile Projects

Deepika Badampudi[1], Samuel A. Fricker[1], and Ana M. Moreno[2]

[1] Blekinge Institute of Technology, 371 79 Karlskrona, Sweden
[2] Universidad Politécnica de Madrid, 28660 Boadilla del Monte, Madrid, Spain
deba10@student.bth.se, samuel.fricker@bth.se,
anamaria.moreno@upm.es

Abstract. Many large and distributed companies run agile projects in development environments that are inconsistent with the original agile ideas. Problems that result from these inconsistencies can affect the productivity of development projects and the timeliness of releases. To be effective in such contexts, the agile ideas need to be adapted. We take an inductive approach for reaching this aim by basing the design of the development process on observations of how context, practices, challenges, and impacts interact. This paper reports the results of an interview study of five agile development projects in an environment that was unfavorable for agile principles. Grounded theory was used to identify the challenges of these projects and how these challenges affected productivity and delays according to the involved project roles. Productivity and delay-influencing factors were discovered that related to requirements creation and use, collaboration, knowledge management, and the application domain. The practitioners' explanations about the factors' impacts are, on one hand, a rich empirical source for avoiding and mitigating productivity and delay problems and, on the other hand, a good starting point for further research on flexible large-scale development.

Keywords: Inductive process improvement, large-scale agile development, grounded theory.

1 Introduction

Agile methods promise lightweight, fast, and nimble development of software solutions [1]. The values and principles of agile methods suit project environments particularly well that are characterized by small, competent, and collocated teams that aim at creating rapid value with small products for well-collaborating customers. The methods' rapid and continuous feedback from customer to development team allows a shared understanding to emerge, rather than requiring requirements to be pre-determined and specified up-front.

Many organizations are appealed by the idea of generating rapid value with emergent requirements. However, when attempting to use agile methods for large-scale product innovation, these organizations discover misalignments between method and environment [29]. Large scale implies distributed collaboration, coordination

H. Baumeister and B. Weber (Eds.): XP 2013, LNBIP 149, pp. 180–194, 2013.

among teams, and the presence of many stakeholders that need to be satisfied in addition to the project customer. Product and technology novelty imply competence gaps, potentially both for customer and project team [15]. Misalignments affect project success negatively or lead to failure [9].

To improve project performance, companies invest in process improvement. Such learning organizations actively collect experience and modify their behavior to reflect the insights they have gained [16]. In mature areas, such process improvement is often based on prescriptive frameworks, such as CMMI [10], that benchmark industry best practices. When best practices for specific improvement goals have not been established yet, inductive approaches are used to guide process improvements [5, 27]. An inductive approach exposes past experience and allows the organization to learn from it. If they are attractive enough, the results from inductive process development ultimately become part of prescriptive benchmarking frameworks.

This paper reports early results of such inductive process improvement that aimed at enhancing productivity and reducing delays of large-scale agile development in a particular software development organization. The organization enabled large-scale software product innovation for a multi-national company, a market and technology leader in multiple industry sectors. The organization noticed a misalignment of project needs for predictability and dependability with agile practices. It used inductive process improvement to assess and improve the productivity of their development projects. The assessment elicited challenges and their impact on project roles to identify how to avoid these challenges and to mitigate their effects. The results are a condensed rich description of real-world experiences that enables evidence-based definition of a prescriptive framework to diagnose and improve agility for large-scale software product innovation.

The remainder of this paper is structured as follows. Section 2 describes related work and motivates the research. Section 3 describes the research method. Sections 4 and 5 characterize and discuss the results. Section 6 summarizes and concludes.

2   Related Work

Many organizations feel pressure to produce more at lower costs [23]. Productivity improvements require software projects to reduce development cost, while still ensuring that solutions are technically correct and satisfactory to stakeholders. Usually, this is achieved by increasing development efficiency and avoiding rework. Productivity is also closely related to predictability. Wrong estimates and scheduling problems increase the error rate of investment decisions [12]. Productivity problems and delays affect the company's bottom line because market share erodes rapidly and the market is entered with a little attractive product [3].

A variety of factors affect productivity and delays. The ability to plan is a key determinant: requirements engineering, prototyping, and reuse reduce the need for error correction and rework [2, 3]. Requirements engineering, in particular, enables effort estimation, project negotiation, progress tracking, and high test coverage [12]. Project management problems such as customer and management changes, unrealistic project plans, staffing problems, and inability to track problems early lead to delays [17].

Other determinants are software architecture, team size, and tooling. Software architecture limits the number of developers that can effectively work together on a software solution [7]. Small teams with better programmers are more productive than large teams [3]. Tools, finally, have positive or negative effects on productivity [6].

Many companies believe that agile methods effectively address productivity problems, in particular because they enable continuous change instead of costly upfront requirements specifications [23]. Some companies were successful: phenomenal productivity was achieved with a shared backlog, shared code ownership, and joint daily Scrum meetings even in globally distributed development [32, 33]. Productivity improvements were also reported in other studies [8].

Productivity suffers if methods are used in an incompatible environment, however. Agile methods shift success determinants from good planning to frequent releases and strong communication [9]. This shift is difficult for companies that are used to heavyweight sequential processes [25] and companies that are confronted with interdependent teams and stakeholders located at different locations [9]. Challenges appear in development and management processes [4, 11]. However, they can be addressed with appropriate practices for improving communication, sharing knowledge, managing trust, and adapting processes [22, 28].

Companies that have adopted agile practices and discover that their development environment is incompatible have limited support for improving development performance. An enabler for identifying effective practices is to understand the development context and how it enables, respectively inhibits success [19]. Without such knowledge, projects outside the agile "sweet spot" [21] feel forced to change again the development method and, due to lack of alternatives, will probably fall back to the old traditional way of development, losing some of the benefits that agile frameworks can provide.

3   Research Methodology

Our work aimed at understanding productivity impediments of projects for large-scale software product development. The here presented embedded multi-case study [34] was part of an inductive process development effort [27] in a software development organization of a multi-national company. The effort aimed at improving the organization's agile development practices by capturing the experience of the employees. Members of multiple projects were interviewed to identify challenges in the application of agile techniques. Grounded theory [31] was used to analyze the impact of these challenges on the various roles involved in the software projects and to understand how productivity problems can be avoided and mitigated. The cause-effect form of the resulting analysis not only supports the specific process improvement, but also represents an empirical basis for the definition of a situational framework with guidelines for flexible large-scale development.

To understand the challenges of the agile projects and the impacts of these challenges, the following research questions were posed:

- RQ1: Which challenges led to productivity problems and delays?
- RQ2: How were the involved project roles affected by these challenges?

Data collection and analysis proceeded iteratively and in parallel. The collected data was analyzed to build a model of causes and effects for the observed challenges. Information needs from the analysis indicated the roles that needed to be interviewed. For example, if an interviewee mentioned a challenge in a particular activity, then the project role responsible for that activity was selected for the next interview. Our industry partner's quality manager identified relevant projects and interviewees to ensure representativeness for the organization and the application domains of the developed software products. A total of 14 representatives for the following roles were selected: product manager, global project manager, architect, integration manager, technology manager, scrum master, developer, and tester. A brief description of each role is provided in the next section. The data collection continued until the saturation point where no new data about the challenges could be obtained.

Semi-structured interviews [30] were used for data collection. During the interviews, the purpose of the study was explained and open-ended questions about challenges and the impact of the challenges were asked. The initial questionnaire was continuously refined on the basis of the analysis results and the information needs discovered during the analysis. Each interview lasted approximately 120 minutes. The interviews were recorded and transcribed.

The transcribed data was analyzed using grounded theory [31] by following the steps iteratively. *Pre-coding:* we have identified the parts of our transcripts that pertained to challenges and impacts. *Open coding:* we have defined codes to label the identified challenges, their causes, and their impacts. Each challenge and impact then was described from the interviewees' perspectives in terms of its characteristics (Table 1). *Axial coding:* we connected challenges with conditions that gave rise to the challenges (Table 2) and the impacts of the challenges (Tables 3 and 4). *Selective coding:* we then identified the central traits of the observed large-scale challenges and discussed them in relation to previous literature and potential solutions.

Flexible research is confronted with the following threats to validity [30]: reactivity, respondent bias, researcher bias, reliability, and generalizability.

Reactivity refers to the way in which the researcher's presence alters the behavior of the subjects involved in the research. This threat to validity was addressed by letting the interviewing researcher stay at the development organization for a prolonged period of time and develop trusted relationships with the interviewees.

Respondent bias refers to the risks of obtaining answers that respondents judge are those the researchers want and of having information withheld that can be used against the respondents. This threat to validity was reduced by aligning the study goals with the interests of the study participants: understanding how to improve their development processes. To check correctness of the obtained answers, one of the researchers studied the company's standard processes and participated as observers in project meetings. Further threat reduction was achieved by triangulating the data among the interviewees.

Researcher bias refers to the preconceptions and assumptions the researcher brings into the study. Researcher bias could have manifested in the selection of the projects and interviewees. This threat to validity was reduced by letting the quality manager of the organization, who was interested in correct and useful results, select the projects and the interviewees and review the questionnaire. The open-ended interview questions allowed the interviewees to share answers they judged to be important.

Reliability refers to how carefully the research was performed and how honestly the results were presented. Reliability was achieved by following the above-described research design, by transcribing all interviews, by managing coding results with a qualitative analysis tool, and maintaining a chain of evidence.

Generalizability refers to how far the obtained results are applicable and valid. To support generalization beyond the studied organization we developed a model of challenges, causes, and impacts that can be used for generating hypotheses about determinants for productivity and delays in large-scale software product development. In addition, the results were compared with related work to indicate consistency and differences with previous state of knowledge.

4   Results

4.1   The Development Organization

We studied a development organization of a Global 500 company. The company served a large number of markets with a widely diversified portfolio of products, systems, and services. Many of the products were built on leading technologies and contained a significant amount of software.

The development organization developed software solutions with projects requested by product managers. Many of these solutions were established for 5 to 10 years and represented critical parts of products and larger systems that included both hardware and software. The largest software had approximately 5 million lines of code. The products and services targeted customers in a number of industry sectors. They were managed by product managers that worked remotely and acted as product owners to the development projects. The projects were globally distributed with 25 to 100 members allocated to up to 10 Scrum teams and located at up to 4 development sites. Important roles of the Scrum teams were the Scrum master responsible for a team's work process, the developers responsible for component design and implementation, and the testers responsible for quality assurance. Important members of the global project teams were the product manager responsible for product success, the project manager responsible for coordinating the Scrum teams in the global project, the architect responsible for overall product design, the integration manager responsible for composing the overall product, and the technology manager responsible for the development organization. An independent organization verified compliance to regulations.

The development organization had adopted agile development processes, in particular Scrum, for over 5 years and followed agile practices like short iterations, daily stand-up meetings, pair programming, and test-first development. Kano analysis was used for prioritization at the project level and planning poker for development iterations. State-of-art tools were used to manage the product repository that included requirements, agile project management, code, and testing artifacts.

The projects were not implementing Scrum to the letter. Deviations were due to compliance, business practices, and distribution of teams. FDA regulations imposed documentation and traceability requirements, and external testing of the product was not possible until the entire product was ready. Most projects had contracts signed early, and workshops disrupted the regular flow of work. These deviations were one source for the challenges the study discovered.

4.2 Challenges That Affected Productivity and Delays

The practitioners reported a wide range of challenges they perceived affected development productivity and timeliness of software releases. The challenges related to requirements creation and use, collaboration, knowledge, and the product repository. Table 1 gives an overview of the most problematic productivity and delay-affecting challenges that have been reported by the interviewees.

Table 1. Challenges that affected productivity and delays in the agile projects (*italics*: quotes)

Category	Challenge	Characteristics
Requirements Creation	Requirements Quality (RQ)	*Sometimes requirements are not mature enough. If a new technology needs to be implemented, then the requirements are not always well understood.*
	Non-functional Requirements (NFR)	*Sometimes product managers are not fully aware of the non-functional requirements. Also the demonstrations do not demonstrate the NFRs. This comes as a defect when the product goes into system testing.*
	Estimates (ES)	*If the project is for 2 years, it is ok to have estimates much bigger. They might be more than even a man month. In the last step where we plan the single sprint they should be down to single days.*
	Competitors' Influence (CI)	*Time-to-market is influenced by the competitors. It may happen that the competitors come up with a similar product. Then the product needs to release earlier with at least the same features like the competitors to avoid sales loss.*
Requirements Use	Requirements Selection (RS)	*How to split the requirements, how to phase them across different phases of the project, I would say, continues to be a challenge.*
	Requirements Stability (RV)	*When there is a change, it takes a couple of sprints to align everything together. The impact of change can be felt for a longer time*
	Testing Completeness (TC)	*Incomplete testing is another aspect. Some workflows are not fully tested.*
	Integration (IN)	*Global integration reports defects for skipped functionality. This happens because some other team changes something which was not available to us for testing and that has cost us the defect.*
	Clarity of Done (CD)	*Perspective of developers and product managers differ sometimes due to poor understanding of requirements. What we consider done is not considered done by product manager sometimes*
Collaboration	Communication Quality (CQ)	*Communication is another aspect as all team members are not in the same place. The communication between the engineering project head and the product manager is less.*
	Decision-making (DM)	*All the key stakeholders from all teams should be involved in release planning along with the product manager and customer. That would lead to development of a concrete plan.*
	Team Dynamics (TD)	*The scrum masters have own motives in completing their tasks.*
	Test Infrastructure (TI)	*When the developers finish the development the scrum server is not available for testing.*
	Team Stability (TS)	*Sometimes resources leave the project. Then recalculations need to be done. The project may take 15 months instead of 10 months.*
Knowledge	Domain and Technology Knowledge (DTK)	*Using a new technology without evaluating it could be a potential risk that can cause a plan to get derailed.*
Product Repository	Progress Measurement (PM)	*Testing may result in re-implementing the user story. This is not always updated to the release backlog.*
	Documentation Quality (DQ)	*Developer pairs code without writing comments because they know each other. But a third person faces lot of issues.*

A majority of the challenges related to requirements creation or use. The creation of clear, mature, and complete-enough requirements that are correctly estimated and lead to a stable project and a well-integrated accepted solution was here as important as in other software development efforts. The use of an agile process did not change this need. The challenges RQ, NFR, ES, and RV are consistent with those reported by studies of large-scale market-driven requirements engineering [20]. New challenges were CI and CD that reflected the importance of product management decisions. Connected to the agile development process were RS, TC, and IN that were due to splitting complex requirements and implementing them stepwise.

The next important group of challenges related to collaboration, knowledge, and the product repository. The collaboration challenges CQ, DM, and TD and the product repository challenges PM and DQ are well-known global software development challenges [18]. The challenge of domain and technology learning DTK is well-known in product innovation [24]. New challenges were the problems of test infrastructure TI and team stability TS. None of these challenges were removed by the agile processes.

4.3   Causes for the Challenges

The practitioners suggested that the challenges were caused by six conditions present in the environment of the development projects. The rationales for why the causes gave rise to the challenges characterize the misalignment of the organization's characteristics and how the agile processes were implemented. Table 2 gives an overview.

Table 2. Conditions that gave rise to productivity and delay-affecting challenges (*italics*: quotes)

Condition	Challenge	Rationale
Project Complexity	Requirements Quality (RQ)	*If a new [complex] technology needs to be implemented then the requirements are not always well understood.*
	Requirements Stability (RV)	*Requirements changes might also come from the development teams. Sometimes a team realized that they needed support from other teams or other components.*
Multiple Teams	Integration (IN)	*Other teams change something which was not available to us for testing and that has cost us the defect.*
	Clarity of Done (CD)	*People don't want to report yellow or red. If you have many teams that all report green, but still have open tasks, this does not give a correct indication of work done*
	Test Infrastructure (TI)	*It happens that the team is ready for beta testing but the beta sites are not available for testing as other teams use the same site.*
	Progress Measurement (PM)	*Teams do not always updated requirements that result from defects to the [global] release backlog. As a result release burndown gives a wrong indication on the project progress.*
Multiple Sites	Communication Quality (CQ)	*Lack of communication across locations. Time zones are different. This causes delay when queries need to be answered.*
	Decision-making (DM),	*Sometimes meetings are not done jointly due to time differences. Then only the minutes of meeting are shared after the meeting.*
	Team Dynamics (TD)	*Every scrum group would have their own priorities to finish their tasks. This creates more problems when teams are multi-site.*

Table 2. (*continued*)

Condition	Challenge	Rationale
Product Characteristics	Non-functional Requirements (NFR)	*There is no denial that NFRs like scalability are ignored in agile projects.*
	Documentation Quality (DQ)	*Test cases need to be written at a later stage as a cleanup process due to FDA regulations.*
	Requirements Selection (RS)	*How to split the requirements, how to phase them across different phases of the project, I would say, continues to be a challenge.*
	Testing Completeness (TC)	*Due to FDA regulations external testing is only done at the end of release and not after each sprint.*
Knowledge Limitations	Domain and Technology Knowledge (DTK)	*If the domain is not understood there could be lot of errors.*
	Estimates (ES)	*It depends how mature the team is. There are overestimations because of which the team needs to stretch.*
	Integration (IN)	*The involved people are still learning about the system. We want to be more efficient and have better quality of the integrated product.*

Product complexity, multiple teams, and multiple sites were conditions related to the scale of the development effort. The development was highly parallel and introduced a need for coordinating teams with joint meeting, shared documentation, consistent progress measurement, and a joint product repository. Shared resources such as test infrastructure needed to be managed. Perturbations, such as requirements changes, perturbed the development streams that needed to be stabilized again.

NFR, RS, and TC were challenges due to misalignments of the agile process with product characteristics. NFR cut across implementation activities of many iterations and were not easily handled with backlogs. Similarly, implementation with short iterations required splitting features, such as the support of a workflow, into multiple parts even-though they would have been preferred to be implemented as a whole. The product domain was regulated and imposed constraints on development documentation and process such as traceability and certification tests.

Deep knowledge of the domain, technologies, the product, and the development organization was needed for effective development. The unavoidable learning was accompanied with estimation and product quality problems.

4.4   Impact of Challenges on Productivity and Delay of Scrum Teams

The Scrum team members reported that the challenges caused problems in project planning, in shared understanding (SU) and coordination between the team, other teams, and stakeholders, and in software quality assurance (SQA). Table 3 gives an overview of the impact of the challenges on the Scrum teams.

Table 3. Impact of Challenges on Scrum Team (*italics*: quotes).

Role	Challenge	Impact	Rationale / Mechanism
Scrum Master	Requirements Quality (RQ)	**Planning:** Planning uncertainty and overestimation.	*There are overestimations when requirements not clear or they are missing.*
	Estimates (ES)	**Planning:** Overestimation.	*If I didn't estimate the size of the feature or predict the feature to be unstable then my schedule gets extended.*

Table 3. (*continued*)

Role	Challenge	Impact	Rationale / Mechanism
Developer	Estimates (ES)	**Planning:** Inadequate time budget for implementation.	*Estimates from unqualified people do not match real effort.*
	Requirements Stability (RV)	**Planning:** Deviations from software design and project schedule.	*The reasons for deviation are evolving requirements and some technical challenges.*
	Decision-making (DM)	**Planning:** Project plan was not concrete enough.	*Involvement of all the key stakeholders from all teams ... will lead to development of a concrete plan.*
	Test Infrastructure (TI)	**Planning:** Deviations from project schedule.	*Also external factors affect the schedule. Developers finish the development, but the scrum server is not available for testing.*
	Domain or Technology Knowledge (DTK)	**Planning:** Deviations from project schedule.	*Using a new technology without evaluating it could be a potential risk that can cause a plan to get derailed.*
	Communication Quality (CQ)	**SU and Coordination:** Coordination problems and misunderstandings between stakeholders and developers.	*We lack communication across locations. Time zones are different. This causes delay when queries need to be answered. They think about dependencies, but forget to tell.*
	Decision-making (DM)	**SU and Coordination:** Team coordination and component consistency problems.	*Workshops should be conducted by having all stakeholders in one place.*
	Domain or Technology Knowledge (DTK)	**SU:** Software design conflicts between teams at different sites.	*The European architects are not aware of the latest technology and still implement [the old] concepts in new solutions. We learned SE much later with new technology. So we have a problem in accepting that.*
	Documentation Quality (DQ)	**SU:** Code understanding difficulties and delayed code changes and bug fixing.	*Developer pairs code without writing comments because they know each other. But a third person faces lot of issues.*
	Clarity of Done (CD)	**SQA:** Failed acceptance of features.	*Perspectives of developers and product managers differ sometimes. What we consider done is not by product manager.*
Tester	Requirements Selection (RS)	**Planning:** Varying test effort between sprints with ineffective use of test resources. Re-work of tests.	*During the sprints the test cases are written just for requirements without considering the [whole] workflow ... When the workflow starts coming, the test cases have to be modified to a large extent.*
	Decision-making (DM)	**SQA:** Insufficient alignment of software design and tests.	*Testers don't always get into design discussions because they are pre-occupied with testing the previous sprints.*

Most of the planning problems were visible in the uncertainty of estimates and plans that led to inadequate time budget and deviations from project schedule. They affected Scrum masters and developers. The uncertainties were caused by unclear and unstable requirements, insufficient qualification, competence, and participation of decision-makers, and scarce shared resources. Testers were confronted with another kind of planning problem. Splitting the implementation of requirements over multiple releases led to uneven distribution of effort and to re-work of test cases.

The problems in shared understanding with other teams and with stakeholders were encountered by developers. These problems were visible in misunderstandings and coordination problems that led to inconsistent design and development results and ultimately resulted in re-work. The problems were caused by challenges of insufficient knowledge, communication, documentation, and participation in decision-making.

The quality assurance problems were encountered by developers and testers. Software and tests were insufficiently aligned and features failed acceptance by stakeholders and users. These problems were caused by problems in shared understanding and insufficient participation in decision-making had to be corrected with re-work.

4.5   Impact of Challenges on Productivity and Delay of Global Project Teams

The managers and architects indicated that the challenges caused problems in plan quality, in development capacity, in coordination between teams, in shared understanding between teams and stakeholders, and in software quality assurance. Table 4 gives an overview.

Table 4. Impact of Challenges on Global Projects (*italics*: quotes)

Role	Challenge	Impact	Rationale / Mechanism
Product Manager	Competitors' Influence (CI)	**Planning:** Changes in time-to-market and priorities.	*The competitors come up with a similar product. Then the product needs to release earlier with at least the same features.*
	Team Stability (TS)	**Planning:** Re-planning with scope reduction or deadline postponement.	*[When project members leave] the management does not have budget for additional head count. In that case the deadline is increased or the scope reduced.*
Project Manager	Testing Completeness (TC)	**Planning:** Underestimated effort for bug-fixing.	*The external testing is only done at the end of a release and not after each sprint. It might reveal that the algorithm is not fully tuned to real world cases. Another 2 or 3 weeks are spent on adjusting the product.*
	Communication Quality (CQ)	**SU:** Misunderstandings between product and project managers and remote team members	*The reason for delay is lack of clarity at each development step - design, coding, and testing. This is because of limited communication across multiple sites.*
	Team Dynamics (TD)	**Coordination:** Coordination problems between teams.	*Typically interdependency is not really considered. Every scrum group has its own priorities to finish its tasks.*

Table 4. (*continued*)

Role	Challenge	Impact	Rationale / Mechanism
	Progress Measurement (PM)	**Coordination:** Coordination problems among development teams.	*Re-implementation due to bugs or changes from customer is not updated to the release backlog. Some scrum teams may not be aware of the changes.*
Architect	Non-functional Requirements (NFR)	**Planning and SQA:** Defect discovery in system testing or feature delivery. Late costly changes.	*Demonstrations do not demonstrate the NFRs. This comes as a defect in large scale testing or in test of the system limits. This requires change of design, which is costly.*
	Requirements Stability (RV)	**Planning and Coordination:** Solution redesign during development. Plan changes. Increased coordination effort.	*Changes in NFRs caused refactoring of design and code.*
	Integration (IN)	**SQA:** Irreproducible defects at integration testing and difficult root-cause analysis.	*Other components may have caused the defect. We see a trend that defects at this stage are not reproducible or consistent. Fixes for these defects are not easy.*
Integration Manager	Integrations (IN)	**Capacity:** Not enough people working on integration	A dedicated integration team was not setup until last year: *there are not enough people working on it as the people who are involved are still learning about the system.*
	Communication Quality (CQ)	**Coordination:** Incomplete awareness of dependencies.	*Even though at some instance they think about dependencies then they may forget to tell. Then we don't find out.*
Technology Manager	Estimation (ES)	**Capacity:** Teams overloaded with work.	*Actual work is much more than people would think.*
	Requirements Stability (RV)	**Capacity:** Congested backlogs.	*The impact of change can be felt for a long time.*
	Clarity of Done (CD)	**Coordination:** Wrong understanding of real progress.	*If all [teams] report green but they still have some open tasks then at the end to the management it is all green.*

Many of the problems at the global project level were not visible at the Scrum team level and related to enabling and coordinating the teams and integrating their results. Problems of shared understanding were less a concern than on Scrum team level. Planning problems were experienced at a similar extent, but with different causes.

The planning problems affected first product managers, project managers, and architects. Market changes and resource problems led to scope and deadline changes. Requirement changes and failed external regulatory tests led to redesign, delays, and increased coordination effort. Related were capacity problems that were stated by the integration and technology managers. The learning process and repercussions of changes congested backlogs, overloaded teams, and introduced delays.

Coordination problems were mentioned by all interviewed roles except the product managers. Sub-optimized plans, inconsistent reporting, insufficient communication, and requirements changes caused misaligned work, inconsistent work results, and wrong understanding of real progress. The communication challenges also introduced problems of shared understanding between management and remote teams. Together with ignored and unstable NFR they led to hard problems in quality assurance.

5 Discussion

Many of the reported challenges were well known. They represented a selection of challenges reported in market-driven requirements engineering [20], global software engineering [18], and innovation [24]. Agile development did not change importance of these challenges. Instead it added the previously hidden angle of product management and introduced new problems such as those due to stepwise implementation of complex requirements.

The development organization showed a need for predictability, dependability, stability, and effective use of an appropriate amount of resources. On a global level, it turned to solutions offered by planning, coordination, and communication. The complexity of the products and of the organization, however, led to the described challenges that generated productivity problems and delays. The problems generated by these challenges differed depending on the organizational level. The Scrum teams struggled mainly with plan stability and adherence, shared understanding, and quality assurance. The global projects battled mainly with project plans, enabling and coordinating the Scrum teams, and integrating results.

The study results were partially consistent with previous research on determinants for productivity and delays. Many determinants of the studied projects were the same as the determinants of pre-agile projects [2, 3, 12, 17]. Requirements could only be stabilized when the product and product use were clear enough. Unclear requirements, limited knowledge of domain, technology, and the organization, and communication problems led to uncertain estimates, unstable plans and integration, and quality problems with the consequent need for rework.

Determinants that were not reported by the subjects to be problematic were team sizing [3] and tooling [6]. They seemed to have been adequately addressed by the organization.

The study discovered new determinants that affected productivity and delay: stability of markets and organization, consistency of the development process with product characteristics, and support of complexity of the organization. Releases of competitive products and personnel fluctuation affected scope, deadlines, and capacity. Complex requirements, regulations that imposed documentation and product certification, and separation of product development and maintenance were difficult to handle with the chosen agile approach. Shared understanding, collaboration between teams, and consistent reporting were addressed unsatisfactorily, especially because they led to costly ripple effects.

Solutions are known that can help to avoid many of the challenges and mitigate their impact on productivity problems and delays. For example, an approach to stabilizing requirements is structured handshaking between stakeholders and development teams with implementation proposals [13]. Implementation proposals allow focusing design and prototyping on critical features and stabilizing the concerned requirements with stakeholder feedback. Sufficient coverage of requirements with implementation proposals increased reliability of project plans.

Requirements structuring with feature trees modularizes specifications and plans according to alternative decision options [14]. Such modularization reduces planning complexity, simplifies progress reporting, and integrates backlogs of individual teams in a consistent manner.

Collocation of some members of distributed teams with scrum masters and product owners and regular, well-prepared global scrum team meetings improves shared understanding and team coordination, and reduces integration problems [33]. Other collections of practices exist and provide concrete approaches for addressing challenges related to scaling agile development [22].

The overall development throughput can be improved by capturing the flow of software development by tracking the lifecycle stage of features and visualizing progress with cumulative flow diagrams [26]. This specific approach can be used as an early warning system and for identifying bottlenecks.

The list of solutions is by far not exhaustive. Selection of an appropriate combination of practices and evaluation of their effects is the concern of the next process improvement steps at the studied organization. Research towards understanding the fundamental principles of productivity and delays in large-scale agile development will support that work.

6   Conclusions

This paper presented the results of an empirical study that examines the challenges that affected productivity and delays encountered in large-scale agile development of a global product company. Data was collected from 14 interviewees and covered 8 roles in 5 relevant projects.

In relation to RQ1, which challenges led to productivity problems and delays, 17 challenges were identified that were caused by project and organizational complexity, by product characteristics, and by knowledge limitations. Many of the challenges were well known, but have not been removed by the agile development process. Instead, the agile focus added new problems such as those due to stepwise implementation of complex requirements.

RQ2 asked how the involved project roles were affected by these challenges. The interviewees identified 28 mechanisms of how the challenges affected the roles. The problems at the global project level were mostly about enabling, planning, and coordinating the Scrum teams and integrating their results. The problems at the Scrum teams level were about shared understanding, planning, and quality assurance.

Interestingly, the organization did not abolish planning for their large projects. Instead, consistent with previous research on productivity and delays, it wanted predictability, dependability, stability, and effective use of resources. Known determinants for productivity and delays were confirmed and new ones related to software product management, process-product alignment, and process-organization alignment discovered.

In sum, the study describes an in-depth analysis of an organization that has adopted agile processes for large-scale product development, discovered misalignments of this approach with the project context, and intends to adjust its processes to improve productivity and delays. The results are a basis for selecting appropriate solutions and for better understanding principles of productivity and delays with future theoretical and empirical studies.

Acknowledgments. This work was funded by The Knowledge Foundation in Sweden under a research grant for the Blekinge Engineering Software Qualities (BESQ) project. We would like to thank our anonymous industry partner for enabling the here reported research.

References

1. Abrahamsson, P., et al.: Agile software development methods: Review and analysis, vol. 478. VTT Publications, Espoo (2002)
2. Basili, V.R., Briand, L., Melo, W.: How Reuse Influences Productivity in Object-Oriented Systems. Communications of the ACM 39(10), 104–116 (1996)
3. Blackburn, J., Scudder, G., Van Wassenhove, L.: Improving Speed and Productivity of Software Development: A Global Survey of Software Developers. IEEE Transactions on Software Engineering 22(12), 875–885 (1996)
4. Boehm, B., Turner, R.: Management Challenges to Implementing Agile Processes in Traditional Development Organizations. IEEE Software 22(5), 30–39 (2005)
5. Briand, L., El Emam, K., Melo, W.: An inductive method for software process improvement: concrete steps and guidelines. In: El Emam, K., Madhavji, N. (eds.) Elements of Software Process Assessment & Improvement. Wiley-IEEE Computer Society (2001)
6. Bruckhaus, T., et al.: The Impact of Tools on Software Productivity. IEEE Software 13(5), 29–38 (1996)
7. Cain, J., McCrindle, R.: An Investigation into the Effects of Code Coupling on Team Dynamics and Productivity. In: 26th Annual International Computer Software and Applications Conference (COMPSAC 2002), Oxford, UK (2002)
8. Cardozo, E., et al.: SCRUM and productivity in software projects: a systematic literature review. In: 14th International Conference on Evaluation and Assessment in Software Engineering (EASE 2010), Keele, UK (2010)
9. Chow, T., Cao, D.-B.: A survey study of critical success factors in agile software projects. Journal of Systems and Software 81(6), 961–971 (2007)
10. CMMI Product Team, CMMI for Development, Version 1.3. Carnegie Mellon University (2010)
11. Cohn, M., Ford, D.: Introducing an Agile Process to an Organization. IEEE Computer 36(6), 74–78 (2003)
12. Damian, D., et al.: Requirements payoff: An empirical study of the relationship between requirements practice and software productivity, quality and risk management. University of Victoria (2003)

13. Fricker, S., et al.: Handshaking with Implementation Proposals: Negotiating Requirements Understanding. IEEE Software 27(2), 72–80 (2010)
14. Fricker, S., Schumacher, S.: Release Planning with Feature Trees: Industrial Case. In: Regnell, B., Damian, D. (eds.) REFSQ 2011. LNCS, vol. 7195, pp. 288–305. Springer, Heidelberg (2012)
15. Garcia, R., Calantone, R.: A Critical Look at Technological Innovation Typology and Innovativeness Terminology: A Literature Review. The Journal of Product Innovation Management 19(2), 110–132 (2002)
16. Garvin, D.: Building a Learning Organization. Harvard Business Review 71(4), 78–91 (2000)
17. Genuchten, V.: Why is Software Late? An Empirical Study of Reasons For Delay in Software Development. IEEE Transactions on Software Engineering 17(6), 582–590 (1991)
18. Herbsleb, J., Moitra, D.: Global Software Development. IEEE Software 18(2), 16–20 (2001)
19. Hoda, R., et al.: Agility in Context. In: OOPSLA/SPLASH 2010, Reno/Tahoe, Nevada, USA (2010)
20. Karlsson, L., et al.: Requirements Engineering Challenges in Market-Driven Software Development - An Interview Study with Practitioners. Information and Software Technology 49(6), 588–604 (2007)
21. Kruchten, P.: Scaling Down Large Projects to Meet the Agile Sweet Sport. In: IBM developerWorks. IBM (2004)
22. Leffingewell, D.: Scaling Software Agility: Best Practices for Large Enterprises. Addison-Wesley (2007)
23. Lindvall, M., et al.: Agile Software Development in Large Organizations. IEEE Computer 37(12), 26–34 (2004)
24. Lynn, G., Morone, J., Paulson, A.: Marketing and Discontinuous Innovation. California Management Review 38(3), 8–37 (1996)
25. Nerur, S., Mahapatra, R.K., Mangalaraj, G.: Challenges of Migrating to Agile Methodologies. Communications of the ACM 48(5), 73–78 (2005)
26. Petersen, K., Wohlin, C.: Measuring the flow in lean software development. Software Practice and Experience 41(9), 975–996 (2010)
27. Pettersson, F., et al.: A practitioner's guide to light weight software process assessment and improvement planning. Journal of Systems and Software 81(6), 972–995 (2007)
28. Ramesh, B., et al.: Can Distributed Software Development be Agile? Communications of the ACM 49(10), 41–46 (2006)
29. Reifer, D., Maurer, F., Erdogmus, H.: Scaling Agile Methods. IEEE Software 20(4), 12–14 (2003)
30. Robson, C.: Real World Research: A Resource for Social Scientists and Practitioner Researchers, 2nd edn. Blackwell Publishing (2002)
31. Strauss, A., Corbin, J.: Basics of Qualitative Research: Techniques and Procedures for Developing Grounded Theory. SAGE Publications (1998)
32. Sutherland, J., et al.: Fully Distributed Scrum: Linear Scalability of Production between San Francisco and India. In: Agile Conference (AGILE 2008), Toronto, Canada (2009)
33. Sutherland, J., et al.: Disributed Scrum: Agile Project Management with Outsourced Development Teams. In: 40th Hawaii International Conference on System Sciecnes, Hawaii, USA (2007)
34. Yin, R.K.: Case study research: Design and methods. SAGE Publications (2008)

Continuous Release Planning in a Large-Scale Scrum Development Organization at Ericsson

Ville T. Heikkilä[1], Maria Paasivaara[1],
Casper Lassenius[1], and Christian Engblom[2]

[1] Department of Computer Science and Engineering,
Aalto University, Helsinki, Finland
{ville.t.heikkila,maria.paasivaara,casper.lassenius}@aalto.fi
[2] Oy LM Ericsson Ab, Kirkkonummi, Finland
christian.engblom@ericsson.com

Abstract. Scrum development at large-scale requires a release planning process that supports the agile way of working and planning. Most of the existing release planning processes are plan-driven and ill suited for a large Scrum organization. This case study describes how release planning was conducted in a 350-person Scrum development organization with over 20 teams at Ericsson in 2011, and the related challenges and benefits. Data was collected with 39 interviews which were transcribed, coded and analysed. The release planning process was continuous and characterized by regular scoping and prioritization decisions, and by incremental elaboration of features. The challenges were the overcommitment caused by external pressure, managing non-feature specific work, and balancing between development efficiency and building generalist teams. The benefits were the increased flexibility and decreased development lead time, waste eliminated in the planning process, and increased developer motivation.

Keywords: release planning, scrum, scaling agile, case study.

1 Introduction

The Scrum agile software development method [1] has become mainstream in the software development community [2]. Scrum was originally created for small co-located teams [1]. Scrum emphasizes face-to-face communication [1], which puts a limit on the maximum practical size of the development team [3]. The early normative Scrum literature provided little guidance for the long-term planning of software, as the focus was on the planning and development of software one iteration (sprint) at a time in a single team, single project context [1]. However, large development organizations soon started to adopt Scrum practices [2]. In large organizations, there are multiple levels of planning which are performed on different time horizons and by different actors [4,5,6]. We adopt a three-level planning model where the levels are *strategic planning*, *release planning* and *operational planning*. Strategic planning is the interface between business

H. Baumeister and B. Weber (Eds.): XP 2013, LNBIP 149, pp. 195–209, 2013.

management and development and it is performed on a long term, multi-release time horizon [4]. Release planning, in agile software development context, is concerned with deciding the feature content of the next release and on planning how to most efficiently create that content [7]. Operational planning is concerned with how the implementation of the features is achieved on a day-to-day basis [5]. The early Scrum literature describes operational planning in depth, superficially covers release planning, and almost completely ignores strategic planning [1].

One way to scale a Scrum development organization is to employ multiple small Scrum teams [6,8,9]. In a such organization, the strategic planning is mostly agnostic towards the development method [4] and the operational planning can follow the Scrum practices [1]. However, release planning must support the Scrum development organization by providing goals and direction on how the release should be constructed [4]. Although successful release planning is an important success factor in agile software development projects [10] and a challenging aspect of agile adoption in market-driven product development [11], there is very little empirical research literature of large-scale agile release planning. Thus, there is a clear need for empirical research that describes how release planning is conducted in large agile organizations. To start filling this gap in the empirical research, we conducted a case study in a large organization that had adopted Scrum. The case organization was a node development organization of Ericsson. The specific research questions were:

RQ1: What was the release planning process?
RQ2: What were the challenges related to the release planning process?
RQ3: What were the benefits of the continuous release planning process?

The rest of this paper is organized as follows: We first review existing related work on release planning in large-scale agile development organizations in Section 2. We describe our research methods in Section 3. We describe the case organization in Section 4. In Section 5, we describe the results of the case study. In Section 6, we discuss the case and threats to the validity of our results. Finally, in Section 7, we provide conclusions and directions for future work.

2   Release Planning in Large-Scale Agile Development

Most release planning research has focused on proposing mathematical optimization models [12]. This approach has resulted in models which either are too simple to be useful in practice, or so complex that practitioners find it difficult to provide the necessary input values and find it hard to trust the output, as they cannot comprehend the process that created it [13,14,15]. In addition, the models typically contain assumptions which do not hold in many software development organizations; the models assume a common understanding of requirements, while in reality such understanding arises thorough continuous knowledge generation and sharing. The models assume that the requirements selection criteria are stable, while in reality the criteria and their weights may change over time. The models assume that dependencies between requirements are clearly

Table 1. Details of the data collection

Interviews	39 (Finland 28, Hungary 11)
Roles[a]	Middle and upper managers (6), Agile coach (1), Scrum Masters (6), Developers (13), Line managers (3), Product owners (7), Technical specialists / architects (5)
Interview lengths	Managers & the coach: 2-3h, others: 1-2h

[a] Total of 41 roles. Two interviewees had dual roles.

defined and pairwise, while in reality the dependencies are often unclear and complex. Finally, the models assume that development capacity is the main constraint, while in reality combined domain and system knowledge often is the critical resource [15].

The existing empirical research on release planning in large-scale agile development is scarce. When using Scrum, large-scale release planning can be performed in joint release planning sessions where all development teams and other stakeholders come together to plan the next release [6,16].

3   Data Collection and Analysis

Our case was purposefully selected, as it provided an opportunity to perform an information rich study [17,18] in a large organization with a long history of developing a complex product. The organization had adopted Scrum gradually over the 18 months preceding the interviews, which made the project an excellent candidate for the study. We first interviewed nine people who had managerial roles (who were our *key informants* [18]). They provided us with an overview of the organization history, goals, growth, structure and the planning process used in the organization. To enable the triangulation of data sources [17], the rest of the interviewees had different roles, belonged to different Scrum teams and had different amounts of experience. All interviews were voice-recorded. The first three authors conducted the interviews. We selected the *general interview guide* approach [17] in order to maintain adaptability to the roles and individual experiences of the interviewees while simultaneously making sure that the relevant topics were explored. We updated the interview guide constantly based on new insights from the previous interviews [17]. We asked the interviewees to describe their own experiences of how the release planning process worked and the successes and challenges in the release planning process. Details of the data collection are shown in Table 1.

The interviews were transcribed by a professional transcription company. We coded the interviews with a process that was inspired by the grounded-theory method [19]. During the coding process, we combined related concepts into new concepts and categories using the constant comparison technique [19]. In total, we coded 625 passages (with some minor overlap). Finally, we extracted passages related to categories of planning and organization and re-read all the passages to construct the descriptions of the release planning process and the challenges and benefits related to it. The challenges and benefits included in the results were perceived as the most important by multiple interviewees from multiple roles in the organization.

4   The Case Organization

4.1   Background

This paper is based on a case study of an Ericsson node development unit in 2011. The unit developed a large systems product consisting of both software and hardware. The product was a single node which handled specific type of traffic in telecommunications networks. The development of this product had started over ten years ago and at the time of the study it was used by operators all over the world, while the further development of the product still continued. The focus of this paper was on the organization that developed the software of the product.

The organization begun the process improvement initiative in 2009. The existing, plan-driven process worked quite well, but the management wanted to decrease the development lead time, improve flexibility, increase motivation of the developers, and increase the efficiency of quality assurance. The management studied different options and chose Scrum as a best fit for their needs. They started with one pilot Scrum team to test the approach. Soon a few more teams were created, and in quick succession the rest of the Scrum teams were formed. At the time of the interviews in 2011, all of the over twenty development teams, spread across two sites in Finland and Hungary, had been using Scrum for almost a year. The transformation did not stop there and the way of working was continuously improved, as reflected by the interviewees who called the transformation a "journey".

Before the transformation, the development had been arranged as a traditional plan-driven project organization. The release planning had begun two years before the release date when the scope of the next release was decided by the product management. Technical specialists then created an implementation plan for the requirements and the plans were handed to the developers for implementation. When the implementation was ready, the software was put thorough multiple stages of testing and verification, and finally shipped as a part of the generally available products and as software updates.

4.2   Case Organization Structure

The development organization and its stakeholders are illustrated in Figure 1. In the rest of this section, we describe the roles and responsibilities of the members of the case organization.

Product Owner Team. The organization of product owners deviated from the basic Scrum model [1]. Instead of having team-specific product owners, a product

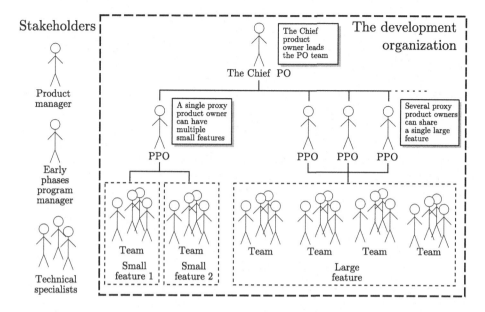

Fig. 1. The case organization structure

owner team (PO team) had been created to accommodate the large number of teams and the globally distributed structure of the organization. The PO team consisted of a Chief product owner (Chief PO) and ten proxy product owners (PPOs). The whole PO team was jointly responsible for the feature development to mitigate personnel risks. The PPOs rotated between teams when features were completed. Based on the size of the features, one PPO could work with two of cross-functional teams when both teams were developing their own small features, or a group of two to three PPOs could take collectively responsibility of one large feature developed by several teams. The Chief PO was responsible for managing the PO Team. The Chief PO acted as an arbiter between the development organization and the stakeholders external to the development organization. The main task of the PO team was to manage and synchronize the work of the development teams.

Development Teams. The Scrum development organization was arranged around Scrum development teams [1]. These teams of 6-7 persons were originally formed with the goal of having all the needed competence for end-to-end development in each team. However, the managers soon realized that this goal would be very challenging to achieve with a large, over ten-year-old product, since the different areas of the product required very specific technical knowledge. Thus, the development teams, in practice, were usually assigned features that were best suited for the competence and previous experience of the team members. The teams had different amounts of experience of Scrum development practices and of working in a cross-functional way. The teams on both sites were located near each other to allow the teams to easily visit each other.

Stakeholders. There were several stakeholders that had an important role in the release planning process, but who did not belong to the development organization. A product management function was responsible for the long term planning of the product from the business perspective. A single product manager (PM) was responsible for the software part of the product and she was also the main point of contact between the development organization and the product management. The PM mostly communicated with the Chief PO although the other members of the development organization could contact the PM directly, if required. In addition, there was an early phases program manager who was responsible for managing the early phases of the release planning process. The product management and the development organization were assisted by technical specialists who were people with extensive knowledge of telecommunication technology.

5 Results

In this section, we present our results. In Section 5.1, we describe the work items, decision makers and process steps of the release planning process. We describe challenges found in the case in Section 5.2 and benefits created by the release planning process in Section 5.3.

5.1 Release Planning Process

The new continuous release planning process, depicted in Figure 2, contained five feature decisions, F0 to F4. The decisions were made by two steering groups, which both had weekly meetings. Decisions F0-F2, which were made by *the portfolio steering group*, belonged to the *early phases* where the feasibility, profitability and risk of the feature were studied and no actual feature implementation was performed. Decisions F3-F4 were made by *the development steering group*.

The public releases of the software were tied to the calendar year. Two major versions of the software and two smaller maintenance updates of the software were published each year. The new development model would have allowed more frequent public releases, but the customers preferred the aforementioned release schedule. The contents of each release were tentatively planned by the product management. The actual contents of a release were based on the features that were completed in time. Following the F-process, those features which had passed the F4-milestone could be included. In the rest of this section, we describe the steps, the planning artefacts, and the stakeholders of the release planning process in detail.

Work Items. The case organization had three level work item hierarchy. The levels were called *features*, *epics* and *user stories*. All three level work items were stored in the product backlog, which was in an electronic backlog management tool Jira.

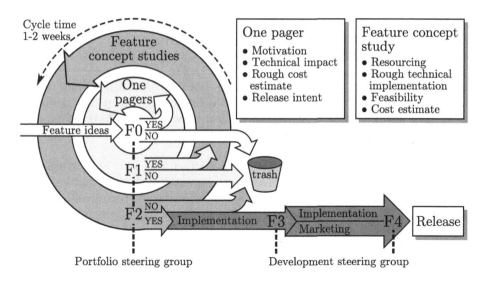

Fig. 2. The release planning process

Features were the main way that requirements were managed in the new process. The Chief PO was responsible for maintaining and prioritizing the product backlog on the feature level. The size of features varied considerably from a single team for a couple of months to a year for ten teams.

Epics were split from features. Epics were large, semi-independent functional requirements that produced value on their own. Each epic was typically team-specific. The purpose of the epic-level was to decrease dependencies between teams working on the same feature by grouping related user stories, and to provide a view to the multi-sprint development plan of the feature. Epics were split into user stories by the PPO(s) responsible for the feature together with the team responsible for the epic in the team's bi-weekly grooming sessions. The user stories were also estimated in the grooming sessions. The teams had a physical sprint backlog which contained the team's user stories.

Portfolio Steering Group. The portfolio steering group consisted of representatives from all stakeholders of the development organization, including the product manager, the Chief PO, the early phases program manager and the technical specialists. The group made decisions related to the early phases of feature development. Any number of F0-, F1- and F2-decisions could be made in a single portfolio steering group meeting, which were held once a week.

Development Steering Group. The development steering group included the Chief PO and the product manager. Selected PPOs and other stakeholders from the organization could also participate in the meetings if deemed necessary. The group made decisions during the implementation of the feature. Any number of F3- and F4-decisions could be made in a single development steering group meeting, which were held once a week.

F0-Decision. The first step in the F-decision process was the F0-decision. Before the F0-decision, the product manager and the early phases program manager had to have a very rough idea of the feature. When time was right, the early phases program manager presented the feature idea in a portfolio steering group meeting. The steering group then decided to either take the feature into development, to postpone it, or to abandon it. If the feature was postponed, it would be brought into F0-decision later on. If the feature was taken into development, the creation of a one pager could begin.

One Pager. The one pager described on an abstract level what the feature was and why it was needed, including the rough estimates of the cost and business impact of the feature, and the intended release which would tentatively include the feature. The goal was to fit all the information on a single presentation slide, hence the name one pager. The early phases PM had the official responsibility of creating the one pager, but in practice it was written by a technical specialist. The maximum effort of writing the one pager was one or two days, and the time given to the writing was two weeks.

F1-Decision. The F1-decision could be made after the one pager was ready. The Chief PO presented the one pager to the group. The portfolio steering group then decided to either to abandon the feature or to create a feature concept study (FCS). If the portfolio steering group decided to create the FCS, the group could then decide either to initiate the FCS immediately or to postpone it, based on how urgent and large the feature was. In case the FCS was initiated immediately, the steering group selected a PPO and team(s) for writing it. If the FCS was postponed, the assignment would be made in a later portfolio steering group meeting. If the feature was not abandoned, the feature was added to the product backlog and prioritized by the Chief PO.

Feature Concept Study. The writing of the feature concept study begun after the F1-decision to initiate it had been made. The purpose of the FCS was to provide the information that was needed to decide whether the feature should be implemented. The FCS was written by a virtual team consisting of a PPO, who was primarily responsible for the study, and members from one or several teams. The virtual team members were typically from the teams that would be assigned to implement the feature. The virtual team was assisted by the technical specialists if required. Having developers to contribute to the FCS was a notable change from the previous planning process where the developers did not contribute to requirements planning. The length and the writing time of a FCS varied by the size of the feature, but the goal was to get the writing done in under two weeks.

F2-Decision. The F2-decision was the last step in the early phases program. When the feature concept study was ready, the Chief PO presented it to the portfolio steering group, which then decided to either take the feature into development or to abandon it. If the feature was taken into development, it was given a non-binding target release. The Chief PO had the option to postpone the beginning of the implementation if he though that there was more important work and the target release could be reached nevertheless. Otherwise, the team(s) begun the development of the feature immediately.

Feature Implementation. The implementation of a feature could officially begin after a F2-decision to implement the feature was done and when the Chief PO decided it was time to start the implementation. Typically, the implementation was started by the PPO and the team(s) that created the FCS. In large features, more teams were added during the implementation when they become available. When the feature neared completion, the number of teams was reduced to one or two teams that were responsible for finalizing the feature, and the rest of the teams were freed to develop other features. On the team level the planning was performed mostly following the basic Scrum process [1].

F3-Decision. When the implementation of a feature was close to completion, the Chief PO proposed F3-decision in the development steering group, which meant that the Chief PO gave a commitment for the completion date of the feature. If the development steering group agreed to the commitment, a F3-decision was made by the group, which meant that marketing of the feature could begin. Otherwise the feature needed to be further developed before the F3-decision.

F4-Decision. When a feature was implemented, tested and integrated into the product, the Chief PO proposed a F4-decision in the development steering group. The steering group could then make a F4-decision which meant that the feature could be included in the next (or a later) public release of the product.

5.2 Challenges

Overcommitment Caused by External Pressure. According to the interviews, the product management still worked in the "old world" way. They requested long-term feature development plans from the PO team, which were not available in the new release planning process, and pressurised them to give premature feature commitments when the release date was approaching. This caused overcommitment by the development organization and decreased the flexibility of the development.

> *... perhaps the product management is not in the new way of working, it easily goes with the old model that we plan one big release ... it feels like we plan a big future release and see what can fit in it.* – A proxy product owner

The case organization tried to mitigate this issue in two ways. First, they tried to improve the predictability of the development by increasing the detail level of FCS's, and by increasing the amount of slack in effort estimates. Second, they created the concept of a minimum marketable feature, which was the set of functionality they could commit to delivering very probably by the next release.

Managing Non-feature Specific Work. In the previous, plan-driven development model the responsibilities of the project management were clearly defined. In the new model, the PO team assumed the responsibility of feature definition and management, but it was unclear who took care of the other project management tasks. These included the handling of the system planning, non feature specific problem reports, system documentation, and external change requests. The PO team had started to have regular meetings where they addressed such issues although it was contrary to the their originally planned responsibilities.

> *Every week we notice things that are not taken care by anybody, that somebody took care of when we had the project organization. ... For example the product documentation that is not directly related to any feature.*
> – A proxy product owner

An additional problem was the prioritization of system improvement work. All features, epics and user stories originated from the product backlog. The developers had difficulties getting system improvement included into the backlog, and if they got it in, they had difficulties getting it included in a development sprint. They also had difficulties finding time to perform system improvement work, as implementing features was implicitly prioritized higher. The development organization attempted to mitigate this issue by making each team take in at least one system improvement user story every sprint.

> *... it is very difficult to participate in things affecting the whole organization or the testing of the whole product, because I have the sprint backlog and I have to get the sprint done first and then if there is time I can perform those things.*
> – A developer

Balancing between Development Efficiency and Building Generalist Teams. Initially the goal of the development organization was to create cross-functional generalist teams that could implement features in all components of the software. However, they quickly realized that many components were technically very difficult and required years of experience to completely understand. This had, in several occasions, caused very long lead times (one to half a year) before a team could implement anything useful in a component. Thus, the portfolio steering group had started mostly assigning features to teams that had the best pre-existing competency in the affected components. Balancing between the development efficiency and building generalist teams was seen difficult especially near the release date when the pressure to get features completed was mounting.

> *... building the competencies has been one of the biggest challenges. ... we have very difficult products where the transfer [of knowledge] is very challenging, it cannot be done in a couple of sprints, it requires several months, in practice. We've had to yield in that, we had to give it to the best [team] ...*
> – A scrum master

5.3 Benefits

Increased Flexibility and Decreased Development Lead Time. In the previous model the release planning was conducted during the first six moths of the two-year project. The changes that could be made to the release after the first six months were typically very small, as they needed to pass thorough a tardy change management process. In the worst case, a feature had over three year lead time from a customer request to a public release.

> ... *[previously] releasing one package took 18-24 months. In the beginning we performed this system planning which took maybe half an year. And if you did not get the right contents in the release during the first half a year ... it was immensely difficult to get any changes into the project. ... If some essential functionality was missing from it, we missed the train, I had to wait to the end of the current project and then the two years after [that]. Which was a very long time* – The product manager

The new process was seen as improvement to the flexibility of development. The new release planning process allowed making changes to the contents of the release on a relative short notice. The feature development schedule was no more tied to the release schedule, which immensely decreased the lead time of the feature development.

> *Now it is like, okay, let's add it to the list. And no worries about where we are going with the change. It's there and in a way nothing was changed even though a new thing was added to the list. I think it is a really good improvement. The flexibility is on another level.* – The product manager

Eliminating Waste in the Planning Process. The general concept in the process was that in the F0-F2 steps the sunk costs would be relatively small, and thus early identification of too expensive or infeasible features would save development resources. In addition, by employing the minimum marketable feature concept, the case organization was able to concentrate on developing the most important parts of the features.

> *What is good in it [the F-decision process] is that ... it in a way divides the decision making, which is a good thing. We can cut it [the feature] at any point, ... if we see that the feature passes the time window or otherwise. It gives structure to the decision making and enables us to make smaller decisions and in that way separate the feature decision from the release decision.* – A manager

Increased Developer Motivation. The developers were included in the feature planning starting from the early phases, which allowed them to contribute to the planning and gave them the visibility to the big-picture of the feature. This increased the motivation of the developers.

> ... *one of the product management involved in the [feature] travelled here to [Hungary] and had a one-day workshop. Why [the feature] is needed for the customer, what information they get, what kind of reasoning [is] behind this feature. ... It was a motivation boost for the team, to see that what they are doing is really, means something for the [customers].* – A developer

6   Discussion

6.1   RQ1: What Was the Release Planning Process?

Before the agile transformation, the releases were planned by project managers as traditional projects with set resources, schedule and goals. In the new agile process, the release planning was a continuous process where features were initiated based on the availability of resources and the priority of the feature. The release planning process was characterized by regular scoping and prioritization decisions and incremental elaboration of the features before the implementation. The release planning was a collaborative action and the developers took part in the feature planning in early phases of the feature elaboration. Our results support Benestad's and Hannay's observations on release planning [15]. In contrast, most of the proposed models for software release planning treat release planning as an activity that is either performed at the beginning of the release project or over lengthy iterations during the release project and conducted by a few authoritative decision makers in isolation [12,14]. The structure of the development organization was similar to the structure proposed by Leffingwell [6]. However, Leffingwell proposes that the tentative contents of each release should be planned on the user story level in the beginning of each release project [6].

6.2   RQ2: What Were the Challenges Related to the Release Planning Process?

The product management expected precise long-term plans from the development organization. After the transformation, such plans were not created. Many developers would have preferred detailed implementation plans, but such plans were not created any more. Both issues are symptoms of friction between the previous plan driven process and the new agile process. The longing for detailed implementation plans will likely disappear as the developers become more experienced in planning. The conflict between an agile development organization and a plan-driven product management is a recognized challenge in large-scale agile development [2,20]. By employing the minimum marketable feature concept, the case organization was able to provide relatively reliable long term plans without sacrificing flexibility. Although the minimum marketable feature concept is not new in the software development management literature [6,21], it was employed in the case in a novel way to combine long-term planning with flexibility.

There were many tasks which the development teams did not have the competency to perform, for example system level documentation and system level technical planning. In addition, the development of some components required extensive experience and specialized skills. Identifying who should perform such work was a challenge in the case. Initially, Scrum guidance emphasised true cross-functional teams [1]. Several authors of later normative agile development guidance have taken the stance that in large, complex systems there is a place for limited specialization both on the system level and the team level [6,9,22], and our results support this notion.

6.3   RQ3: What Were the Benefits of the Continuous Release Planning Process?

The biggest benefit from the new release planning process was the drastically decreased feature development lead time. The lead time decreased, approximately, from a minimum of two years to a minimum of three months. The short lead time was enabled by the continuous nature of the release planning process and by the flexibility of the Scrum development organization. The short lead time increased the responsiveness of the case organization to customer requests, which created a clear competitive edge [23].

Another benefit was the reduced planning waste. According to the product development queue theory [23], unnecessary inventory is a form of waste that should be eliminated. Compared with the previous, plan driven-process, the incremental elaboration of features in the early phases of the release planning process drastically decreased the inventory of plans and technical specifications waiting on a shelf to be implemented.

The results indicated that software developer's motivation increased because they were included in the decision making and given understanding of the big picture. The existing research on developer motivation [24] supports this result.

6.4   Generalizability and Threats to Validity

In the discussion about the validity of this research, we rely on the definitions of validity and reliability proposed by Yin [18]. Internal validity is not relevant, as this research was neither explanatory nor causal [18]. The main threat to the construct validity of this research was the accuracy of the descriptions. To increase the construct validity, we interviewed multiple persons for each role in the case organization, if possible. The interviews were coded and analysed by the first author. To increase the construct validity, the second and the third author reviewed the analysis. Furthermore, the fourth author of this article was one of our key informants and he also reviewed the analysis.

The external validity of a case study concerns the domain to which the results can be generalized [18]. Based on our study, we can create a hypothesis of the significant characteristics of the domain. First, the system under development was large, multifaceted and technically demanding. Second, the product and release management organizations worked in a plan-driven way and were separate from the development organization. Third, the number of development teams was relatively large. Fourth, the development was distributed on two sites. The results are likely generalizable to single site development, but it difficult to hypothesize how generalizable the results are when the development is distributed on three or more sites.

The main threat to the reliability [18] of this research is the variability in the data collection. The data collection was conducted using the general interview guide approach [17], which introduced variability to the topics discussed in the interviews. However, the large number of interviewees and multiple interviewers allowed data source and investigator triangulation [17] which increased the reliability of the results.

7   Conclusions and Further Work

Release planning is a crucial task in market-driven requirements engineering [11]. Large development organizations have increasingly started adopting agile software development methods [2]. The traditional, plan-driven release planning models are not well suited for agile development organizations where scoping decisions must be made constantly and detailed requirements analysis is performed alongside the implementation [14]. If the release planning process does not support the agile development organization, the development organization will not be able to work efficiently towards the high level goals of the company.

Our case study provides a detailed description of how a large-scale Scrum organization in Ericsson performed release planning, and of the challenges and benefits related to the release planning process. The continuous release planning process is characterized by regular scoping and prioritization decisions, and by the incremental elaboration of features. The challenges were the overcommitment caused by external pressure, managing non-feature specific work and balancing between development efficiency and building generalist teams. The benefits were the waste eliminated in the planning process, the increased flexibility and the decreased development lead time. Our study contributes to the growing knowledge base on scaling agile software development methods.

We will continue to study the case organization as the Scrum development organization becomes more mature and all the stakeholders have had time to adjust to the new development and planning processes. Specifically, we are interested in studying how the product management organization is changed to better work with the Scrum development organization. In addition, it would be interesting to study how other large organizations that have adopted agile development methods perform release planning.

Acknowledgment. We would like to thank Oy LM Ericsson Ab for making this study possible and all the anonymous interviewees for providing valuable contributions to this research. We would like to thank the TiViT Cloud Software Finland-program for funding this research.

References

1. Schwaber, K., Beedle, M.: Agile software development with Scrum. Prentice-Hall, Upper Saddle River (2002)
2. VersionOne, Inc.: 6th Annual "State of Agile Development" Survey (2011)
3. Cockburn, A.: Agile software development. Addison-Wesley, Boston (2002)
4. Rautiainen, K., Lassenius, C., Sulonen, R.: 4CC: A framework for managing software product development. Eng. Manag. J. 14(2), 27–32 (2002)
5. Cohn, M.: Agile estimating and planning. Prentice Hall Professional Technical Reference, Upper Saddle River (2005)
6. Leffingwell, D.: Agile software requirements: lean requirements practices for teams, programs, and the enterprise. Addison-Wesley, Upper Saddle River (2011)

7. Ruhe, G., Saliu, M.O.: The art and science of software release planning. IEEE Softw. 22(6), 47–53 (2005)
8. Schwaber, K.: The enterprise and scrum. Microsoft Press, Redmond (2007)
9. Augustine, S.: Managing Agile Projects. Prentice Hall Professional Technical Reference, Upper Saddle River (2008)
10. Chow, T., Cao, D.B.: A survey study of critical success factors in agile software projects. J. Syst. Softw. 81(6), 961–971 (2008)
11. Fogelström, N.D., Gorschek, T., Svahnberg, M., Olsson, P.: The impact of agile principles on market-driven software product development. J. Softw. Maint. Evol.-R. 22(1), 53–80 (2010)
12. Svahnberg, M., Gorschek, T., Feldt, R., Torkar, R., Saleem, S.B., Shafique, M.U.: A systematic review on strategic release planning models. Inform. Softw. Tech. 52(3), 237–248 (2010)
13. Carlshamre, P.: Release planning in market-driven software product development: Provoking an understanding. Requir. Eng. 7(3), 139–151 (2002)
14. Jantunen, S., Lehtola, L., Gause, D.C., Dumdum, U.R., Barnes, R.J.: The challenge of release planning. In: Proceedings of the Fifth International Workshop on Software Product Management, pp. 36–45 (2011)
15. Benestad, H.C., Hannay, J.E.: A comparison of model-based and judgment-based release planning in incremental software projects. In: Proceeding of the 33rd International Conference on Software Engineering, pp. 766–775. ACM, New York (2011)
16. Heikkilä, V., Rautiainen, K., Jansen, S.: A revelatory case study on scaling agile release planning. In: Proceedings of the 36th Euromicro Conference on Software Engineering and Advanced Applications, pp. 289–296. IEEE Computer Society (2010)
17. Patton, M.Q.: Qualitative research and evaluation methods, 3rd edn. Sage Publications, Thousand Oaks (2002)
18. Yin, R.K.: Case study research: design and methods, 4th edn. Sage Publications, Thousand Oaks (2009)
19. Adolph, S., Hall, W., Kruchten, P.: Using grounded theory to study the experience of software development. Empir. Softw. Eng. (2011)
20. Lyon, R., Evans, M.: Scaling up pushing scrum out of its comfort zone. In: Proceedings of the Agile 2008 Conference, pp. 395–400 (2008)
21. Denne, M., Cleland-Huang, J.: The incremental funding method: Data-driven software development. IEEE Softw. 21(3), 39–47 (2004)
22. Larman, C., Vodde, B.: Practices for scaling lean & agile development: large, multisite, and offshore product development with large-scale scrum. Addison-Wesley, Upper Saddle River (2010)
23. Reinertsen, D.G.: Principles of product development flow: second generation lean product development. Celeritas Publishing, Redondo Beach (2009)
24. Beecham, S., Baddoo, N., Hall, T., Robinson, H., Sharp, H.: Motivation in software engineering: A systematic literature review. Inform. Softw. Tech. 50(9-10), 860–878 (2008)

Micro Patterns in Agile Software

Giulio Concas, Giuseppe Destefanis,
Michele Marchesi, Marco Ortu, and Roberto Tonelli

Department of Electrical and Electronic Engineering (DIEE)
University of Cagliari
Cagliari, Italy
{concas,giuseppe.destefanis,michele,
marco.ortu,roberto.tonelli}@diee.unica.it

Abstract. In this paper we present a study on micro patterns in different releases of two software systems developed with Object Oriented technologies and Agile process. Micro patterns are design decisions in code that can be easily automatically recognised. Gil and Maman introduced the concept to support providing objective assessment of design decisions [1]. They catalogued 27 micro patterns that capture a variety of programming practices in Java. Micro patterns can be a useful metrics in order to measure the quality of software by showing that certain categories of micro patterns are more fault prone than others, and that the classes that do not correspond to any category of micro patterns are more likely to be faulty. In our study we present some empirical results on two case studies of systems developed with Agile methodologies, and compare them to previous results obtained for non Agile systems. In particular we have verified that the distribution of micro patterns in a software system developed using Agile methodologies does not differ from the distribution studied in other systems, and that the micro patterns fault-proneness is about the same. We also analyzed how the distribution of micro patterns changes in different releases of the same software system. We demonstrate that there is a relationship between the number of faults and the classes that do not match with any micro patterns. We found that these classes are more likely to be fault-prone than the others even in software developed with Agile methodologies.

Keywords: agile, micro pattern, data mining, object oriented programming.

1 Introduction

Software quality metrics [20] aim measuring how much a software is good especially from the point of view of being error-free and easy to modify and maintain. Software quality metrics tend to measure whether software is well structured, not too simple and not too complex, with cohesive modules that minimize their coupling. Many quality metrics have been proposed for software, depending also on the paradigm and languages used there are metrics for structured programming, object-oriented programming, aspect-oriented programming, and so on. In this

H. Baumeister and B. Weber (Eds.): XP 2013, LNBIP 149, pp. 210–222, 2013.

paper, we will focus on micro patterns metrics. Micro patterns are design decisions in code that can be easily and automatically recognized. Gil and Maman introduced the concept to support providing objective assessment of design decisions [1]. They catalogued 27 micro patterns that capture a variety of programming practices in Java, from inheritance, to data encapsulation, to the emulation of typical practices of procedural programming. The 27 micro patterns proposed by Gil and Maman were shown by them to be present in 75 % of classes they analyzed. Some of those patterns are regarded as anti patterns [10] representing practices that are considered to be poor design practice although it is important to emphasize that there is no agreement about which micro patterns are considered anti patterns. Thus classes can be divided into 2 categories: MP (Micro Patterns) and NMP (no Micro Pattern) namely those that match one or more of the 27 micro patterns, and those that do not match any micro patterns. Given the purpose of micro patterns, a question naturally arises as to whether there is a relationship between the use of different patterns and the quality of the code. In particular there are no studies investigating the diffusion and the distribution of micro patterns in software systems developed using Agile methodologies [2].

In this work we will present the possible use of micro patterns metrics to indirectly assess the quality of the developed software, by showing the relationship between micro patterns and faults and in this context, we assess the ability of micro patterns to discriminate the usage of Agile practices. We present results on different releases of two software systems on two industrial case-study. We understand that the presented evidence is anecdotal, but with real software projects it is very difficult to plan multi-project researches of this kind. This is because software houses tend to be very secretive about their projects. We hope that other researchers will try to replicate the presented results on similar projects whose data they can access. The target of our research is the evolution of a software project consisting of the implementation of floss-AR, a program to manage the Register of Research of universities and research institutes. floss-AR was developed with a full object-oriented (OO) approach and released with GPL v.2 open source license. The second system is a Web application, which has been implemented through a specialization of an open source software project, jAPS (Java Agile Portal System) [6], that is a Java framework for Web portal creation. This system is certified as a software developed using Agile methodologies.

In order to verify the use of Agile methodologies during the development phases of the analyzed systems, we submitted a questionnaire to the developers such as to have greater knowledge about Agile methodologies used.

We decided to organize our paper answering to the following research questions:

- **RQ1:** Do software systems developed with Agile methodologies have a different distribution of micro patterns with respect to non Agile open source systems?
- **RQ2:** Is the micro patterns faults-proneness the same for Agile and non Agile software?
- **RQ3:** Does the micro patterns distribution change during software evolution? If yes, how?

2   Related Works

After the work of Gil and Maman that defines the catalog of the micro patterns [1], several works have appeared in this field. Arcelli and Maggioni suggest a novel approach for the detection of micro patterns which is aimed at identifying types that are very close and similar to a correct micro patterns implementation, even if some of the methods and/or attributes of the type do not comply with the constraints defined by the micro patterns [4]. The new interpretation is based on the number of attributes (NOA) and the number of methods (NOM) of a type. Similar studies to those discussed in our work have been conducted for design patterns [5]: Heuzeroth et al. presented an approach to support the understanding of software systems by detecting design patterns automatically using static and dynamic analyses [7]. Aversano et al. report an empirical study showing that for three open source projects, the number of defects in design-pattern classes is in several cases correlated with the scattering degree of their induced crosscutting concerns, and also varies among different kinds of patterns [8]. Destefanis et al. [3] analyzed the relationship between faults and the remaining 25% of classes that do not match with any micro pattern. They found that these classes are more likely to be fault-prone than the others. Tasharofi et al. [14] provide a set of high-level process patterns for Agile development which have been derived from a study of seven Agile methodologies based on a proposed generic Agile Software Process. These process patterns can promote method engineering by providing classes of common process components with can be used for developing, tailoring, and analyzing Agile methodologies. Concas et al. in [13] studied and discussed the evolution of the classical software metrics and their behavior related to the Agile practices adoption level. The authors show that, in the reported case study, a few metrics are enough to characterize with high significance the various phases of the project. Consequently, software quality, as measured using these metrics, seems directly related to Agile practices adoption.

3   Methodology

The goal of this paper is to investigate the possible relationship between Agile methodologies and micro patterns. We submitted to the developers of the floss-AR software system, a questionnaire in order to evaluate the effective use of Agile methodologies in the early stages of software development [17]. We developed a custom Java tool, based on Gil and Maman's research [1] in order to extract from the software systems analyzed the data relative to the micro patterns distribution. We tested our tool on the data-set used in [1] finding the same results. The tool works in two steps:

- the first step consists in parsing the source code and in generating a series of files containing information relative to the various classes, fields, methods, calls and so on;
- in the second step the tool calculates the presence of the micro patterns for each class of the analyzed system, using the files produced in the first step.

The tool uses the definitions given by Arcelli and Maggioni described in [4]. The class is assigned to only one micro pattern, the one with the highest GSR (Global Similarity Ratio). GSR is a real number between zero (complete absence of the micro pattern) and one (presence of the micro pattern as defined in [1]). Intermediate values indicate a partial presence of the micro pattern. Each software system analyzed is characterized by a GSR matrix where each row represents the value for a class and each column contain a GSR value for each micro pattern. The correlation between columns of the GSR matrix provides important information about the relationship between different micro patterns, for example if the matching of one micro pattern with a class implies the matching of an other micro pattern with the same class. We analyzed the two systems developed using Agile methodologies and we have studied the distribution and the evolution of micro patterns through different releases.

The micro patterns catalog contains several categories that in the literature are considered like anti patterns [12] as descriptive of bad programming practices not related to the object orientation techniques.

In [3] Destefanis et al. show that there are other micro patterns categories prone to fault and that the classes of a software system that does not belong to any category of micro patterns are more prone to faults. In this paper we analyzed the different releases of the floss-AR system in order to verify if:

- also in this case there is a relationship between the number of faults and anti micro patterns;
- there is a relationship between number of faults and micro patterns more fault prone;
- there is a relationship between number of faults and classes that do not belong to any micro patterns category.

The analysis cannot have statistical significance (because it is performed on a single system), but it is however interesting and a good starting point to further studies. To establish the link between source code and fix operation we adopt the traditional heuristics proposed by Bachmann and Bernstein [11]:

1. Scan through the change logs for bug report in a given format (e.g. fix bug, fix issue and so on).
2. Exclude all false-positive bug numbers (e.g. r420, 2009-05-07 10:47:39 -0400 and so on).
3. Check if there are other potential bug number formats or false positive number formats, add the new formats and scan the change logs iteratively.
4. Check if potential bug numbers exist in the bug- tracking database with their status marked as fixed.

Based on these heuristics we mine the source code repository (such as CVS and SVN) for commit that fixed a bug. Knowing how many time a class have been debugged and knowing the micro patterns associated (if any) to the class we could then evaluate the fault proneness of micro patterns for the system analyzed.

4   Results

In this section we present the results of the survey to developers and on the analysis performed on the source code of the Agile systems. In particular we show how the Agile development impacts on the micro patterns statistics, and on the fault proneness of micro patterns, anti patterns and the set composed by the classes that do not match with andy micro patterns of the catalog (no micro patterns category: NMP).

4.1   Survey

The results of the survey clearly show that Agile development has been applied for the floss-AR system. Tabs. 1 2 3 resume the survey's results.

Table 1. floss-AR developers survey (5 developers)

Question	Very good	Good	Discrete	Adequate	Not adequate
How would you describe the collaboration of the team?	4	1	0	0	0

Table 2. floss-AR developers survey (5 developers)

Question	Yes	No
The collaboration inside the team increased the productivity?	5	0
Did you take part in developing the whole system?	3	2
Do you have favourite programming styles?	2	3
Have the project decisions been discussed together with the team?	5	0
Did you interact directly with the customer?	4	1
Did you use refactoring?	5	0

The questions are divided in three groups according to the format of the possible answers. The first question requires an answer with 5 possibilities, in the second set the questions are posed in a YES or NO form, while in the third set the questions require a short sentence answer.

For developing floss-AR the following Agile practices have been applied:

- Pair programming
- Stand Up Meeting
- Refactoring
- On Site Customer

According to further discussions with the developers team, we are also able to identify four main phases of development:

Table 3. floss-AR developers survey (5 developers)

Question	Answer
Which Agile methodologies did you use during development?	 • Pair Programming • Stand Up Meeting • Refactoring • On Site Customer
How often did you interact with the customer?	1-2 times per month
How often did you use refactoring?	2-3 times per month

- Phase 1 (Initial Agile): a phase characterized by the full adoption of all practices, including testing, refactoring and pair programming. This is the phase leading to the implementation of a key set of the system features. In practice, specific classes to model and manage the domain of research organizations, roles, products, and subjects were added to the original classes managing the content management system, user roles, security, front end and basic system services. The new classes include service classes mapping the model classes to the database, and allowing their presentation and user interaction.
- Phase 2 (Cowboy Coding): this is a critical phase, characterized by a minimal adoption of pair programming, testing and refactoring, because a public presentation was approaching, and the system still lacked many of the features of competitors' products. So, the team rushed to implement them, compromising the quality.
- Phase 3 (Refactoring): an important refactoring phase, characterized by the full adoption of testing and refactoring practices and by the adoption of a rigorous pair programming rotation strategy. The main refactorings performed were Extract Superclass, to remove duplications and extract generalized features from classes representing research products, and corresponding service classes, and Extract Hierarchy applied to a few big classes, such as an Action class that managed a large percentage of all the events occurring in the user interface. This phase was needed to fix the bugs and the bad design that resulted from the previous phase.
- Phase 4 (Mature Agile): Like Phase 1, this is a development phase characterized by the full adoption of the entire set of practices, until the final release.

4.2   Source Code Analysis

We next report the results on how Agile methodologies can impact on the micro patterns distribution and on the fault proneness of the code. In Tabs. 4 5 we report the micro patterns distributions for each release of the floss-AR and Japs systems, in order to show how such distributions evolve from one release to the next.

Table 4. jAPS micropattern distribution (%)

MP	1.0	1.2	1.4	1.6	1.6.2	1.8	1.8.2	2.0
DESIGNATOR	2.14	1.79	2	3.3	3	4.32	6.83	9.6
TAXONOMY	0	0	0	0	0	0	0	0
POOL	0	0	0	0.55	0.54	0.27	0	0.35
JOINER	0	0	0	0	0	0	0	0
FUNCTIONPOINTER	27.1	23.3	27.5	18.7	19.5	18.1	16.7	7.18
FUNCTIONOBJECT	0.71	6.1	0	2.2	2.7	1.89	2.02	1.22
COBOLLIKE	0	0	0	0.27	0.27	0.81	0.75	0.5
STATELESS	0.71	0	1	0.82	0.82	1.08	1.01	1.22
COMMONSTATE	0	0	0	0	0	0	0	0.17
IMMUTABLE	0	3.2	0	0.82	0.82	0.81	0.75	0.87
RESTRICTEDCREATION	0.35	0.4	0.33	0.55	0.54	0.54	0.5	0.17
SAMPLER	0	0	0	0	0	0	0	0
BOX	4.64	15.4	3.98	0.27	0.27	0.27	0.25	1.4
COMPOUNDBOX	7.5	10	12.3	7.1	17.9	7.02	6.83	11.9
CANOPY	0	0	0	0	0	0	0	0
RECORD	0	0	0	0	0	0	0	0
DATAMANAGER	0.35	0.35	0	0	0	0	0	0
SINK	15.3	3.9	15.6	4.14	3.5	2.7	2.78	2.45
OUTLINE	0	0	0	0	0	0	1.0	0.35
TRAIT	0	0	0	0	0	0	1.3	1.1
STATEMACHINE	0.71	0	0.66	0.82	0.82	0.54	0.5	5.4
PURETYPE	0	0	0	0	0.5	0.8	0.3	0.2
AUGMENTEDTYPE	0	0	0	0	0	0	0	0
PSEUDOCLASS	0	0	0	0	0	0	0	0
IMPLEMENTOR	0	0.71	0.3	0.27	0.27	0.27	0.25	0.35
OVERRIDER	0	0	0.3	0.82	0.82	0.54	0.5	0.87
EXTENDER	25	27.9	27.5	36.1	35.9	37.2	34.6	25.1
TOTAL	84	73	85.7	77	76.6	76.4	74.4	75.1

Both systems respect the Gil and Maman statement that about 75% of classes belong to at least one micro pattern. This means that micro patterns are good descriptors also for software developed with Agile methodologies. The distributions of micro patterns among classes roughly respect the same proportions found for software developed with traditional methodologies [3]. In fact previous results show that Extender, Sink and Function Pointer are the most common micro patterns, while Taxonomy, Pool, Sampler and Record are almost absent. One key point is the behavior of anti patterns, which are indicators of bad programming practices [19]. The overall anti patterns behavior is captured by Function Pointer, because classes belonging to others anti patterns, like Pool or Record, are a very small fraction of the total number of classes. Such behavior is displayed in Fig.1 (left side), which shows an overall decreasing trend in the usage of anti patterns. This suggests that the constant application of Agile methodologies during software development across different releases may impact

Table 5. floss-AR micro patterns distribution (%)

MP	CA	SAR	SS	OS	2.1.1
DESIGNATOR	1.5	1.5	1.6	1.38	0.9
TAXONOMY	0	0	0	0	0
POOL	0.2	0.2	0.36	0.3	0.76
JOINER	0	0	0	0	0
FUNCTIONPOINTER	20.2	19.7	22.8	17.8	13.31
FUNCTIONOBJECT	2.5	2.4	2	4.45	1.53
COBOLLIKE	0.17	0.17	0.14	0.46	0.13
STATELESS	0.4	0.3	0.29	1.07	2.57
COMMONSTATE	0.2	0.2	0.14	0.15	0.06
IMMUTABLE	0.2	0.2	0.14	0.76	0.06
RESTRICTEDCREATION	0.1	0.1	0.29	0.30	0.06
SAMPLER	0	0	0	0	0
BOX	2	2	3.21	0.15	13.79
COMPOUNDBOX	7.9	8.2	7.45	10.4	12.61
CANOPY	0	0	0	0	0
RECORD	0	0.2	0	0.2	1.6
DATAMANAGER	0	0	0	1.68	1.74
SINK	18.9	18.6	17.2	3.53	14.77
OUTLINE	0	0	0	0.3	1.1
TRAIT	0.33	0.3	0.29	1.2	0.13
STATEMACHINE	0.17	0.17	0.29	0.15	0.06
PURETYPE	0	0	0	0.3	0.1
AUGMENTEDTYPE	0	0	0	0	0
PSEUDOCLASS	0	0	0	0	0
IMPLEMENTOR	1.7	1.22	1.46	2.61	0.69
OVERRIDER	0.33	0.34	0.29	1.07	0.2
EXTENDER	28.4	28.8	27.7	28.4	16.58
TOTAL	85.1	84.8	85.8	75.5	81.6

positively the software quality, carrying as side effect the reduction in the use of bad programming practices.

4.3 Micro Patterns and Faults

Next we examine the relationship among micro patterns and faults in the floss-AR releases. The top part of Tab. 6 shows the distribution of faulty classes among non micro patterns (NMP) and micro patterns (MP). It must be noted that NMP classes are only 25% of the total classes, and nevertheless they own the larger percentage of faulty classes, except for the last release, where the percentage of faulty classes is the same as the percentage of NMP in the entire release. This result for the first four releases is in agreement with those reported in [3], where NMP own most of the faults. This means that software developed through the adoption of Agile methodologies does not differ from other software

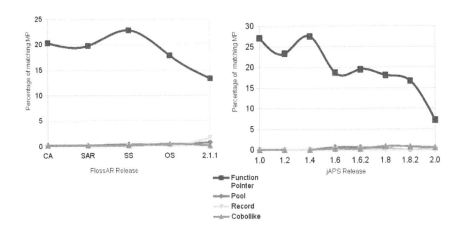

Fig. 1. Left side: floss-AR - Right side: Japs

Table 6. FlossAR fault-prone analysis

		OS(%)	CA(%)	SAR(%)	SS(%)	2.1.1(%)
Distribution of faulty classes	NMP	63.12	62.41	71.63	70.92	23.4
among NMP and MP	MP	36.87	37.58	28.36	29.07	76.59
Percentage of MP faults						
Fault Percentage of AMP		12.76	12.05	7.8	7.8	23.4
Fault Percentage of fault-prone MP faults		18.43	14.89	11.34	13.47	32.62
Fault Percentage of other MP		5.67	10.63	9.21	7.8	20.56

with respect to such distribution. The result for the last release is somehow unexpected, and we cannot explain it with the data at our disposal. Further analysis are needed in order to understand the reasons for this inversion in the fault proneness.

The bottom part of Tab. 6 shows how faults are distributed among the different MP categories: anti micro patterns (AMP), fault-prone MP, and other MP, where fault prone MP are identified by the analysis performed in [3]. Also in this case the total percentage of faulty classes in the last release is different than in previous releases, but the distribution among AMP, fault prone MP, and other MP is again respected. These results confirm that also in Agile systems the most fault prone micro patterns are Extender and Compound Box, and that also the AMP classes are more fault prone than others.

4.4 Discussion

According to these results, we can now answer to the research questions:

RQ1: Do software systems developed with Agile methodologies have a different distribution of micro patterns with respect to non Agile open source systems?

The answer to this research question is negative. According to tabs. 4, 5, the distributions of classes across micro patterns is roughly the same described in [3], where 8 systems were analyzed. They are very similar for both Japs and floss-AR, in all the releases analyzed. This result suggests that the use of Agile methodologies and programming practices does not influence the distribution of micro patterns in the classes.

RQ2: Is the micro patterns faults-proneness the same for Agile and non Agile software?

The answer to this question is positive except for the last release of floss-AR. Comparing the results obtained for the first 4 releases of floss-AR analyzed (Tab. 6, top part) NMP classes are by far the most fault prone classes. The more detailed analysis reported in Tab. 6 (bottom part) shows that among the classes matching with at least one micro pattern the Extender and Compound box micro patterns as well as the anti patterns are the most fault prone. This result confirms the findings reported in [3] and shows that the fault prone micro patterns distributions in Agile software is similar to the one found in systems developed without the adoption of Agile methodologies.

RQ3: Does the micro patterns distribution change during software evolution? If yes, how?

The answer to this research question is not univocal. In general we have shown that across all the releases the micro patterns distribution remains the same, with the exception of the anti patterns classes. In fact we found a decrease of the percentage of anti patterns classes in both systems across the releases. This may be related to the continuous adoption of Agile methodologies during development and maintenance.

5 Threats to Validity

Threats to construct validity are related to the Agile methodologies not used during the system's development (like TDD and continuous integration). This may influence our conclusion that the use of agile methodologies may improve software quality, given that agile development has been adopted partially. Another threat to construct validity is related to the relationship between micro patterns and faults. We assume, based on previous works, that MP are related to software defectiveness. This result has not been generalized to all software systems, thus not necessarily the micro patterns catalogue is directly related to software defectiveness. Nevertheless we believe that our work can build a first step in this direction. Threats to internal validity are related to the fact that with different values of micro patterns could be possible to observe different correlations. Threats to external validity are related to generalization of our conclusions. With regard to the system studied in this work we considered only open source systems written in Java, and this could affect the generality of the discussion and thus our results are not representative of all environments or programming languages. Commercial software is typically developed using different platforms and technologies, with strict deadlines and cost limitation, and by developers with different experiences. This might result in different micro patterns distributions, which is another threat for the external validity. Another threat regards the relationships among anti patterns and faults, which has been studied only for the floss-AR system. Finally we have another threat to conclusion validity: there is not an estimated error on the recognition of a particular micro pattern for a given class.

6   Conclusions

The goals of this research were the analysis of micro patterns distribution in Agile open source software and the analysis of the relationship between MP-NMP and faulty classes. We used the Java tool discussed in [3] in order to extract the data relative to the micro patterns distribution in the two Agile software system studied.

For the floss-AR system we analyzed the change log for bug report and extracted fix operation according to the traditional heuristic proposed in [11]. We also submitted to the floss-AR developers team a questionnaire in order to evaluate the effective use of Agile methodologies, while for Japs this is certified on the web site [6].

Our analysis shows that the micro pattern distribution among classes is the same for the two systems, and remains roughly the same as the one found in non agile systems. Thus the adoption of agile methodologies does not influence such distribution. For example, Gil and Maman statement's that about 25% of classes does not match with any micropattern, is confirmed also in the two agile systems analyzed, for all the releases.

The analysis of fault prone classes shows that in agile systems the Extender and Compound box micro patterns are fault prone, as well as the AMP classes. In particular the most fault prone classes are those not belonging to any micro pattern. The last release of floss-AR represents an exception to this rule, even if the percentage of faulty classes belonging to NMP (23.4%), is still larger than the percentage of NMP classes in all the systems (18.4%).

Finally we found that the micro patterns distribution across the releases is unchanged, with the exception of the anti pattern classes, which displays a decreasing trend.

We can conclude that micro patterns may be helpful to evaluate the quality of an Agile software project during the development process. A tool like the one used in the present work could be used in order to monitor the different stages of development, and possibly to control the temporal evolution of each category of micro patterns. It can be seen from our empirical results that classes that do not correspond to any micro patterns are more fault-prone and this supports that the use of a design methodology increases the quality of the code. Considering the natural adaptiveness of Agile development it could be useful to monitor the evolution of the most fault-prone micro patterns in order to increase the software quality and decrease the amount of defects.

Acknowledgment. This research is supported by Regione Autonoma della Sardegna (RAS), Regional Law No. 7-2007, project CRP-17938 LEAN 2.0

References

1. Gil, J.Y., Maman, I.: Micro pattern in Java Code. In: Proceedings of the 20th Object Oriented Programming Systems Languages and Applications, San Diego, CA, USA, p. 97116 (2005)
2. Agile Manifesto, http://www.agilemanifesto.org
3. Destefanis, G., Tonelli, R., Tempero, E., Concas, G., Marchesi, M.: Micro Pattern Fault-Proneness. In: 2012 38th EUROMICRO Conference on Software Engineering and Advanced Applications (SEAA), pp. 302–306. IEEE (September 2012)
4. Arcelli, F., Maggioni, S.: Metrics-based Detection of Micro pattern to improve the Assesment of Software Quality. In: Proceedings of 1st Symposium on Emerging Trends in Software Metrics (ETSM 2009), Italy (May 2009)
5. Gamma, E., Helm, R., Jhonson, R., Vlissides, J.: Design Pattern: Elements of Reusable Object-Oriented Software. Addison Wesley (1995)
6. JAPS: Java agile portal system, http://www.japsportal.org
7. Heuzeroth, D., Holl, T., Hogstrom, G., Lowe, W.: Automatic Design Pattern Detection. In: IWPC 2003 Proceedings of the 11th IEEE International Workshop on Program Comprehension (2003)
8. Aversano, L., Cerulo, L., Di Penta, M.: Relationship between design pattern defects and crosscutting concern scattering degree: an empirical study. IET Softw. 3(5), 395–409 (2009)
9. Dorairaj, S., Noble, J., Malik, P.: Understanding Team Dynamics in Distributed Agile Software Development. In: Wohlin, C. (ed.) XP 2012. LNBIP, vol. 111, pp. 47–61. Springer, Heidelberg (2012)
10. Bloch, J.: Effective Java Programming Language Guide. Addison-Wesley (June 2011)
11. Bachmann, A., Bernstein, A.: Software process data quality and characteristics: a historical view on open and closed source projects. In: IWPSE-Evol 2009 Proceedings of the Joint International and Annual ERCIM Workshops on Principles of Software Evolution (IWPSE) and Software Evolution (Evol) Workshops. ACM (2009)
12. Destefanis, G., Tonelli, R., Concas, G., Marchesi, M.: An analysis of anti micro patterns effects on fault proneness in large Java systems. In: Proceedings of the 27th Annual ACM Symposium on Applied Computing, pp. 1251–1253. ACM (March 2012)
13. Concas, G., Marchesi, M., Destefanis, G., Tonelli, R.: An empirical study of software metricsfor assessing the phases of an agile project. International Journal of Software Engineering and Knowledge Engineering 22, 525–548 (2012)

14. Tasharofi, S., Ramsin, R.: Process Patterns for Agile Methodologies. In: Ralyté, J., Brinkkemper, S., Henderson-Sellers, B. (eds.) Situational Method Engineering: Fundamentals and Experiences. IFIP, vol. 244, pp. 222–237. Springer, Boston (2007)
15. Martin, R.C.: Agile Software Development: Principles, Patterns, and Practices. Prentice Hall PTR, Upper Saddle River (2003)
16. Empirical studies of agile software development: A systematic review. Tore Dyba, Torgeir Dingsoyr. SINTEF ICT, S.P. Andersensv. 15B, NO-7465 Trondheim, Norway
17. Hoda, R., Noble, J., Marshall, S.: How much is just enough?: some documentation patterns on Agile projects. In: Proceedings of the 15th European Conference on Pattern Languages of Programs, EuroPLoP 2010, Article 13, 13 pages. ACM, New York (2010)
18. Martinez, J., Diaz, J., Perez, J., Garbajosa, J.: Software Product Line Engineering Approach for Enhancing Agile Methodologies. In: Abrahamsson, P., Marchesi, M., Maurer, F. (eds.) XP 2009. LNBIP, vol. 31, pp. 247–248. Springer, Heidelberg (2009)
19. Bloch, J.: Effective Java Programming Language Guide. Addison-Wesley (June 2011)
20. Chidamber, S.R., Kemerer, C.F.: A metrics suite for object oriented design. IEEE Transactions on Software Engineering 20(6), 476–493 (1994)

Feature Usage Diagram for Feature Reduction

Sarunas Marciuska, Cigdem Gencel, Xiaofeng Wang, and Pekka Abrahamsson

Free University of Bolzano-Bozen
Marciuska@inf.unibz.it,
{Cigdem.Gencel,Xiaofeng.Wang,Pekka.Abrahamsson}@unibz.it

Abstract. Feature creep, if not managed well, cause software bloat. This in turn makes software applications become slower. Currently, software industry urgently requires mechanisms and approaches to reduce unnecessary or low value features. In this paper, we introduce a modelling notation, so called Feature Usage Diagram, and an approach to identify and visualize the required information for decision makers when reducing features. We conducted a case study using a real web application to validate and evaluate the Feature Usage Diagram elements and notation. The results showed that the Feature Usage Diagram is easy to learn and understand. Moreover, by visualising useful information, it has potential to support developers when making decisions for feature reduction.

Keywords: feature creep, feature reduction, feature usage, feature location, concern graphs, latent lattice.

1 Introduction

The family of agile and lean methods have been increasingly adopted by many companies in the past decade. The main focus of these methods is to build systems in such a way that allows the software products to reach market in a shorter time and respond to changes more quickly [1]. However, feature creep [2,3] to existing systems is a significant problem that agile and lean methods have not suggested adequate practices and techniques to tackle. In fact, recent studies [13] indicate that 30 to 50 percent of features contained in many software products have no or marginal value. Usually, such features, after being added during the life cycle, loose value in time.

Unmanaged feature creep can cause software bloat [4], which in turn makes a computer application become slower and therefore, requires higher hardware capacity. Software bloat also increases cost for maintenance. One of the most recent example of software bloat is Nokia Symbian 60 smartphone platform. The feature set of the system grew so much that it was too expensive to maintain it, and therefore, it was abandoned [14].

Currently, lean start-up [5,6] software business development methodology tackles the feature creep problem by finding a minimum viable product that contains only essential and the most valuable features. Feature driven development [30] tries to address the feature creep problem by focusing on features that

H. Baumeister and B. Weber (Eds.): XP 2013, LNBIP 149, pp. 223–237, 2013.
© Springer-Verlag Berlin Heidelberg 2013

have the highest value for customers. However, not all companies start development from scratch and use feature driven development methodology. And even
if they do, it is not easy to determine the value of a feature to make a decision.
Therefore, there is an urgent need [14] to define mechanisms and approaches for
feature reduction.

To the best of our knowledge, there is no approach that deals with the feature reduction problem completely. Most of the methods and techniques in the
literature could be applied to address only some parts of the problem (such as
feature identification and location). Furthermore, as they were not specifically
developed for feature reduction purposes, they require improvements to be useful
in this context (see Section 2 for a review of these approaches).

In this paper, our focus is on presenting the required information about features for informed decision making in feature reduction. We introduce an approach and a modelling notation, so-called Feature Usage Diagram, to visualise
the features, their relations, and attributes (such as information about the usage
of each feature by the users to indicate one dimension of value that is stated
as significant [31] for feature reduction). We also present a case study which we
conducted to evaluate the usefulness of the Feature Usage Diagram for feature
reduction purposes in practice.

This paper is structured as follows: Section 2 discusses the related work. Section 3 presents the Feature Usage Diagram. Section 4 provides details of the
case study and the results. Section 6 concludes the work and gives future work
directions.

2   Related Work

Feature reduction involves identifying features, locating them, determining the
value of each, and then systematically removing the ones with less value from
the software (see Fig. 1).

In this section we present the related work, which in some way deals with
different parts of the feature reduction problem, even though not particularly
developed for these purposes, but could be helpful for the aims of this study.
We identified related studies in three areas: feature identification and location,
feature usage monitoring and feature visualization.

2.1   Feature Identification and Location

For feature reduction, decision makers require to know the features, their locations and relations in between. As locating features depends on identifying the
features as an initial step, we present related work for feature identification and
location together under this subsection. A recent systematic literature review on
feature location [11] categorizes the existing techniques as below:

1. **Dynamic** [15,16,17]. These techniques use dynamic analysis to locate the
   features during runtime. Developers provide a scenario, and then links between different elements of the scenario are generated during runtime.

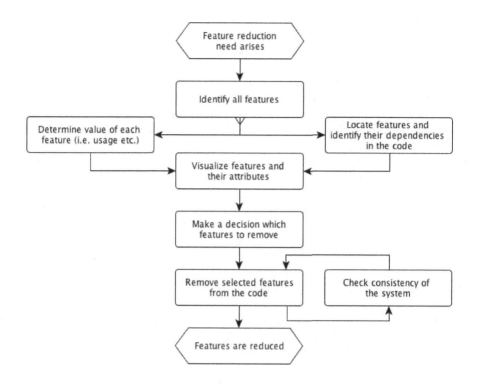

Fig. 1. A Generic Feature Reduction Process

As a result, a graph is generated that shows which classes and methods are called for each part of the scenario. The main advantage of these techniques is that it shows exactly which parts of the code are called during the execution time.

2. **Static** [18,19,20]. These techniques use static analysis to locate features from the source code. The code is statically analysed and then the dependencies between features are explored. Finally, developers validate the nodes and connections in the graph. The main advantage of these approaches is that they do not require executing the system in order to create a dependency graph. In addition, the results present detailed information such as relations between variables and methods.

3. **Textual** [21,22,23,24,25]. Textual analysis examine the textual parts of the code to locate features. Developers provide query with feature descriptions and the method using information retrieval and language processing techniques checks the variables, classes, method names, and comments to locate them. The main advantage of these techniques is that they map real features to code.

4. **Historical** [26,27]. Historical techniques use information from software repositories to locate features. The idea is to query features from comments, and

then associate them to the lines that were changed in that commit. The main advantage of these techniques is that they can map features to a very low granularity of the source code, that is to exact lines.

Even though most of the existing techniques are promising for our purposes, none of them or their combinations provide a solution for automatic and complete feature set identification as they were not designed for this purpose from the beginning. Dynamic feature location techniques rely on user predefined scenarios, so they cannot generate a complete features set if the given scenario is not complete. Static analysis generate a set of features dependent on the source code, so they involve a lot of noise (i.e. variable names that do not represent features). Textual and historical approaches depend on the developer queries and the textual attributes of the source code. Due to these limitations of the current techniques, we decided to manually identify features and their relations for the case study presented in Section 4.

2.2   Feature Usage Monitoring

Another significant information for feature reduction is the value of each feature. In this work, we focus on only one dimension of value: usage of features by users (i.e. which feature was used by whom and when). Other dimensions will be tackled in the future work.

There are two commonly applied methods to monitor how users use the features of a system: 1) extend the software with code that is responsible for monitoring, or 2) design an application that intercepts all events triggered by the observed system when it is used.

The main issue using the former method is that the added piece of software increases the complexity of the overall software. In addition, depending on the country where the software is used, the hidden data collection about users activities might violate the privacy laws. Existing tools that use the second approach (such as OpenSpan Desktop Analytics [9] and Google Analytics [10]) overcome afore mentioned limitations, because they do not modify the software that is being monitored. However, such tools are able to show only which applications are running on an operating system or web browser. They do not provide any details related to the feature usage.

Another set of tools such as Microsoft Spy++ [8], or the method presented by Atterer et al. [7] provide detailed information on how users use a system by monitoring activities of users, such as mouse clicks and key strokes. However these tools collect too much noise, because they were not created with the aim to identify the usage of the features. For example, such tools catch the events raised by random mouse clicks which do not change the behaviour of the system. Then it becomes difficult to automatically filter out the noise and determine which unique features were executed. Having all of those limitations in mind we decided to create custom tool that identifies the feature usage in the case study presented in Section 4.

2.3   Feature Visualization

The decision makers require not only that the important information is captured, but also visualised in a proper way for practical reasons. Therefore, we reviewed related work for features visualisation. Most of this work come from software product line engineering and feature location fields.

The software product line approaches visualize features by Feature Diagram [28,29] that expresses commonality and variability within the domain (see Fig. 2). Feature Diagram shows hierarchical relations between features and displays information related to the whole product line, but not for each product. Therefore, this diagram is not useful for our purposes in this paper.

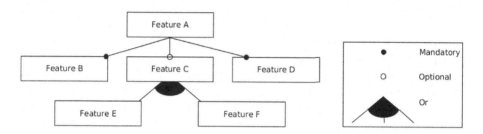

Fig. 2. Feature Diagram

Existing feature location techniques visualize the output of their result using a concern graph [19], or concept lattice [25]. The concern graph displays the classes, methods and variables of the system and their relation (see Fig. 3). However, such visualization does not represent the features that system users are using. For example, class or method might cover several features, while a variable might represent only a part of a feature. Therefore, this graph is also not useful for our purposes.

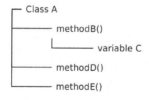

Fig. 3. Concern Graph

The concept lattice (see Fig. 4) represents not only code related parts of the system, but also concepts that can be related to the front end features.

This diagrams contains two layers: feature representation layer and code representation layer. The feature layer represents the scenarios or user queries.

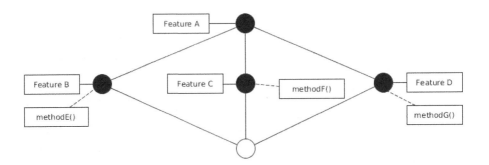

Fig. 4. Concept Lattice

The code layer represent the code dependencies associated to those features identified by feature location techniques.

In the ideal case, the concept lattice could represent the complete features list and their relationships. However, to have only such diagram for visualizing the usage of features is not enough, because it does not include usage related attributes in the feature layer. In addition links between features are not directed (that is, users can access feature B from feature A, but not vice versa). In this study, we extended the feature layer of concept lattice in order to overcome these limitations and developed the Feature Usage Diagram.

3   Feature Usage Diagram

To provide the required information as an input to decision making for feature reduction in an understandable and practical way, we developed a diagram and associated notation, called the Feature Usage Diagram (see Fig. 5).

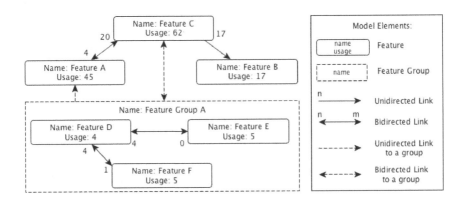

Fig. 5. Feature Usage Diagram

The main model elements of the Feature Usage Diagram are: Feature, Feature Group, Directed Link among Features and Directed Link to Feature Group. We present each of the model elements and their attributes in the following paragraphs.

3.1   Feature

Feature is one of the key elements in feature reduction. In this work we adopt the definition of feature presented by Eisenbarth et al. [12] – "a feature is an observable unit of behaviour of a system triggered by the user". For example, a case where a user has to enter his email, password and press login button in order to login is different from the case where system remembers his credentials and he has just to press a login button in order to login. In the first scenario we can observe that user used three features, while in the second only one, even though the final state was the same (that is, the user logged into the system). In the example provided in Fig. 5 the Feature Usage Diagram presents six features in total.

Attributes of Feature Element: Each Feature has two attributes: Feature name and Feature usage. Feature Name shows the name of a Feature. Feature Usage shows how many times a Feature was used. This attribute provides one of the key information for feature reduction decision. Features that have small relative feature usage values indicate that software might need to go for feature reduction. For example, if a feature is used one hundred times while others are used millions of times, then the first feature should be considered for removal, because it has a relatively small usage in comparison to the other system features. Fig 5 shows that feature A was used 45 times, because it is indicated in its usage attribute.

3.2   Directed Link between Features

Directed Link between Features represents an access path between two Features. It can be uni-directed, or bi-directed. If there is a way to access feature B from feature A and there is no way to access Feature A from Feature B it means that the link between those features is uni-directed A − > B. On the contrary, if there is a possibility to reach Feature B from Feature A and vice versa, then the link A < − > B is bi-directed. The example presented in Fig. 5 contains three bi-directed links between Feature A and Feature C, Feature D and Feature E, and Feature D and Feature F. The remaining directed links have single direction.

Attributes of Directed Link between Features: Link Cardinality attribute on each Directed Link shows how many times a Feature, which the link is pointing to, was accessed from another Features. For feature reduction it provides an important information about the ways how users are using the features. It might reveal unexpected links that are not used, or are not necessary. Therefore, expert might decide to remove those links from the system. In the example provided in Fig. 5, the Link Cardinality value on the link between feature B and feature C shows that Feature B was accessed from a Feature C 17 times.

3.3 Feature Group

Feature Group element is created to group Features that have the same access to the Features that are outside the group. In this way, the Feature Usage Diagram could be represented at a higher level of abstraction, and thus more understandable. The idea is based on the fact that if a system has n Features and those Features are not grouped, then in the worst case there could be $n * (n-1)$ Uni-Directed Links among those Features. Therefore, each k groups of the size m reduces the worst case complexity to $(n - k * (m-1)) * (n - 1 - k * (m-1)) + k * m * (m-1)$. For example, if we have 100 Features, then in the worst case we need to consider $100 * 99 = 9900$ Directed Links. However, if it is possible to group those Features to 10 Feature Groups in such a way that each group contains 10 similar Features, then we need to consider only $90 + 900 = 990$ Directed Links. In this case, the complexity would decrease 10 times. In the example provided in Fig. 5 there is one Feature Group named "Feature Group A". It contains 3 Features: Feature D, Feature E, and Feature F.

Attributes of Feature Group: Group Name attribute is used to name a Feature Group.

3.4 Directed Link to Feature Group

Directed Link to feature Group shows how a Feature Group is connected to other Feature Groups, or Features. These links do not have any attributes, but if the grouping would be removed then all the features of the group would inherit this link. For example, in Fig. 5 grouping container has a uni-directed link to Feature A. This means that Feature D, Feature E and Feature F have uni-directed link to Feature A as well. Obviously, by removing the Feature Group, the Feature Usage Diagram would be extended with inherited links and cardinality attributes on these links, and thus the complexity of the diagram would increase. During the case study (see in Section 4) we discovered that in some situations it is useful to draw a Cyclic bi-directed Link on the corner of a Feature Group and leave all the Features within it disconnected. It means that all Features within that group have Bi-directed Links among each other (see Fig 6 Menu Items group).

4 Case Study Conduct

We conducted a case study to evaluate the Feature Usage Diagram. We selected the case application as the nextrailer.net web based movie recommender system that has 20 daily users. During the time of the case study, the system contained approximately 30 Features and 200 Directed Links between them.

Our research questions were as follows:

1. **RQ1:** – Is the Feature Usage Diagram easy to learn and understandable to use?
2. **RQ2** – Is the Feature Usage Diagram notation complete to represent features and their dependencies (nothing is redundant or missing)?
3. **RQ3:** – Is the visualised information on the Feature Usage Diagram useful for decision making in feature reduction?

RQ1 and RQ2 were answered in Phase 1 and RQ3 in Phase 2.

We used a purposive sampling when choosing the case study participants. 12 Computer Science students (MSc and PhD students in the Free University of Bolzano) participated in the first phase of the case study. The participants were heterogenous with respect to their programming and modelling experience in industry (experience levels varied from a few years to more than ten years). Furthermore, they were from 6 different nationalities with different backgrounds. In the second phase, 3 developers of the case application were the participants of the case study.

4.1   Phase 1

In the first phase of the case study, we gave a brief introduction of the Feature Usage Diagram notation to the participants, and provided them detailed material about the notation in a printed form (see Section 3). We asked them to draw a Feature Usage Diagram for the nextrailer.net website, leaving usage and cardinality attributes empty.

The participants used the Google Drawing graphical editor. During the session, we observed how the participants were modelling the given system and took notes. For each participant, we measured the time to complete the Feature Usage Diagrams. At the end of the case study we collected the diagrams. Before the case study, the first author of this paper draw the Feature Usage Diagram for the case application in order to be able to compare the relative learning time of the participants (RQ1).

To investigate whether the participants understood and correctly used the notation to model the Features, Feature Group elements and Directed Links (RQ1), we introduced 3 developers of the nextrailer.net website the notation and asked them to come up with a complete and correct version of the diagram. We then compared the diagrams drawn by the participants to this version. At the end, we made an unstructured interview with each participant to answer our RQ2.

4.2   Phase 2

In the second phase, we designed a JavaScript library and inserted it in nextrailer.net website in order to fill the final complete and correct version of the Feature Usage Diagram with the usage information. The library was designed to intercept all "on click" events raised by DOM elements that have title attribute.

In the next step, the developers of the system were asked to insert unique title attributes on each element that correspond to the features. The following information was sent to our server when the users use the system: The IP address of the user that triggers the event, the timestamp of the event, and the title attribute of the event. Having this information, we could determine which relation of the Feature Usage Diagram was executed to determine the cardinality information. For example, if Feature B is triggered after Feature A, then we draw a uni-directed link from Feature A to Feature B and increased the cardinality value for the link.

We collected usage data for 30 days. Then we wrote a script that parsed the database and computed the usage information for each feature (links between features and cardinality of the links). Later, we inserted these information to the correct version of Feature Usage Diagram and interviewed the developers to answer RQ3.

5   Results and Analysis

Phase 1: Our first observation was that the participants did not use the additional material about the notation provided before the case study saying that the short introduction given at the beginning of the session was sufficient. On average, it took 25-30 minutes to complete the Feature Usage Diagrams of the nextrailer.net website. There was not high variation among the completion time per participant and the participants used only 5-10 minutes more than the first author of this paper who completed the same task in about 20 minutes. These indicated that the Feature Usage Diagram notation was easy to learn (RQ1).

After reviewing the collected Feature Usage Diagrams from the participants, we observed that all the participants could identify the Features and Feature Groups. However, most of the diagrams were missing a number of Directed Links between Features (20-30 percent). In addition, some of the models contained few non exiting links. When we interviewed the participants to investigate the reasons, they reported that these were analysis mistakes and therefore not related to any misunderstanding about the introduced notation. Thus, we concluded that the Feature Usage Diagram notation is understandable to use (RQ1).

Then we interviewed the participants by asking whether the elements of the Feature Usage Diagram were complete for representing the Features and their relations (RQ2). A few participants suggested using the same notation for the Directed Links to Features and the Directed Links to Feature Groups as they thought these links were redundant. We explained that the attributes on the Directed Links will be populated during the second phase based on which links are abstracted and will be inherited, and which represent the lowest granularity. Then the participants agreed with using different notation for these elements.

Some of the participants reported that most of the Features in the Feature Groups were connected with each other with Bi-directed Links and a special notation for such situations would be more practical. During the case study one participant added Cyclic Bi-directed Link on a Feature Group, meaning that all Features inherit this link (see Fig 6 Menu Items group). We decided to incorporate this suggestion in the Feature Usage Diagram notation (see in Section 3.4).

The biggest challenge reported by the participants was to model Features that change state (that is, in some case Features and their Links are visible at the website, while in other cases they are hidden). In this situation, we suggested to model Features as if they are always visible, because the state of a Feature can be detected by analysing the usability scenarios. For example, if such a Feature is used it means that all scenarios when this Feature is hidden should be excluded.

In addition, several participants mentioned that a modelling tool support would be much more practical. They indicated that such a tool could verify whether the Feature Usage Diagram contains duplicates as well. Moreover, they stated that a tool could allow to collapse the elements to show the relationship between Features and Feature Groups at a higher granularity level or expand them to see at a lower granularity. And by means of a tool, they said that it would also be possible to partially automatically generate the Feature Usage Diagram from the website, which then would require validation by the developers.

Phase 2: The fragment of the final version of the Feature Usage Diagram agreed upon by the developers at the beginning of Phase 2 is presented in Fig. 6. The fragment of this diagram populated with the usage information attributes is presented in Fig. 7.

During the interviews, all developers mentioned that the Feature Usage Diagram would be very useful for making a decision for feature reduction (RQ3). However, they also added that there were other aspects of value which should

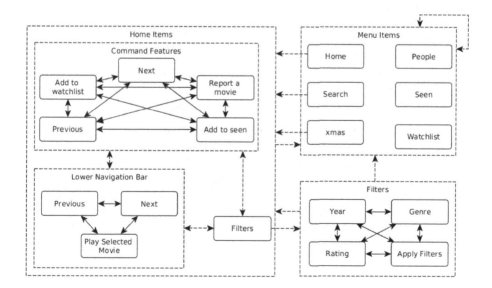

Fig. 6. Fragment of nextrailer.net Feature Usage Diagram chosen by developers

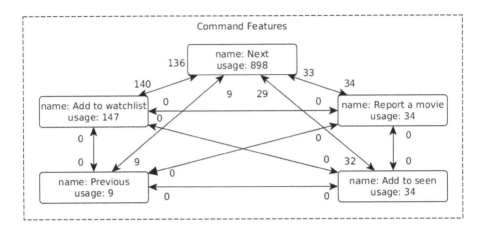

Fig. 7. Fragment of nextrailer.net Feature Usage Diagram with usage attributes

be taken into account as well. For example, the features Login and Report are valuable for the company as these collect important information for the company, but these features are not used by many users. In addition, the developers pointed out that a Feature could appear to be rarely used if it is hidden and is not easy to notice. Nevertheless, the developers said that having such information is very useful for value maximisation reasons by relocating those features to other places. Finally, the developers added that cardinality information is important to understand usage patters and having such information would help in making decisions for how to modify a system, generating more value and understanding the impact of such modifications.

5.1 Threats to Validity

We discuss the validity threats of this study according to the categorization suggested by Runeson and Host for case studies [32]: 1) Construct validity, 2) Internal validity, 3) External validity, and 4) Reliability.

Construct Validity. Construct validity refers to what extent the operational measures represent what is investigated according to the research questions. To answer the RQ1, we measured the time spent by each participant to learn the notation and draw the Feature Usage Diagram for the case application. One possible threat could have been previous knowledge of some participants which could affect the learning time. Therefore, none of the participants were introduced to the Feature Usage Diagram before the case study conduct. In order to measure how easy to learn the notation, we compared the amount of time spent by each participant to that of the first author of this paper to get a relative figure.

Another potential threat was due to how we evaluated the model elements in the Feature Usage Diagrams drawn by the participants. We compared the results to a correct and complete version agreed upon by the developers of the case application. Here, one validity threat could have been if the agreed upon version would have had errors. To mitigate this threat we used subject triangulation, that is we asked 3 developers to separately draw the Feature Usage Diagrams, and then by cross-checking to come up with a final agreed version.

Another validity threat could have been that the participants interpreted the interview questions not in the same was as the researchers really meant. To mitigate this, we had a discussion with each participant about what we meant by each term we used in our questions (e.g 'usefulness' in RQ3).

Internal Validity. Internal validity concerns the causality relation between the treatment and the outcome, and whether the results do follow from the data. In our case, one threat could have been related to background of participants of the study. We chose the participants by making a background check to ensure that that they have minimum skills in Computer Science to be able to understand the concepts. We could not totally control the domain knowledge of the participants that could have an effect on the time spent for task completion. However, as there was not a high variation among the participants, we believe that this did not affect the results of this study significantly.

External Validity. External validity refers to what extent it is possible to generalise the findings to different or similar contexts. One validity threat could have been the small number of participants in the sample. As the participants selected were heterogeneous with respect to their programming and modelling experience in industry, we believe that the results of this study can be generalized to some extent. On the other hand, as we conducted only one case study using a web application, we do not know how much the results are generalisable to other type of applications. Further case studies are required.

Reliability. Reliability reflects to what extent the data and the analysis depend on the specific researchers. Two of the operational measures used in this study are objective. Therefore, we do not see a validity threat for the interpretation and analysis of these measures. However, a validity threat might have been due to interpretation of the answers of the participants. To mitigate this threat, we validated with each participant how we interpreted their answers.

6   Conclusions

In this paper, we introduce a new diagram to visualise the Features, their relationships and their usage information. The results of the case study indicates that the Feature Usage Diagram elements and notation is easy to learn by novice users. The features and and their dependencies could be captured completely following the notation.

Furthermore, the case study showed that the Feature Usage Diagram has potential to aid developers in decision making for feature reduction purposes as information on usage of the features is stated to be one of the important value aspects of features.

As future work, we plan to investigate other aspects of feature value and extend the Feature Usage Diagram to incorporate these aspects as well. We will explore how usage can be maximized by relocating features in different places of a system. We will also apply feature Usage Diagram to analyse complex systems with a high number of features, to better understand the usefulness of our approach.

In addition, we aim to develop a tool to support developers when drawing Feature Usage Diagrams. In addition, we will explore the ways how to automatically generate a part of the diagram.

References

1. Highsmith, J.A.: Agile software development ecosystems. Addison-Wesley Professional (2002)
2. Davis, F.D., Venkatesh, V.: Toward preprototype user acceptance testing of new information systems: implications for software project management. IEEE Transactions on Engineering Management (2004)
3. Senyard, A., Michlmayr, M.: How to have a successful free software project. In: Proceedings of the 11th Asia-Pacific Software Engineering Conference, pp. 84–91 (2004)
4. Xu, G., Mitchell, N., Arnold, M., Rountev, A., Sevitsky, G.: Software bloat analysis: Finding, removing, and preventing performance problems in modern large-scale object-oriented applications. In: Proceedings of the FSE/SDP Workshop on Future of Software Engineering Research (2010)
5. Ries, E.: The Lean Startup: How Today's Entrepreneurs Use Continuous Innovation to Create Radically Successful Businesses. Journal of Product Innovation Management (2011)
6. Taipale, M.: Huitale – A Story of a Finnish Lean Startup. In: Abrahamsson, P., Oza, N. (eds.) LESS 2010. LNBIP, vol. 65, pp. 111–114. Springer, Heidelberg (2010)
7. Atterer, R., Wnuk, M., Schmidt, A.: Knowing the user's every move: user activity tracking for website usability evaluation and implicit interaction. In: Proceedings of the International Conference on World WideWeb (2006)
8. Microsoft Spy++, http://msdn.microsoft.com/en-us/library/aa264396 (v=vs.60).aspx (last visited on the November 27, 2012)
9. OpenSpan Desktop Analytics, http://www.openspan.com/products/desktop_analytics (last visited on the November 27, 2012)
10. Google Analytics, http://www.google.com/analytics (last visited on the November 27, 2012)
11. Dit, B., Revelle, M., Gethers, M., Poshyvanyk, D.: Feature Location in Source Code: A Taxonomy and Survey. Journal of Software Maintenance and Evolution: Research and Practice (2011)
12. Eisenbarth, T., Koschke, R., Simon, D.: Locating Features in Source Code. IEEE Computer (2003)
13. Ebert, C., Dumke, R.: Software Measurement. Springer (2007)
14. Ebert, C., Abrahamsson, P., Oza, N.: Lean Software Development. IEEE Software, 22–25 (2012)
15. Eisenberg, A.D., De Volder, K.: Dynamic Feature Traces: Finding Features in Unfamiliar Code. In: Proceedings of 21st IEEE International Conference on Software Maintenance, Budapest, Hungary, pp. 337–346 (2005)

16. Bohnet, J., Voigt, S., Dollner, J.: Locating and Understanding Features of Complex Software Systems by Synchronizing Time, Collaboration and Code-Focused Views on Execution Traces. In: Proceedings of 16th IEEE International Conference on Program Comprehension, pp. 268–271 (2008)
17. Edwards, D., Wilde, N., Simmons, S., Golden, E.: Instrumenting Time-Sensitive Software for Feature Location. In: Proceedings of International Conference on Program Comprehension, pp. 130–137 (2009)
18. Chen, K., Rajlich, V.: Case Study of Feature Location Using Dependence Graph. In: Proceedings of 8th IEEE International Workshop on Program Comprehension, pp. 241–249 (2000)
19. Robillard, M.P., Murphy, G.C.: Concern Graphs: Finding and describing concerns using structural program dependencies. In: Proceedings of International Conference on Software Engineering, pp. 406–416 (2002)
20. Trifu, M.: Using Dataflow Information for Concern Identification in Object-Oriented Software Systems. In: Proceedings of European Conference on Software Maintenance and Reengineering, pp. 193–202 (2008)
21. Petrenko, M., Rajlich, V., Vanciu, R.: Partial Domain Comprehension in Software Evolution and Maintenance. In: International Conference on Program Comprehension (2008)
22. Marcus, A., Sergeyev, A., Rajlich, V., Maletic, J.: An Information Retrieval Approach to Concept Location in Source Code. In: Proceedings of 11th IEEE Working Conference on Reverse Engineering, pp. 214-223 (2004)
23. Grant, S., Cordy, J.R., Skillicorn, D.B.: Automated Concept Location Using Independent Component Analysis. In: Proceedings of 15th Working Conference on Reverse Engineering, pp. 138–142 (2008)
24. Hill, E., Pollock, L., Vijay-Shanker, K.: Automatically Capturing Source Code Context of NL-Queries for Software Maintenance and Reuse. In: Proceedings of 31st IEEE/ACM International Conference on Software Engineering (2009)
25. Poshyvanyk, D., Marcus, A.: Combining formal concept analysis with information retrieval for concept location in source code. In: Program Comprehension, pp. 37–48 (2007)
26. Chen, A., Chou, E., Wong, J., Yao, A.Y., Zhang, Q., Zhang, S., Michail, A.: CVSSearch: searching through source code using CVS comments. In: Proceedings of IEEE International Conference on Software Maintenance, pp. 364–373 (2001)
27. Ratanotayanon, S., Choi, H.J., Sim, S.E.: Using Transitive changesets to Support Feature Location. In: Proceedings of 25th IEEE/ACM International Conference on Automated Software Engineering, pp. 341–344 (2010)
28. Benavides, D., Trinidad, P., Ruiz-Cortés, A.: Automated reasoning on feature models. In: Pastor, Ó., Falcão e Cunha, J. (eds.) CAiSE 2005. LNCS, vol. 3520, pp. 491–503. Springer, Heidelberg (2005)
29. Czarnecki, K., Helsen, S., Eisenecker, U.: Staged configuration using feature models. In: Nord, R.L. (ed.) SPLC 2004. LNCS, vol. 3154, pp. 266–283. Springer, Heidelberg (2004)
30. Palmer, S.R., Felsing, M.: A practical guide to feature-driven development. Pearson Education (2001)
31. Smith, J.B., Colgate, M.: Customer value creation: a practical framework. The Journal of Marketing Theory and Practice, 7–23 (2007)
32. Runeson, P., Host, M.: Guidelines for conducting and reporting case study research in software engineering. In: Empirical Software Engineering, pp. 131–164 (2009)

The Effect of Complexity and Value
on Architecture Planning in Agile
Software Development

Michael Waterman, James Noble, and George Allan

Victoria University of Wellington, New Zealand

{Michael.Waterman,kjx,George.Allan}@ecs.vuw.ac.nz

Abstract. A key feature of agile software development is its prioritisation of responding to changing requirements over planning ahead. If an agile development team spends too much time planning and designing architecture then responding to change will be extremely costly, while not doing enough architectural design puts the project at risk of failure. Striking the balance depends heavily on the context of the system being built, the environment and the development teams. This Grounded Theory research into how much architecture agile teams design up-front has identified system complexity as an important factor in determining how much planning a team does up-front, while system size, although related to complexity, has a much less direct impact. Furthermore, when determining how much design to do up-front, value to the customer can be a more important factor than overall development cost. Understanding these factors can help agile teams to determine how much up-front planning is appropriate for the systems they develop.

Keywords: Software architecture, agile software development, Grounded Theory.

1 Introduction

A software architecture represents the high-level structure and behaviour of a software system [1] and can be difficult to change once development has started [2]. Architecture is about planning ahead – getting the design of the system right and avoiding costly refactoring during development. On the other hand, one of the key features of agile software development is the ability to respond to changing requirements in preference to planning ahead [3]. There is therefore a tension between up-front architecture design and agile methods. Many agile teams deal with this tension through just enough up-front design to allow development to begin [4]. How much just enough is depends on the context, where context is made up of technical factors, environmental factors and the team itself.

This paper presents results from ongoing research that examines the relationships between complexity and size, value and cost, and the effects that they have on how much architectural planning teams do up-front. Understanding

H. Baumeister and B. Weber (Eds.): XP 2013, LNBIP 149, pp. 238–252, 2013.

these factors can help agile teams to determine how much up-front planning is appropriate for the systems they develop.

Following this introduction, section 2 discusses the problem of architecture planning in agile development, section 3 describes the research methodology used (Grounded Theory), section 4 presents the findings of this research and section 5 discusses the results in context of the literature. Section 6 discusses the limitations of the research, and finally section 7 concludes the paper.

2   Background

2.1   The Tension between Agile and Architecture

There are many definitions of software architecture. Kruchten defined software architecture as "the set of significant decisions about the high level structure and the behaviour of the system" [1]; Booch extended this by noting 'significant' can be measured by the cost of change [2]. We can therefore summarise architecture as comprising the planning and design decisions that are made up-front and are difficult to change once development has started. Examples of architectural decisions are the choice of technology stack (including the development frameworks), architectural styles or patterns and the system's high level components.

Delivering *value* to the customer and other stakeholders lies at the heart of being agile; many of the twelve principles of the agile manifesto directly relate to delivering value earlier and faster [3]. Scrum and XP maximise value by prioritising tasks according to business priorities [5,6], and Lean places high importance on value streams and eliminating waste [7,8].

Agile methods focus on value through delivering software frequently, responding to changing and evolving requirements in preference to planning ahead, delivering quality, and simplicity [3]. Behind its ability to respond to changing and evolving requirements is the principle of 'the simplest thing that will work', or YAGNI – 'you ain't gonna need it': any additional work, such as developing features that *might* be required, will be wasted if those features never actually make it into the final product [6].

Architecture design is often seen as contrary to the philosophy of YAGNI, delivering little immediate value to the customer [9]. Agile developers therefore often avoid or minimise architectural planning [10], with the architecture being either neglected entirely or only implicitly defined. Too little architecture may lead to an *accidental architecture* [11] – one that has not been carefully thought through – and may lead to gradual failure of the project, while on the other hand too much architecture planning will at best delay the start of development, and at worst lead to expensive architectural rework if the requirements change significantly.

The agile principle of YAGNI is therefore in tension with architectural planning.

2.2   The Subjectivity of Up-Front Architecture Decision-Making

Agile methodology instructions generally advise developers to deal with the tension between agile and architecture by designing just enough architecture to start development, with the rest being completed during development as required [4,12,13]. How much is just enough depends heavily on context, with context depending on environmental factors such as the organisation and the domain, as well as specific factors such as project size, criticality, business model, architecture stability, team distribution, governance, rate of change and the age of system [9]. More than this however; context also includes social influences [14], such as the background and experience of the architects. Booch and Fairbanks noted that a particular system may have more than a single correct architecture [15,16], and two architects are likely to produce different architectures for the same problem with the same boundaries [14]. Taylor described architecture as being as much about 'soft' (subjective) factors as it is about objective design [17].

2.3   The Effect of Size on Up-Front Planning

Boehm undertook a study [18] using the COCOMO II model [19] in which he demonstrated a relationship between the level of up-front architectural effort and the overall development effort (and hence cost). This study showed that up-front architectural effort is a compromise between the amount of time spent planning up-front and the amount of time spent on rework caused by doing too little, with a 'sweet spot' at the overall minimum cost. The location of this sweet spot is highly dependent on the context of the system; Boehm's study illustrated the impact of the size of the system, with a larger system requiring more time spent resolving architectural issues than a smaller system for any given level of up-front planning. This difference is due to the diseconomies of scale of software development [18].

Figure 1 shows that an increase in size from 100 KSLOC (thousand equivalent source lines of code) to 10,000 KSLOC increases the up-front planning sweet spot from around 20 per cent of the total effort to around 40 per cent of the total effort.

2.4   The Research Gap

There has been very little empirical research on the relationship between software architecture and agile development to date [20]. Breivold et al. performed a survey of the literature and concluded that studies have been small, diverging, and in some cases, performed in an artificial setting [20]. Dybå and Dingsøyr also noted the need for more knowledge of software development in general, particularly through empirical studies [21]. This lack of research does not mean that it is not an important issue: at the XP2010 conference, how much architectural effort was rated as the second-equal most burning question facing agile practitioners [22].

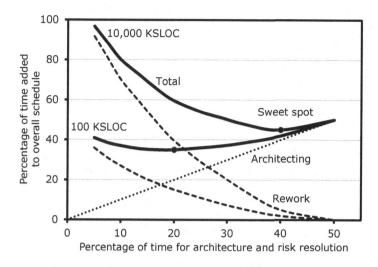

Fig. 1. The effect of system size on the up-front architecture sweet spot, from Boehm [18]

This paper presents results from ongoing research that helps address this gap by investigating the relationships between complexity and size, value and cost, and how they affect how much architectural planning teams do up-front. These results can be used to guide agile development teams when making decisions on how much up-front architecture design and planning is appropriate for systems they develop.

3   Research Method

This research into up-front architecture uses the qualitative Grounded Theory methodology [23]. Qualitative methods such as Grounded Theory are used to investigate people, interactions and processes. As noted above, architecture is very dependent on the architects themselves and the development teams. Qualitative research is generally *inductive* – it develops theory from the research, unlike *deductive* research which aims to prove (or disprove) a hypothesis or hypotheses. Because of the scarcity of literature on the relationship between architecture and agile methods [20], an inductive methodology that will develop a new hypothesis is more suitable for this research. We selected Grounded Theory because it is a systematic and rigorous method [24] that allows researchers to develop a *substantive* theory that explains the processes observed in a range of cases [25].

3.1   Data Collection

In this research, we collected data primarily through face-to-face semi-structured interviews with agile practitioners who design or use architecture, or who are otherwise architecture stakeholders. Participants were typically architects, developers, project leaders/managers and customers, and are all involved with business-type applications. We collected additional data in the form of documentation and discussions by email and telephone to seek further information or clarifications on earlier interviews.

3.2 Data Analysis

The first step of data analysis, *open coding*, can begin as soon as the first data is obtained. In open coding, phenomena in the data are methodically identified and labelled using a code that summarises the meaning of the the the data [26].

As open coding progresses, emerging codes are compared with earlier codes; codes with related themes are aggregated into higher levels of abstraction called *concepts*. This process, called *constant comparison* [27], continues at the concept level, with similar concepts being aggregated into a third level of abstraction called *categories*. Categories are the highest conceptual elements of Grounded Theory analysis; a Grounded Theory research project may have hundreds of different codes but will typically have no more than four or five categories [28]. The relationships between the categories are analysed and focused using *selective coding*; a dominant category emerges as the *core category*, which becomes central to the emerging theory. Throughout the analysis process, *memos* – free form notes ranging anywhere in size from a sentence to several pages – are written to record thoughts and ideas about developing relationships between codes, concepts and categories, and to aid the development of the theory [29].

Grounded Theory uses iteration to ensure a wide coverage of the factors that may affect the emerging theory [26]: later data collection is dependent on the results of earlier analysis. Data collection and analysis continue until *saturation* is reached, which occurs when no new insights are learned, and all variations and negative cases can be explained [30].

We can illustrate the Grounded Theory process with an example from this research. One participant commented that they had regular tax law changes that meant regular changes to their requirements:

> "You've got your taxation changes coming in on specific dates throughout the year, so those are generally around our release dates, because we have to stay compliant with that." (P3, development manager)

We coded this as 'having regulatory changes'.

Similarly another participant commented on the pharmaceutical regulations that affected his company's product:

> "The regulations keep changing every six months." (P23, senior manager)

We also coded this as 'having regulatory changes'.

Codes that had similar themes to this example included 'having changes in usage patterns or system load', 'requirements evolving' and 'understanding of requirements changing'. We combined these similar codes into a concept called 'having unstable requirements'. Figure 2 shows the relationship between the underlying codes and 'having unstable requirements'.

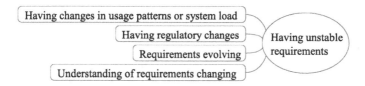

Fig. 2. An example of a concept emerging from its codes

We have analysed thirty two interviews to date. Participants were gathered through industry contacts, agile interest groups and through direct contact with relevant organisations. Almost all participants were very experienced developers, and most were also very experienced in agile development. Organisation types vary from development consultancies, government departments, mass-market product developers and single contractors. Different types of agile development are included, with most participants using Scrum; other methods included XP, Lean and bespoke methods. Most participants adapted their processes to some extent to suit their team or customer's requirements. The inclusion of this range of participants and systems enables the research to include the effects of different factors on architecture decision making.

We asked participants to select a project that they had been involved with to discuss during the interview. Types of projects varied hugely, from green fields to system redevelopment, from standalone systems to multi-team enterprise systems, and from start-up service providers and ongoing mass market product development to bespoke business systems. Systems varied from highly critical systems such as air traffic control and health record management, to business critical systems such as banking and retail, through to largely non-critical administration and entertainment broadcast systems. We also obtained documentation where possible to corroborate the interview data.

To maintain confidentiality, the participants are referred to using codes P1 to P32. A summary of participants and their projects are listed in table 1.

4   Findings

This paper presents findings on the effects that complexity and size have on up-front effort, and on using value rather than cost to determine how much effort a team should put into architectural planning. An earlier paper [29] captured the effects of architectural frameworks and templates, and the architects' experience, on the amount of up-front effort required in architectural design.

We used the Grounded Theory category "complexity over size" to form the basis for part of these results. This category consists of the concepts "indicators of complexity", "up-front effort affected by complexity of system" and "up-front effort affected by size of system" (figure 3a). The concept "indicators of complexity" in turn emerged from the codes "complexity leading to multiple frameworks", "frameworks reducing architectural complexity", "legacy systems

Table 1. Participant summary

	Role	Organisation type	Domain	Agile methods	Team size or no. of teams	Duration	System description
P1	Developer	Government agency	Health	Single developer	1 team member	6 months	Web-based, .NET
P2	Dev./ architect	Start-up	E-commerce	Scrum	3 team members	Ongoing	.NET, cloud-based
P3	Dev. manager	Vendor	Human resources	Scrum	3 teams	Ongoing	Web-based, .NET,
P4	Director of architec- ture	Government dept.	Digital archiving	Scrum	5 developers	Ongoing	Java, rich client, suite of standalone tools
P5	Coach/dev. manager	Start-up	Entertainment	Scrum/ kanban	Various	N/A	Various
P6	Man. Dir./ lead dev.	Vendor	Telecoms	Informal, iterative	1–3 developers	Ongoing	Suite of standalone applications
P7	BA	Telecoms operator	Telecoms	Scrum	12 team members	1 year+	Suite of web-based services
P8	Lead developer	Government dept.	Digital archiving	Scrum	4–14 team members	1 year+	Ruby on Rails, Java back-end
P9	Developer	Financial services	Telecoms	Bespoke	2–24 team members	3 years	Web-based system
P10	Coach	Multinat. hardware vendor	Transport	Scrum/XP	500–800 developers	Several years	Large distributed web-based system
P11	Architect	Government	Government services	Scrum	8 team members	Several years	Web-based services, .NET
P12	Senior developer	Service provider	Financial services	Scrum	6–7 developers	7 months	.NET, suite of web-based applications
P13	Architect	Government	Health	Scrum	12 team members	4 years	Monolithic .NET app
P14	Architect	Government	Animal health	Scrum	6–8 team members	18 months	.NET, large GIS component
P15	Customer	Start-up service provider	Retail (electricity)	Scrum	7 developers	Ongoing (3 years)	Ruby On Rails
P16	CEO/chief engineer	Start-up	Retail (health)	XP	5 team members	5 months	Ruby On Rails
P17	Manager/ coach	Government	Statistics	Scrum	6 dev + admin	2–3 years	Web-based, PHP using DAO pattern
P18	Dev. manager	Multinat. hardware vendor	Health	Scrum	15 team members	Ongoing (>2 years)	Web-based, Java platform
P19	Dev. manager	Start-up service provider	Retail (travel)	Lean	4 developers	Ongoing (<1 year)	PHP/Symfony, Javascript/Backbone
P20	Coach and trainer	Independent consultant	N/A	Scrum	N/A	N/A	N/A
P21	Manager/ coach	Service provider	Retail (publishing)	Scrum	3 teams; 40 total	Several years	.NET, Websphere Commerce, SAP, others.
P22	Senior manager	Service provider	Contact man- agement/marketing	Scrum/XP	More than 40 total	N/A	.NET
P23	Senior manager	Vendor	Pharmaceut- ical	Own methods	3 teams	Ongoing	Various web based, client/server
P24	Customer	Start-up service provider	Retail (electricity)	Scrum	7 developers	Ongoing (3 years)	Ruby On Rails web applications
P25	Team lead	Service provider	Banking	Scrum	1 team	Ongoing	.NET, single tier web
P26	Team lead	Government	Water management	Scrum	8 team members	1 year	.NET, web based, 7 tier
P27	CEO/coach	Start-up service provider	Retail (electricity)	Scrum	7 developers	Ongoing (3 years)	Ruby On Rails
P28	Technical lead	Service provider	Broadcasting	Scrum	42 team members	N/A	Python with Django, CMSs for multiple websites
P29	Dev. manager	Banking	Banking	Kanban	20 team members	Ongoing	Web based, AJAX, interface to mainframe
P30	Consulting architect	Service provider	Telecoms	Scrum	7 team members	2 years+	Python with Django and Twisted, NoSQL
P31	Enterprise architect	Government	Transport	Bespoke	7 team members	13 week pilot	Web services, SOA using .NET/WCF
P32	Software dev. director	Vendor	Government	FDD, kanban	N/A	N/A	N/A

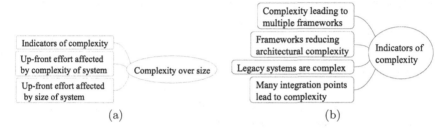

Fig. 3. (a) the category "complexity over size" emerging from its concepts; (b) the concept "indicators of complexity" emerging from its codes.

are complex" and "many integration points lead to complexity" (figure 3b). The other concepts likewise emerged from their respective codes; they are not listed here for the sake of brevity.

4.1   The Effect of Complexity on Up-Front Architecture Effort

Participants reported that the complexity of a system is an important determinant of how much architecture planning a team does up-front. System complexity is caused by demanding requirements and quality attributes, and results in design decisions that are intertwined and have multiple dependencies [31]. Complexity may extend or break the limits of the development frameworks being used, and therefore increases the decision-making effort required to select appropriate frameworks and tools, and to design a suitable architecture. A less complex system will require less effort and a less sophisticated design.

For example, a participant in this research described how complexity affects up-front architectural effort in his work:

> "Typically, [the length of the start-up phase] depends on the complexity."
> [...] "The project that I am working on now is not a very complex architecture. For that I don't think we need a visual modelling tool – just a simple whiteboard or flipchart with coloured Post-Its can work." (P21, manager/agile coach)

Participants noted that complexity can often be indicated by the need to use bespoke components and libraries, by the need to use multiple technologies, having many integration points, and by having to work with legacy systems. These are explored below.

Bespoke Components: Modern vendor frameworks such as .NET, Hibernate and Ruby on Rails provide standard solutions to problems, reducing the up-front effort required to build a system, and enabling architectural changes to be made with a lot less effort [29]. Frameworks are used by development teams to greatly reduce the amount of up-front architecture and development effort required, particularly in business-type applications, with participants commenting that they did not need to make as many architectural decisions when using modern frameworks:

"You choose the proper plug-ins and then you get the functionality that you are looking for." (P16, CEO)

What used to be considered architectural decisions ten years ago are now sometimes considered design decisions, or even simply configuration decisions:

"Those [structural] decisions can be very emergent nowadays; I don't think they're nearly as intractable" (P29, development manager).

Frameworks, however, cannot always provide a complete solution. There are frequently parts of systems that cannot be implemented using components or libraries from the frameworks and have to be designed and developed from scratch. These may be because the problem is unique or because the framework components do not meet non-functional requirements such as performance. Non-framework components increase complexity and result in extra up-front effort as teams first identify the parts of the system that cannot be implemented using pre-built components, and then perform analysis and experiments to come up with satisfactory bespoke replacements:

"There were a number of architectural things that were developed in-house. [...] We wrote our own data binding framework for instance. [...] We did a bit of prototyping, we built the data binding framework that we came up as a result of all of those factors. We had a bit of a go with what Microsoft had off the shelf previously, found it painful and limiting, and felt that it confirmed our decision to go our own way with data binding." (P13, architect)

Multiple Technologies: Like the need for bespoke components, a system with complex requirements may not be able to be implemented entirely using a single vendor framework, and instead may require multiple frameworks to implement the required features and functionality. Not only does selecting these frameworks require extra up-front planning, but setting up automatic testing platforms, continuous integration delivery and other related set up activities become more difficult and require more effort:

"If it's really horribly complex and you've got to request all sorts of bits of infrastructure from all over the show to get it to work then it definitely slows down iteration zero." (P29, development manager)

Legacy Systems: Legacy systems are older systems that were created using outdated techniques and technology [32], and are no longer being 'engineered' but rather are simply patched as requirements change [33] without consideration of the technical debt being incurred [9]. These patches add to the system's complexity [34]:

"Systems become more complex with age. Just the burden of code – entropy over time and all that." (P32, Software Development Director)

Good engineering practices such as simplicity, modularity and high cohesion are eroded, and continuing to develop, or even interfacing with, these entropic legacy systems is a source of complexity that requires more up-front exploration and proofs of concept to ensure that integration is possible.

Integration: Participants identified integration points, or interfaces to external systems, as a major source of complexity in the systems being developed, particularly when the other systems are legacy or are built from different technologies. Integration with other systems require data and communications to be mapped between the systems, which adds to the up-front effort to ensure integration is possible with the technologies being used.

> *"Today's systems tend to be more interconnected – they have a lot more interfaces to external systems than older systems which are typically standalone. They have a lot higher level of complexity for the same sized system." (P14, solutions architect)*

4.2   The Effect of Size on Up-Front Architecture Effort

The size of a system is frequently considered by the literature as a factor in determining how much up-front architectural effort is required [9,18] (section 2.3). Contrarily, the participants in this research reported that size is not as important as complexity:

> *"In my experience, the complexity of an organisation's systems landscape has a greater influence on the amount of fore-thought required than the budget or size of any particular initiative" (P10, agile coach)*

Size may be measured explicitly by using a metric such as lines of code or number of components, or implicitly using a metric such as the project's budget or development time required. Size typically has some correlation with complexity: a small system is usually not very complex, and a large system has the potential for a high level of complexity. The relationship is not linear however; sometimes there may only be a small correlation.

A system, independent of size, may not have any of the sources of complexity described above – bespoke components, integration, multiple technologies and legacy systems – and hence will have a low level of complexity, and will require less up-front architectural effort:

> *"If we have size that just extends the time, it's of little concern to us. It's just a slightly larger backlog, management overhead." (P32, software development director)*

Specifically, a large system that can be implemented entirely using the components and libraries of a framework with an acceptable level of risk is often not very complex, and will require less up-front effort than a similar sized complex system. For example, P27's team was building a large system that had complex requirements and complex functionality, but the team was able to decouple this complexity from the architecture through implementing the system entirely within the boundaries of Ruby on Rails. They were therefore able to build the system with very little up-front planning:

"We talk to a lot of systems, we interface with a lot of systems, we've got customer web requests coming in, we've got iPhone requests coming in, from a software point of view there's a lot of moving parts. The [functionality] is very, very complex – but the physical architecture itself that it sits on is nice and standard. [...] It's a just well adopted Ruby On Rails stack. We deliberately try not to do anything different. Go with what's proven, go with what works. [...] We don't have architectural discussions – we don't need to – the problem's [already] been solved." (P27, CEO/agile coach)

Another participant, P26, described a .NET system that he built as having an 'enterprise-grade architecture' that was too big for the system being built: it had more layers and levels of abstraction than required. Despite this extra size, he believed the extra complexity was minor, describing the additional up-front effort required for this larger architecture designed for a larger system as being minimal, with most of the extra effort coming during development when getting new team members up to speed with the architecture.

Conversely, even a small system may require a lot of up-front planning if it is complex:

"It could have been a very small thing that created a big iteration zero." (P29, development manager)

The use of frameworks to avoid complexity allowed some participants (such as P27) to completely avoid up-front planning, allowing them to increase their agility and respond to change and deliver early value much more effectively.

4.3 Using Value and Cost Minimisation to Determine How Much Up-Front Architectural Effort

Section 2.3 above described Boehm's analysis which uses the minimum effort (and hence cost) to determine the sweet spot of architectural effort. While "cost is always a concern" (P10) in agile development, in some situations agile teams are more concerned about delivering business value to their customer – at the expense of cost.

For many businesses, particularly those building a new commercial mass market product or service, the value of software is the economic value that it adds to the business, and is measured by participants in this research in terms of cash flow or net present value, with early value being provided by early adopters of the service. When faced with a decision of either doing more architectural planning up-front (and delaying the release) or minimising architectural planning (and releasing as early as possible with less functionality), the teams consider which option will provide the most value to the business:

"Today they've got an opportunity for a business idea that might make them some money – if they don't pounce on it it's gone regardless of how clever they think they are." (P26, team lead)

and

"If they [build] the big system, then they will never reach their end customer and make their money." (P22, senior manager)

An early release may be in the form of a Minimum Viable Product [35], which is a marketing experiment – a release with limited functionality designed to determine which features are desirable, rather than a fully functional version of the software.

Focusing on business value and minimising the up-front effort may lead to the need to re-design the architecture later and increase the overall cost. By this stage the customer is in a better position to pay for that rework:

> "Maybe it'll cost a lot more to replace it a year later, but you already have some business..." (P22, senior manager)

and

> "[Designing for a million users] is a problem you can have once you've got a million users and you've got a million users worth of revenue..." (P27, CEO/agile coach)

Agile teams must therefore consider value, and not just cost, as a measure for determining the level of up-front architectural planning the team does.

5   Discussion

This study of agile practitioners has found that the complexity of a system is an important factor in determining how much up-front architecture planning is required. Indicators of complexity include bespoke components, multiple technologies, integration with other systems, and dealing with legacy systems. On the other hand, system size by itself is not a good determinant of up-front effort, a result that is at odds with Boehm's analysis [18], described above in section 2.3. That analysis presented a clear relationship between the up-front architectural effort sweet spot and system size (see figure 1), due to the diseconomies of scale of software development. Boehm's analysis is based on data derived from the COCOMO II cost model, a model released in 1996 that calculates the cost of development of software systems using a complex regression algorithm and historical parameters, calibrated with the experiences obtained from a set of 161 software projects [18].

There may be a number of reasons for the difference between Boehm's result and these findings.

Boehm's analysis did not distinguish between complexity and size. The data that COCOMO II is based on is likely to be from projects from the mid 1990s or earlier. COCOMO II therefore predates modern frameworks that developers currently use to reduce complexity and up-front effort. When considering systems that do not use modern frameworks, there may be a good correlation between size and complexity which allows size to be used as a proxy for complexity.

The importance of the effect of early delivery on value was noted by Boehm in the context of software economics [36]: "The primary value realized may not be in cost avoidance but rather in reduced time to market." COCOMO II, a cost model, does not consider the benefit gained from early delivery of value, simply using cost to determine the sweet spot. Poort and van Vliet similarly proposed a method of determining the level of up-front architecture which is based on prioritising risk and minimising cost [37]. They claimed that stakeholder value is implicit in the presence of the solution's goals and business requirements. However this assumption is not appropriate for agile development, because firstly it assumes that the solution's goals and business requirements do not change after development has started, and secondly it assumes that there is no value in delivering functionality to the end user before development of the entire system has been completed.

Boehm and Turner presented an earlier comparative model similar to figure 1 which had risk exposure (rather than effort) as the dependent (y-axis) variable [38]. Risk exposure included the business risk of delay caused by spending too much time on architectural planning, and is therefore more appropriate for agile development. Higher levels of risk exposure caused by higher levels of up-front planning would cause the sweet spot to move towards the less-planning end of the scale. Poort and van Vliet did not consider business risk [37].

Abrahamsson, Babar and Kruchten [9] listed a number of factors that they suggested can affect the level of up-front planning, including the rate of change of requirements, governance, team distribution, stability of the architecture and the business model. These factors are not discussed in this paper.

6   Limitations

A substantive Grounded Theory is only applicable to the domain being studied [30], and therefore cannot be assumed to be applicable to other contexts, or in general. The result is therefore, to some extent, dependent on the participants selected for the research. For example, these results cannot be applied to embedded software because we did not include any participants who develop embedded software systems.

7   Conclusion

This paper considers the relationships between complexity and size, value and cost, and how they affect how much up-front planning agile teams do.

Previous analysis undertaken by Boehm using the COCOMO II model presents a clear relationship between size and up-front architecture planning. However, results from this research show that the relationship between system complexity and up-front planning is more important than the relationship between size and up-front planning. Complexity, caused by demanding requirements and quality attributes, greatly increases the up-front planning required, and may be indicated by the need to build bespoke components, which are required where the framework does not provide the functionality needed or cannot meet non-functional requirements such as performance, by the need for multiple frameworks, by the need for many integration points with other systems, and by the need to work with legacy systems. While complexity is closely related to size, size in itself does not always directly affect the amount of up-front planning, particularly if the system has a low level of complexity.

The need for architecture planning is in tension with agile's need to respond to changing requirements: too much planning results not only in unnecessary effort but also wasted effort if requirements change, while too little planning leads to more effort to address architectural problems that arise. Therefore the minimum overall cost is sometimes used to determine how much up-front planning a team should do. However, in agile development, the need to provide early value to the customer may override the need to minimise overall cost, if early value will lead to an improved cash flow for the customer. To provide early value, the team may do less up-front planning, potentially with more architectural rework later when the customer's cash flow is more able to support that architectural effort.

Agile teams must consider complexity and value when determining how much architectural design to do up-front. Further results from this research will explore other factors that influence how much up-front design is required.

References

1. Kruchten, P.: The Rational Unified process – an Introduction. Addison Wesley (1998)
2. Booch, G.: Architectural organizational patterns. IEEE Software 25(03), 18–19 (2008)
3. Beck, K., et al.: Agile manifesto (2001), http://agilemanifesto.org/
4. Ambler, S.W.: Agile architecture: Strategies for scaling agile development, http://www.agilemodeling.com/essays/agileArchitecture.html
5. Deemer, P., Benefield, G., Larman, C., Vodde, B.: The scrum primer (2010), http://assets.scrumtraininginstitute.com/downloads/1/scrumprimer121.pdf
6. Beck, K.: Extreme Programming Explained: Embrace Change, 2nd edn. Addison-Wesley Professional (2005)
7. Poppendieck, M., Poppendieck, T.: Lean Software Development: An Agile Toolkit. Addison-Wesley Professional (2003)
8. Coplien, J.O., Bjørnvig, G.: Lean Architecture for Agile Software Development. John Wiley and Sons, Ltd. (2010)
9. Abrahamsson, P., Babar, M.A., Kruchten, P.: Agility and architecture: Can they coexist? IEEE Software 27(02) (2010)
10. Kruchten, P.: Agility and architecture: an oxymoron? In: SAC 21 Workshop: Software Architecture Challenges in the 21st Century (2009)
11. Booch, G.: The accidental architecture. IEEE Software 23(03), 9–11 (2006)
12. Booch, G.: An architectural oxymoron. IEEE Software 27(05), 96 (2010)
13. Avram, A.: 10 suggestions for the architect of an agile team (September 2010), http://www.infoq.com/news/2010/09/Tips-Architect-Agile-Team
14. Bass, L., Clements, P., Kazman, R.: Software Architecture in Practice, 2nd edn. SEI Series in Software Engineering. Addison-Wesley (2003)
15. Booch, G.: The irrelevance of architecture. IEEE Software 24(03), 10–11 (2007)
16. Fairbanks, G.: Just Enough Software Architecture: A Risk Driven Approach. Marshall and Brainerd (2010)
17. Taylor, P.R.: The Situated Software Architect. PhD thesis, Monash University (December 2007)
18. Boehm, B.: Architecting: How much and when? In: Oram, A., Wilson, G. (eds.) Making Software. O'Reilly (2011)

19. Boehm, B.W., Clark, Horowitz, Brown, Reifer, Chulani, Madachy, R., Steece, B.: Software Cost Estimation with COCOMO II with CD-Rom, 1st edn. Prentice Hall PTR, Upper Saddle River (2000)
20. Breivold, H.P., Sundmark, D., Wallin, P., Larson, S.: What does research say about agile and architecture? In: Fifth International Conference on Software Engineering Advances (2010)
21. Dybå, T., Dingsøyr, T.: What Do We Know about Agile Software Development? IEEE Software 26(05), 6–9 (2009)
22. Freudenberg, S., Sharp, H.: The top 10 burning research questions from practitioners. IEEE Software 27(05), 8–9 (2010)
23. Glaser, B.G., Strauss, A.L.: The Discovery of Grounded Theory: Strategies for Qualitative Research. Aldine de Gruyter (1967)
24. Allan, G.: The legitimacy of Grounded Theory. In: European Conference on Research Methods (keynote address) (July 2006)
25. Strauss, A., Corbin, J.: Grounded theory methodology. In: Denzin, N.K., Lincoln, Y.S. (eds.) Handbook of Qualitative Research. Sage Publications, Inc. (1994)
26. Allan, G.: A critique of using grounded theory as a research method. Electronic Journal of Business Research Methods 2 (July 2003)
27. Bryman, A.: Social Research Methods, 3rd edn. Oxford University Press (2008)
28. Glaser, B.G.: The grounded theory perspective III: Theoretical coding. Sociology Press (2005)
29. Waterman, M., Noble, J., Allan, G.: How much architecture? Reducing the up-front effort. In: Agile India 2012, pp. 56–59 (February 2012)
30. Charmaz, K.: Constructing Grounded Theory: A Practical Guide Through Qualitative Analysis. SAGE Publications Ltd. (2006)
31. Jansen, A., Bosch, J.: Software architecture as a set of architectural design decisions. In: WICSA 2005, pp. 109–120 (2005)
32. Bennett, K.: Legacy systems: Coping with stress. IEEE Software 12(01), 19–23 (1995)
33. McGovern, L.: What is legacy code? (2008), http://www.flickspin.com/en/software_development/what_is_legacy_code
34. Lehman, M.: Programs, life cycles, and laws of software evolution. Proceedings of the IEEE 68, 1060–1076 (1980)
35. Ries, E.: The Lean Startup: How Today's Entrepreneurs Use Continuous Innovation to Create Radically Successful Businesses. Crown Publishing Group (2011)
36. Boehm, B., Sullivan, K.: Software economics: a roadmap. In: Proceedings of the Conference on The Future of Software Engineering, ICSE 2000, pp. 321–343. ACM, New York (2000)
37. Poort, E.R., van Vliet, H.: Architecting as a risk- and cost management discipline. In: WICSA 2011, pp. 2–11 (2011)
38. Boehm, B.: Get ready for agile methods, with care. IEEE Computer 35(01), 64–69 (2002)

Author Index